"Struggling for Wings"

"Struggling for Wings"
The Art of James Dickey

Edited by Robert Kirschten

University of South Carolina Press

Copyright © 1997 University of South Carolina

Published in Columbia, South Carolina, by the
University of South Carolina Press

Manufactured in the United States of America

01 00 99 98 97   5 4 3 2 1

Excerpts from James Dickey's poetry © James Dickey and
Wesleyan University Press and used by permission of the University Press
of New England.

Library of Congress Cataloging-in-Publication Data

Struggling for wings : the art of James Dickey / edited by Robert
    Kirschten.
        p.   cm.
    Includes bibliographical references.
    ISBN 1-57003-165-7
    1. Dickey, James—Criticism and interpretation.   I. Kirschten,
Robert, date.
PS3554.I32Z86   1997
811'.54—dc21   97–729

For Jim Dickey
(1923–1997)

Contents

"Struggling for Wings"

Introduction

ROBERT KIRSCHTEN

. . . if you want to understand

Frustration, look up while the moon, which is nothing

But a wild white world,

Struggles overhead: fights to grow wings
For its creatures but cannot get
Creatures to have them. . . .

You don't have to look up, but can look straight

Straight

Straight out   out over the night sea
As it comes in. Do that.
Do it and think of your death, too, as a white world

Struggling for wings.

—James Dickey, "Moon Flock"

In these compelling lines from *The Eagle's Mile* (1990), his most recent and complex book of poems, James Dickey confronts no generalized or abstract conception of "frustration." Instead, in his late sixties, after several near-fatal illnesses and operations, he deals with an extremely concrete, if not compulsive, concern with death. Using the archetype of the moon in conjunction with one of his characteristic examples of mythological animal imagery, Dickey grounds his response to mortality in "a white world // Struggling for wings."[1] With its implicit possibility for flight and thus for uplifting transformation, this compensatory setting is placed against an ultimate, existential morbidity at the poem's end, in which, instead of a "moon flock" (which one deserves yet may find only in the imagination), a human's final destiny is described in another archetype, one that Dickey often pairs with the moon. This time his archetype appears as an opposite: "the ocean / In shock . . . all insanity and necessity" which "is right at you // Coming / hear-tearing // Hair-tearing and coming." Needless to say, especially for James Dickey, the cessation of natural motion ("the ocean / In shock") is the cessation not only of the redemptive imagination but also of life itself. The title of his poem, "Moon Flock," thus signals

1

one power of the animistic mind, figured in a group of birdlike "creatures," which, alas, is tragically doomed, for "the moon . . . fights to grow wings . . . but cannot." Unlike the mystical, pragmatic optimism of his early nature poetry, Dickey's courageous later vision is darker and tougher; it embodies the acknowledgment that, while we aspire to dwell in a "wild white world" in which one is "Struggling for wings," instead, we encounter (and must come to grips with) a disturbing future of "insanity and necessity." This future, ultimately, is that of a "moveless man"—that is, a man of no purposive motion (or, death) (46).

"A wild white world" in which man is struggling for wings is scarcely a new literary battleground for James Dickey. In a chapter entitled "The Pale Horse" from his master's thesis, written in 1950 at Vanderbilt University on Herman Melville's shorter poems, Dickey describes "Melville's prose works and his poems" as "a series of variations on the relation between evil and Fate (or God)."[2] Dickey develops this duality by noting that Melville thinks of Jehovah as "a mixture of the cunning and the awful" and that "the former quality, as it is embodied in the latter . . . is the informing concept of Melville's art" (57). Later, after examining a series of instances in which whiteness appears as a cover for the "cunning" of Fate, Dickey cites several lines from *Moby-Dick*, lines that not only suggest Dickey's chapter title but which focus on whiteness as a fundamental strategy for dramatizing literary "struggle[s]" in Melville's work and, proleptically, in his own:

> Nor even in our superstitions do we fail to throw
> the same snowy mantle round our phantoms; all ghosts
> rising in a milk-white fog—Yea, while these terrors seize us,
> let us add, that even the king of terrors, when personified
> by the evangelist, rides on his pallid horse.
>
> (65)

If whiteness, for Melville, disguises a "snowy," "milk-white" surface that may, at any time, give way to the diabolical cunning of Jehovah's "Fate," likewise, in Dickey's work, "snowy" surfaces give way to a terror-filled world of sanctity and struggle. In his remarkable, most recent novel, *To the White Sea*, whiteness is featured not only in the title, but it also pervades the very surface of nature in a rolling wave of beneficent movement, providing Dickey's narrator with his own set of wings.[3] After falling out of a tree almost to his death, this narrator reflects on the danger and ecstasy of flight in this extended moment of impressive prose-poetry:

> there are things better than life. I was whole in the air, long wings
> left and right, the color of snow, the color of cloud, and I was not
> falling but riding, riding over the whole frozen earth, whiteness
> everywhere under me, the land pushed up in hills and mountains,
> the rivers like white roads made out of white, going through white,

the woods covered with snow, all hanging, all hanging with me, and pure, the whole earth as pure as it could get, and still, real still. All I heard was the air I was in, the wind holding me up in myself, over everything. Pure air: pure, pure. Pure riding. I looked up, and white cloud was there. Where I was, the clouds didn't have to be dark to snow, and these were not dark, but it was snowing, and I climbed up through it on air that was doing it for me, riding, rising, not moving a wing, to be inside the cloud. The wind was making another kind of sound, and I was everywhere . . . I was riding. I was riding in snow and on snow, in the whiteness where whiteness counted for the most it could. It held me that way, and I was riding. (144–45)

Whiteness is also the energizing emblem for the fantastic conversion of an office worker into a migrating albatross in Dickey's long lyric "Reincarnation II." This poem, appropriately enough, begins with a quote from Melville on wings and whiteness while, like the passage cited from *To the White Sea*, carrying its half-human, half-animal subject to a celestial surface of pure, instinctive motion.[4] However tranquil and ecstastic white surfaces appear in his poetry, they have another Melvillian side in Dickey's novel. His American narrator, the downed B-29 tail gunner Sergeant Muldrow, rides a train through the snows of northern Japan in the winter of 1945 to escape his wartime pursuers and arrive safely on the island of Hokkaido in the White Sea. As the sergeant rides through the landscape, he howls like a wolf, and Dickey uses whiteness to throw (in Melville's terms) "a snowy mantle round [the] phantom" of Muldrow's cunning and "diabolical" animal side. Whiteness thus provides a "mantle" of snowy nature that reverses its beneficent appearance and reveals Muldrow as an opposite, yet continuous, moment in the natural landscape of killing and eating, which is an essential part of his—and, as Dickey emphatically points out, our—natural state. Blood and the hunt, two topics powerfully prominent in Melville's classic about the white whale, are also featured here:[5]

Then I was white, and hunting again . . . I had a taste for blood in my mouth, in my whole body—my body that borrowed something from snakes—that was stronger than anything in life, that had more power than the sun and the moon shining together. It was not just being hungry; it was way more than that, a lot more necessary. It was the taste, it was the color of it, the heat. It was what it came from: something alive and now not, the steam rising out of it before you tore it apart to eat. Everything about it was enough to drive you crazy, but you like it and want more, have to have it and will do anything to get it, will go for the color and the heat and the steam a long time after you've eaten all you want, and more. As soon as all the blood was out, you go looking for the next one, to do it again. You? I? Who? What had me was more than I was. I couldn't help myself and didn't want to. All I could do was what it said. (143)

In many ways this alternating pattern of whiteness and blood, of wings and struggle, constitutes not only the central action in *To the White Sea;* just as it does in Melville, it functions as one of the "informing concept[s]" throughout Dickey's poetry and prose. This informing concept is essentially ritualistic, and it contains an even more powerful, redemptive structure than is first apparent. Archetypal in scope, the ground of this ritual depends on a conception of nature which is emblematic. In *Myth and Reality* Mircea Eliade describes this ground and also the mythopoeic genre of Dickey's alternating pattern: "If the World speaks to [man] through its heavenly bodies, its plants and animals, its rivers and rocks, its seasons and nights, man answers it by his dreams and his imaginative life, by his Ancestors or his totems, . . . by his ability to die and return to life, ritually in initiation ceremonies (like the Moon and vegetation), [and] by his power to incarnate a spirit by putting on a mask."[6] In the dreamy world of "plants and animals" and of "rivers and rocks" in *To the White Sea,* Dickey intertwines life, death, and a "return to life" in a dynamic realm that masks an ancient, if not classical, conception of nature. It is no accident that Dickey introduces his novel with a quotation from the Roman poet Lucretius, whose didactic poem of six books, *The Nature of the Universe* (De rerum natura), was written (ca. 58 B.C.E.) in the mode of Epicurean philosophy. Dickey's introductory citation from Lucretius is especially suited to his own war novel, for it vividly describes the fire of a thunderbolt from book 6, "Meteorology and Geology."[7] Yet, just as *To the White Sea* is vastly more than a war novel, Lucretius' discussion in the "Movements and Shapes of Atoms" in book 2 reveals an even more detailed basis for the metamorphic philosophy of death dramatized in Dickey's landscape:

> We see every sort of substance transformed in the same way. Rivers, foliage and lush pastures are transformed into cattle; the substance of cattle is transformed into our bodies; and often enough our bodies go to build up the strength of predatory beasts or the bodies of the lords of the air. So nature transforms all foods into living bodies and generates from them all the senses of animate creatures, just as it makes dry wood blossom out in flame and transfigures it wholly into fire. . . . Death does not put an end to things by annihilating the component particles but by breaking up their conjunction. Then it links them in new combinations, making everything change in shape and colour and give up in an instant its acquired gift of sensation.[8]

The emotional goal of Lucretius' poetic atomism is to free individuals from the superstitions of a state-sponsored priesthood that grandiosely promises that anthropomorphic gods will intervene in human affairs to save believers from death. Dickey's ritualized landscape further develops Lucretius' liberating aim by dramatizing death as such a familiar part of nature that man's attitude toward it—certainly, Muldrow's—no longer intimidates or frightens one into politicoreligious subservience. This is not to say that Dickey's novel is essentially political. Rather, despite its historic, wartime setting, it is profoundly religious and atemporal. If transcending one's fear of death—for example, struggling for wings—has previously been the prerogatives of gods and saints (or even madmen), Dickey invests his hero-predator Muldrow with just such a spiritual, naturalistic immunity by converting Muldrow's adventure into a paradigmatic initiation ceremony. In Dickey's magical, mythological world, ceremonial "nature," no matter how much it appears to be an obsessive and exotic realm of recurring violence, is reinvented by making it, in Eliade's terms, "familiar," "intelligible," and even transparent. This last trait is especially interesting, for Eliade believes that through "recollection and re enactment of the primordial event . . . 'nature' at once unveils and 'camouflages' the 'supernatural'; and this, for archaic man, constitutes the basic and unfathomable mystery of the World."[9] Dickey's mysterious, "supernatural" nature—that is, his primordial paradigm of ritual action, brilliantly camouflaged in *To the White Sea*—may not exactly match Eliade's, but it bears striking similarities. Here is Eliade's version of one paradigmatic act of creation: "The mythico-ritual theme can be reconstructed as follows: '(1) A Supernatural Being kills men (to initiate them); (2) (not understanding the meaning of this initiatory death) men avenge themselves by slaying him; (3) but afterward they institute secret ceremonies related to this primordial drama; (4) the Supernatural Being is made present at these ceremonies through an image or sacred object supposed to represent his body or his voice.' "[10]

Whether in the basic Christian narrative of Christ's death, resurrection, and ascension or in the Near Eastern myth of the Egyptian god Osiris' death, mutilation, and reconstitution, this archetype has been cast and recast over centuries in a vast array of oral and literary cultures. By imitating rather than copying (to use Aristotle's classic distinction) this sacred paradigm, Dickey re-creates a mythological cosmos in which his writing is not static subservience to an archetype. Instead, enabled by myth, Dickey employs his ritual action to transcend the genre of the war story while retaining its dramatic intensity, in a creative endeavor that, to use Eliade's words, is "constantly opening new perspectives to his inventiveness." Dickey's new, ritualized war story thus provides him access to a "supernature" that is not a paeon to human atrocity but, rather, an intensely effective, poetic re-individuation of the ancient cycle of life, death, and renewal-through-death. Such accounts are, as Eliade notes, not morbid but energizing and liberating: "The imitation of paradigmatic acts . . . forces man to transcend his limitations, obliges him to take his place with the Gods and the mythical Heroes so that he can perform their deeds. Directly or indirectly, myth 'elevates' man."[11]

In conclusion, we may observe, as many critics have, that James Dickey has been working in a mythopoeic mode of rebirth and renewal since the very beginnings of his career in the late 1950s. These lines from his first book of poems, *Into the Stone,* published in 1960, vividly signal this early (and current) interest, and they may well stand as a motto for his entire literary enterprise: "elsewhere I have dreamed of my birth, / And come from my death as I dreamed" (*Poems 1957–1967,* 47). No better summary of Dickey's struggle for literary wings, wings that soar brilliantly so often in a mythopoeic mode, may be found than in these poignant words from Ernst Cassirer which conclude his book *Language and Myth.* In this passage Cassirer underscores many of the major values exhibited by Dickey's own commitment to myth and, thus, central reasons for our continuing interest in Dickey's work, both in his poetry and his prose:

> Lyric poetry is not only rooted in mythic motives as its beginning, but keeps its connection with myth even in its highest and purest products. . . . The world of poetry stands apart . . . as a world of illusion and fantasy—but it is just in this mode of illusion that the realm of pure feeling can find utterance, and can therewith attain its full and concrete actualization. Word and mythic image, which once confronted the human mind as hard realistic powers, have now cast off all reality and effectuality; they have become a light, bright ether in which the spirit can move without let or hindrance. This liberation is achieved not because the mind throws aside the sensuous forms of word and image, but in that it uses them both as organs of its own, and thereby recognizes them for what they really are: forms of its own self-revelation.[12]

The history of critical response to James Dickey has also been a struggle for wings. Now in its fourth decade, this response has been, at times, an obsessive struggle of opposites, ranging from high praise to scathing, personal attack that seems to have little to do with his writing. The selections in this book are arranged chronologically to highlight major moments in Dickey's career, including both positive and negative assessments. If Louis Untermeyer thinks that Dickey's *Poems 1957–1967* is "the outstanding collection of one man's poems to appear in this decade," Harry Morris believes that Dickey's use of poetic form in the same book is marked by "incredibly inept management." If William C. Strange believes that Dickey's *Buckdancer's Choice* "displays a breadth of concern and a balance of energies that are notable in themselves," Robert Peters charges that Dickey's "poems . . . generate weakly, . . . plodding along, . . . maddeningly self indulgent" and are based in "sentimentality." Just as issues in law courts are defined by the clash of opposite points of view, these critical struggles, juxtaposed here in the section of reviews, will better help to define what is at stake in Dickey and, ultimately, to let the reader make the final decision about his work.

Another purpose of this book is to offer a focus expanded beyond traditional literary criticism to include that of performance art. Consequently, four essays or interviews deal with ways in which other art forms—music, film, and theater—have discussed Dickey's literary work. Janet Larsen McHughes describes how Dickey's poem "Sleeping Out at Easter" was performed as an orchestral piece. Director John Gallogly and actress Bridget Hanley discuss in considerable detail the long and laborious process of producing "May Day Sermon" for the theater. R. Barton Palmer comments astutely on the differences between the novel *Deliverance* and the film version, directed by John Boorman. Harold Schechter reads *Deliverance* the novel from a psychological point of view, a perspective that is also relevant to one's emotional experience of the movie. Ronald Baughman's article is the best reading now available on Dickey's war poetry and experience. Laurence Lieberman's analysis of "Madness" is the first article-length analysis of this poem, while Patricia Laurence's important, seminal treatment of *Puella* deals with one of Dickey's most neglected books. Dave Smith presents an outstanding overview of the development of Dickey's poetry and assesses his place in southern letters.

Except for Monroe Spears's essay on Dickey as "celestial navigator," none of the other pieces has been collected. All of them are major treatments of Dickey's work, and many are extremely difficult to locate. Neither interview with James Dickey or with John Gallogly and Bridget Hanley, has appeared in print. The University of South Carolina Press, under the direction of Catherine Fry, is to be commended for making these central studies accessible in one volume.

NOTES

1. James Dickey, "Moon Flock," *The Eagle's Mile* (Hanover, N.H.: University Press of New England, 1990), 45; hereafter cited parenthetically in the text.

2. James Dickey, "Symbol and Image in the Shorter Poems of Herman Melville" (Master's thesis, Vanderbilt University, 1950), 56; hereafter cited parenthetically in the text.

3. In fact, we may read *To the White Sea* (New York: Houghton Mifflin, 1993) as a savage commentary and qualification by Dickey of his own dreamy mysticism, just as Melville offers this realistic, if not truculent, commentary on a beneficent Emersonian transcendentalism that does not fully appreciate the lethal depths below the diaphanous surfaces of nature:

> Lulled into such an opium-like listlessness of vacant, unconscious revery is this absent-minded youth by the bleeding cadence of waves with thoughts, that at last he loses his identity; takes the mystic ocean at his feet for the visible image of that deep, blue, bottomless soul, pervading mankind and nature, and every strange, half-seen, gliding beautiful thing that eludes him; every dimly discovered, uprising fin of some discernable form, seems to him the embodiment of those elusive thoughts that only people the soul by continually flitting through it . . . But while this sleep, this dream is on ye, move your foot or hand an inch; slip your hold at all; and your identity comes back in horror. Over Descartian

vortices you hover. And perhaps, at mid-day, in the fairest weather, with one half-throttled shriek you drop through that transparent air into the summer sea, no more to rise forever. Heed it well, ye Pantheists!

(Cited by F. O. Matthiesson, *American Renaissance: Art and Expression in the Age of Emerson and Whitman* [New York: Oxford University Press, 1941], 405)

4. James Dickey, "Reincarnation II," *Poems 1957–1967* (Middletown, Conn.: Wesleyan University Press, 1967); hereafter cited parenthetically in the text. "—the white thing was so white, its wings / so wide, and in those forever exiled waters" (243). In his master's thesis Dickey also cites Melville on the whiteness of the albatross from *Moby-Dick:*

Bethink thee of the albatross, whence come those clouds
of spiritual wonderment and pale dread, in which that white phantom
sails in all imaginations? Not Coleridge first threw that spell;
but God's great, unflattering laureate, Nature.

(Qtd. in "Symbol and Image," 62)

5. Regarding Muldrow's howling on the train, one recalls that in 1975 Dickey wrote a script for the television production of Jack London's novel *The Call of the Wild,* produced by Charles Fries in 1976. On a similar topic Dickey once stated, "The reversion, that's something I've always liked, the business of an animal, an *animal,* that is partially civilized and domesticated going back, reverting" (qtd. in Ronald Baughman, *The Voiced Connections of James Dickey: Interviews and Conversations* [Columbia: University of South Carolina Press, 1989], 108).

6. Mircea Eliade, *Myth and Reality* (New York: Harper and Row, 1963), 143.

7. Lucretius, *The Nature of the Universe,* trans. R. E. Latham (Baltimore: Penguin, 1951). Dickey quotes Lucretius:

This fire was made by nature, and refined
More than all other fires, with particles
Diminutive, quick, and irresistible,
For lightning bolts go through the walls of houses
As voices do, or noise; they go through rocks,
Through bronze, they can fuse bronze and gold together
In a split second; wine evaporates
Under their force from bowls or jars which show
Never a crack; and this occurs because
The heat is so intense it opens up
All of the pores, and, boiling through, it melts
The motes of wine, dissolving them in ways
The sun could not accomplish in a lifetime,
So burning is this force, this flash, this fire.

8. Ibid., 86, 89.

9. Eliade, *Myth and Reality,* 139, 142.

10. Ibid., 103. Each of these points corresponds in some sense to Dickey's novel, and together they could themselves be the basis of an article-length study. For now we may briefly take each point. First, although Muldrow is not identified as a god, he falls from the sky and possesses extraordinary powers of survival, vastly exceeding those of

his antagonists. Second, "men avenge themselves by slaying him" in the extremely powerful final section of *To the White Sea,* especially in the concluding paragraph, in which the soldiers' bullets go through Muldrow in a "red wall." Third, the "ceremony" of "this primordial drama" is nothing less than the entire stylized action of Dickey's novel. Finally, the "Supernatural Being . . . made present at" this ceremony "through an image or sacred object" is Dickey's extraordinary invention of Muldrow's strangely spiritual and disembodied voice, a voice that relentlessly drives forward the author's sacred story.

    11. Ibid., 141, 145.

    12. Ernst Cassirer, *Language and Myth,* trans. Susanne K. Langer (New York: Dover, 1946), 99.

REFERENCES

Baughman, Ronald, ed. *The Voiced Connections of James Dickey: Interviews and Conversations.* Columbia: University of South Carolina Press, 1989.

Cassirer, Ernst. *Language and Myth.* Trans. Susanne K. Langer. New York: Dover, 1946.

Dickey, James. *The Eagle's Mile.* Hanover, N.H.: University Press of New England, 1990.

———. *Poems 1957–1967.* Middletown, Conn.: Wesleyan University Press, 1967.

———. "Symbol and Image in the Shorter Poems of Herman Melville." Master's thesis. Vanderbilt University, 1950.

———. *To the White Sea.* Boston: Houghton Mifflin, 1993.

Eliade, Mircea. *Myth and Reality.* New York: Harper and Row, 1963.

Lucretius. *The Nature of the Universe.* Trans. R. E. Latham. Baltimore: Penguin, 1951.

Matthiessen, F. O. *American Renaissance: Art and Expression in the Age of Emerson and Whitman.* New York: Oxford University Press, 1941.

REVIEWS

Things, Voices, Minds

A review of *Drowning with Others* by James Dickey

THOM GUNN

"The subject of the vision [is] . . . the rhythm of the universe, in which death
and violence are as important a part as their opposites."

In spite of his distrust of concepts and his concentration on the physical,
James Dickey can be connected in scarcely any way with [William Carlos]
Williams. *Drowning with Others* reminded me once or twice, on the contrary,
of such fantasists as Paul Klee and Jean Cocteau. Unlike as he is to them in
temperament, his effects are sometimes similar to theirs, in that he builds
fantasy on a basis of solid physical detail. "The Heaven of Animals" could be
the title of a picture by Klee, for example, and such lines as "My green, graceful
bones fill the air / With sleeping birds" form a Klee-like image, while the melt-
ing of human figures with forms chalked on a blackboard (in "Between Two
Prisoners") is similar to the semi-hallucinatory devices in Cocteau's movies.

His is, by choice, an almost entirely sensuous imagination. On the first
page of the collection occurs this description of a lifeguard swimming under
water searching for a body.

> Like a man who explores his death
> By the pulling of his slow-moving shoulders,
> I hung head down in the cold,
> Wide-eyed, contained, and alone
> Among the weeds,
>
> And my fingertips turned into stone
> From clutching immovable blackness.

The passage pivots on the fourth line, but the rest supports it with the strength
of accurately evoked sensation. There are many such passages in the book:
description charged with feeling, the words sharp, precise, and hard.

If the basis of fantasy is here firmer and more muscular than it is in Klee

An excerpt from "Things, Voices, Minds," originally published in the *Yale Review* 52 (October
1962): 129–38. Reprinted by permission.

or Cocteau, the nature of the fantasy is different also. Dickey's is an effort to make fantasy meaningful, to turn it into vision. The subject of the vision could be very loosely described as the rhythm of the universe, in which death and violence are as important a part as their opposites. The image of the hunter, whether human or animal, recurs frequently. And the basic vision is maybe of participation in this rhythm, a participation which involves a simultaneous loss of identity and a keen awareness of the total process. In fact, Dickey implies that the awareness results from the loss. It will be seen not only how such ideas connect with his dependence on images but also with what other writers of the past he is aligned. A key poem is "The Heaven of Animals," which is executed with a beautiful simplicity and concision and is probably the best poem in the book.

> For some of these,
> It could not be the place
> It is, without blood.
> These hunt, as they have done,
> But with claws and teeth grown perfect . . .
>
> And those that are hunted
> Know this as their life,
> Their reward: to walk
> Under such trees in full knowledge
> Of what is in glory above them,
> And to feel no fear,
> But acceptance, compliance.
> Fulfilling themselves without pain
>
> At the cycle's center,
> They tremble, they walk
> Under the tree,
> They fall, they are torn,
> They rise, they walk again.

It is an almost feudal vision of order: the hunted are as satisfied with their place in creation as the hunters; they are part of "the cycle." Yet the poem is executed with the tenderness of conviction, and one willingly suspends one's disbelief.

There are two weaknesses to this collection. The more serious is that the meter, as in the first quoted passage but not in the second, is almost consistently anapestic tetrameter. Dickey often handles it astonishingly well, but it is a limiting and monotonous meter at best, and I am unable to see why he considers it so attractive. The other weakness arises from his distrust of conceptual language: he makes something of a fetish of images (images are, after all, merely a rhetorical device), and at times one senses that an idea that occurred to Dickey in abstract terms is being *translated,* too deliberately, into images.

The effect in such cases is of indirection, almost of preciosity. Moreover, the images sometimes accumulate too rapidly, and the result of such rapidity is that the accumulation tends to lack meaning, as in much of the lengthy "Dover: Believing in Kings."

It would be a mistake to make too much of the resemblances between Levertov, Creeley, and Dickey, but it seems as if their attitude to style results from an attitude to life, from their trust in "a wise passiveness."

To Dream, to Remember:
James Dickey's *Buckdancer's Choice*

WILLIAM C. STRANGE

"James Dickey's most recent book . . . displays a breadth of concern
and a balance of energies that are notable in themselves and
full of promise for the future."

D ream, memory, and poem are an ancient knot in a web of tempting corre-
spondencies: image and event, possibility and necessity, wish and com-
mandment, future and past. At one time or another and in various measure,
all of these pairs have been used to explain that tense presence which is a
poem, and they are still useful, permitting one to describe handily the tendency
of modern poetry as a shift from memory and its coordinates to dream. Of
course, there are exceptions. Old Ovid seems a poet of the dream, while David
Jones clearly writes for us out of a remarkable memory. Still, our time is distinguished by poet-theorists such as André Breton, who talks of *"l'homme, ce
rêveur définitif,"* and we support with our prizes the *Seventy-Seven Dream Songs*
of John Berryman. And when the drift of Western poetry is seen in large perspective, as the pitch of its weight slips from heroic to lyric, then its direction
is unmistakable. The Greeks called memory the mother of poetry; we moderns
know a deep well of the unremembered where poetry and dreams are born.

James Dickey's most recent book, *Buckdancer's Choice,* stands out sharply
in this context as a collection of modern poems in which one can feel both the
lure of dream and the thrust of memory. In single poems and in the ordering
of the whole, it displays a breadth of concern and a balance of energies that are
notable in themselves and full of promise for the future.

Most simply, *Buckdancer's Choice* can be sorted into one set of recognizably
modern poems that are dreams in fact or in technique and another set of poems
that are "remembered" rather than dreamed. Indeed, this division is so much
a part of this book that quite often a poem from one category will be paired off
with a poem from the other. "Fathers and Sons," for example, consists of two
poems printed together: the first describes a boy asleep and dreaming while his

Originally published in the *Northwest Review* 7 (Fall–Winter 1965–1966): 33–42. Reprinted by
permission.

father dies, and the second a father haunted by his memories of a dead son. Other poems may not be so explicitly joined, but they, too, will draw together to enforce a balance between timeless dream and time remembered. "Pursuit from Under" and "Sled Burial, Dream Ceremony" or "Faces Seen Once" and "The Common Grave" cooperate in this way. However, the most striking moments in the dialectic occur when these opposites meet within one large poem such as "The Firebombing" or within a short and remarkably compressed piece like "The War Wound." One comes to read *Buckdancer's Choice* for such compounding poems as these, but the collection is best met in its simples.

Of the two categories, Dickey's dream poems are by far the less impressive. Sometimes they are too dependent upon other poems, even upon poems from other collections. "Sled Burial, Dream Ceremony" is scarcely intelligible without "Pursuit from Under," and "Fox Blood" drives us all the way back to "Listening to Foxhounds" and "A Dog Sleeping on my Feet" in Dickey's second book, *Drowning with Others*. More often, these poems fail to impress because we know their moves too well. Dreaming transformations of men into appropriate beasts is old hat, though Dickey can vary his tired totems effectively, reporting the metamorphosis as fact when it suits him, as in "Reincarnation," or using it boldly in "Gamecock" to stage a conceit. His style, too, is masterful, reaching with suitable ease to the brittle clarity of nightmare. And his bag of dream tricks contains all the turns of a neo-Freudian rhetoric: condensation, displacement, reversal, etc. Indeed, the more clinical these poems are, the more effective they seem to be. Witness the depth and power of Dickey's conception in "Them, Crying," where compulsion is his subject. In something less than eighty lines he brings to life a truckdriver, "unmarried, unchildlike, / Half-bearded and foul-mouthed," who is drawn irresistibly to the children's ward of a large hospital by the sound of children crying *within him*. Or witness the perfectly realized counterpoint of hallucination and reality in Dickey's presentation of a voyeur in "The Fiend."

> He has learned what a plant is like
> When it moves near a human habitation   moving
>   closer the later it is
> Unfurling its leaves near bedrooms   still keeping
>   its wilderness life
> Twigs covering his body with only one way out   for
>   his eyes into inner light
> Of a chosen window. . . .

The dreams of damaged minds seldom have been rendered better that this. But the real surprise is to find that Dickey can make of these clinical materials poems that are gracious and charming. Such qualities are not common in those whose work is the dream, be they poets or psychoanalysts, and they have been too rare in Dickey's earlier verse. But he broke through with "Cherrylog Road" in his last collection, *Helmets,* and he breaks through in this book with a poem such as "The Celebration."

This last is as clinical a dream poem as one could wish for. Surely, no tenets are more basic to the art of psychoanalysis than these: We all carry within us a record, written in scars, of the inevitable frustrations met by our growing appetites. Of necessity, these frustrations are usually sexual and often involve our parents. Adjustment, maturity, wisdom, or whatever you choose to call the achievement of a sound life, depends in part upon our becoming aware of past pain and its effects in the present, and this past is recovered most easily through the symbols that we dream. Now, Dickey could have tailored "The Celebration" to these propositions. In it the poet describes himself moving through symbols to a quite literal anamnesis of his parents as lovers and then back from this vision of the primal scene to a new sense of himself and his responsibilities in the present. What the poet learns, he feels along the body more than knows—"[I] stepped upon sparking shocks / Of recognition when I saw my feet . . . knowing them given"—but he does try to state what he has recognized as clearly and as directly as he can. He talks of learning to understand

> the whirling impulse
> From which I had been born,
> The great gift of shaken lights,
> The being wholly lifted with another,
> All this having all and nothing
> To do with me.

The final lines of the poem are even more explicit in pointing out the moral of all this seeing: the poet sees and becomes as a consequence "a kind of loving, / A mortal, a dutiful son." It is hard to conceive of a poem more properly psychoanalytic in its recognitions and consequent moralizings.

The details which earn this recognition, making the "whirling impulse" known and truly told within the poem, also are heavy with the modern craft of dreams. In its first lines the poem looks like a phantasmagoria of lust:

> All wheels; a man breathed fire,
> Exhaling like a blowtorch down the road
> And burnt the stripper's gown
> Above her moving-barely feet.
> A condemned train climbed from the earth
> Up stilted nightlights zooming in a track.
> I ambled along in that crowd . . .

Most of us have met such carnal nightmares before, in the *Commedia* or in *The Rape of the Lock,* but this one is distinctly modern. More savage than Pope's, more narrowly psychological than Dante's, this fantasy is twin to the cases reported in Freud's *The Interpretation of Dreams* or to George Grosz's drawings of Berlin. Reason can stumble through this queer pastiche but is sent spinning when we find that all this fantasy is simple fact. The blowtorch-man is a fire-eater in a sideshow, the stripper just that, the condemned train a roller-coaster, and the crowded scene, Lakewood Midway at carnival time. With some care Dickey has led us into his poem, forcing us to see both the literal and the figurative dimensions of its sense, refusing to let us simplify.

In the second stanza Dickey quickly reasserts the figurativeness of the carnival setting. Just in case his realistic explanation of the hallucinatory first stanza may have been too surprising and too distracting, he makes another ride, the dodgem cars, explicitly figurative by using them as one term of a simile: "each in his vehicle half / In control, half-helplessly power-mad / As was in the traffic that brought him." After this reminder, the poem need not be so explicit with its images; Dickey has prepared us for the symbols that he must use. In the literal scene, the poet is walking quietly and alone in the carnival crowd when he sees with surprise that his mother and father are there, "he leaning / On a dog-chewed cane, she wrapped to the nose / In the fur of exhausted weasels." Age and sexuality are finely caught here as the phallic symbols of cane and wrap are modified by their worn, literal substance. More than anything else, it is precisely this shadow of sexual energy in his parents that surprises the poet. They are so old. What can they celebrate? "I believed them buried [that verb is no accident] miles back / In the country, in the faint sleep / Of the old, and had not thought to be / On this of all nights compelled / To follow where they led. . . ."

In the stanza which follows, similar details reinforce this effect of tired fact scarcely covering powerful fancy. His mother carries a teddy bear that is as insistently symbolic as a weasel wrap and dog-chewed cane; she holds it as if it were a child, and it was won for her "on the waning whip" of his father's right arm. The "crippled Stetson" which his father wears may not be so suggestive, except in its bobbing movement, but even here one could cite a section of Freud's dream book headed simply "A Hat as a Symbol of a Man (or of Male Genitals)." The poem's central image, of the old couple riding on a ferris wheel, needs no such footnoting:

>   They laughed;
>   She clung to him; then suddenly
>   The Wheel of wheels was turning
>   The colored night around.
>   They climbed aboard. My God, they rose
>   Above me, stopped themselves, and swayed
>   Fifty feet up; he pointed
>   With his toothed cane, and took in
>   The whole Midway till they dropped,
>   Came down, went from me, came and went
>   Faster and faster, going up backward,
>   Cresting, out-topping, falling roundly.

"The Wheel of wheels" is a perfectly apt description of a ferris wheel, but here it is also an intensive and a symbol. The cane, too, has become ambiguous with a new-old strength, for *toothed* may still mean "dog-chewed," but it suggests "possessing teeth." And all of the verbs that move these lines carry into them a phallic significance that nearly obliterates their letter. The whole passage is rich with a sense that scarcely requires glossing, even though it is this large image that elicits from the poet those attempts at direct statement our analysis began with.

But working our way up to these statements as the poem meant us to, we find that the lesson read is something more than a moral tag at its close. Recognition sparks within and without this poem, for "The Celebration" is peculiarly reflexive. Its images know themselves as they would be known, and the "whirling impulse" this poet sees he teaches us to see, with all the fervent pragmatism of a revivalist. "Believers, I have seen / The wheel in the middle of the air. . . ." Though such language is borrowed from an old faith and testament, with some wit it calls a new generation of dreamers back to the constant task of prophecy: in omens find a responsible joy, and let it find you.

> Believers, I have seen
> The wheel in the middle of the air
> Where old age rises and laughs,
> And on Lakewood Midway became
> In five strides a kind of loving,
> A mortal, a dutiful son.

With this poem and others like it, Dickey seems to be saying to his contemporaries, "Look, I can do it too," and also "Look, how narrow this thing that we have done." "The Celebration" is a first rate product of our time's craft of dreams, but it is also ours in ways that are not so admirable: in the passivity and in the privacy of its vision. Dreams happen to a person, and if you live in and for them, you wait and are paid for your waiting in coin of no man's realm. Clearly, a balanced art demands visions that one chooses as well as those that one is chosen by, and visions *of more than one's self*. Poetry, at least, should be dreams that one can trade in. Concern with the trap of solipsism, that Wordsworth and Sartre both know so well, and concern for a poetry that is performance as well as visitation run throughout *Buckdancer's Choice*. One finds it in certain implications of "The Celebration" 's moral close: in seeing others oblivious of me, I see myself and my responsibilities, my "duty." One finds it in the way that this small book is crammed with the full reality of other persons: generations of family, friends, an old teacher with a bad heart, a truck driver drowning in tenderness, a voyeur, a slaveowner, enemies from an old war, and victims. One finds it in Dickey's appetite for

> those things that, once
> Established, cannot be changed by angels,

> Devils, lightning, ice, or indifference:
> Identities! Identities!

in a context in which these "Identities" are both the mathematics that Mangham teaches and the man that he is as the poet's remembering "establishes" him. One finds it, conversely, in Dickey's reaction to "an angel's too-realized / Unbearable memory-less face." One finds it, particularly, in his sense of memory as counterweight to dream, public and willed, and in such poems as "Buckdancer's Choice."

Intended or not, the use of this poem as title piece flaunts such a book as John Berryman's *Seventy-Seven Dream Songs,* for "Buckdancer's Choice" is a song, too, but not a dream song. It is an old song that minstrels once danced to, shuffling and flapping their arms like stunted wings, and the poem remembers it as it was performed. The poem begins by recalling the poet's mother, "dying of breathless angina" but finding breath and life of a sort in whistling to herself "the thousand variations" of this one song. It also remembers the poet as a boy who "crept close to the wall / Sock-footed, to hear the sounds alter, / Her tongue like a mockingbird's beak / Through stratum after stratum of a tone. . . ." Behind this spot of time lies another evoked by it: the house in which the boy listens is "barnlike, theatrelike," he is "sock-footed," and his mother's whistle calls up in him "a sight like a one-man band, / Freed black, with cymbals at heel, / An ex-slave who thrivingly danced / To the ring of his own clashing light. . . ." Together, these two moments of time past form a metaphor of sorts whose point is most immediately that time does pass. "For years, they have all been dying / Out, the classic buck-and-wing men / Of traveling minstrel shows; / With them also an old woman / Was dying of breathless angina. . . ."

But there are three faces to this metaphor—the minstrel's, the mother's, and the boy's—and only the first two are stained by death. The song speaks for each of them in different ways, proclaiming

> what choices there are
> For the last dancers of their kind,
> For ill women and for all slaves
> Of death, and children enchanted at walls
> With a brass-beating glow underfoot,
> Not dancing but nearly risen
> Through barnlike, theatrelike houses
> On the wings of the buck and wing.

Choices and *risen* are the most difficult terms in this last and fullest statement of the metaphor. Clearly, they are meant to give the image its final shape by opposing the dying mother and the last dancer to the boy who does not die and, apparently, to the poet who remembers him with this poem. The alignment is clear, if not its sense. Why *choices?*

To choose is to be free, and the buckdancer is a freed slave who celebrates his freedom by dancing out "The thousand variations of one song," thriving all the while in the choices of his dance. His dying art remembered frees the woman who is slave to the nearness of her death, for his song is both a literal artifact making it possible for her to partake of a joy her dying body denies her and a kind of emblematic definition of its own use. Joy is the one song, but she simply cannot identify with it; rather, she must achieve her own identity as a kind of thousand-and-first variation of it. Art's long memory has saved for her the fact of joy, but she must join with it, finding herself in her own performance of this joy as a dancer finds identity in the strict measure of his dance or as variations find themselves in a sounding theme.

The boy and the poet who remembers him complete the literal scene by making something nearly heroic out of the invalid's ultimate lyricism. In listening to his mother "warbling all day to herself," the boy reverses the movement from minstrel show to muffled sickroom by transforming the house into a kind of theatre, while the poet remembering this three-personed song in his poem restores it entirely to the public domain so that we, too, may use it. Perhaps this is one justification for the poem's claim that the vanishing dancer and the dying woman are countered by a "risen" boy: the song she appropriates—and what could be more private than the "prone music" of an invalid's whistle?—he takes back for himself and in time performs, that others may for the moment find themselves, and company, in "Buckdancer's Choice."

But *risen* makes figurative sense as well as literal, as it must when it involves even such mimic wings as the buckdancer's elbows suggest. At first glance *risen* looks like more of that southern evangelical baroque that is such an engaging quality of Dickey's imagination, but here I think the religious implications are more precise and more serious. *Risen* is but the end of something that has been building from the first lines of the poem. For example, why should his mother's whistle have split the air into just "nine levels"? Is the number meant to remind us of the nine muses or of the nine heavens through which Dante rose as the blessed were manifest to him under the conditions of space and time? When this same fracted air, in *terza senza rima,* is offered as proving "some gift of tongues of the whistler," the reference is more certainly religious and more illuminating.

Speaking in tongues is described several times in the New Testament. In Acts St. Peter defends the authenticity of the experience in terms which could suggest Dickey's poem: "your sons and daughters shall prophesy, / And your young men shall see visions, / And your old men shall dream dreams" (2:17). However, St. Paul's discussion of the gift of tongues seems more relevant to a reading of Dickey's poem. In I Corinthians 14, he develops at some length the distinction between tongues and prophecy that St. Peter hints at with his young prophets and aged dreamers. According to St. Paul, the man with the gift of tongues speaks in mysteries to his God; his spirit prays, but his understanding is not fruitful unless his words are interpreted for him and for others.

To the unbelievers, speaking in tongues will seem testimony only of madness in the speaker. (In this context, the address "Believers, I have seen . . ." at the close of the "The Celebration" acquires further ironic bite.) Describing his mother's whistle as a gift of tongues, Dickey draws heavily upon St. Paul's conception and even language, for St. Paul calls this a "speaking into the air" and expands his claim with a series of musical metaphors. More important, Dickey's reference seems to involve St. Paul's valuation of the experience: speaking in tongues is a valid gift of the spirit, but the gift of prophecy is much greater. The prophet is a tuned pipe and harp, a certain trumpet; he speaks to all for the sake of all. He is a bearer of public visions. If the old woman has received the gift of tongues, her son hopes for the gift of tuned speech, for the gift of prophecy; and in time he receives it, as this poem testifies most powerfully.

No wonder, then, that Dickey chooses "Buckdancer's Choice" as the title piece for this collection: it is a perfect emblem of the art he would achieve. Modern poetry has been content too long with an invalid's private song. Dickey is reaching once more for the time that was and the time that is to be. He is reaching for prophecy.

Dickey's verbal skills were always considerable; they have grown more sure. In his earlier books the fluent movement of his verse was overwhelmed at times by a surge of anapests, and diction was marred by conventional insincerities. Those poems had a brother dying "ablaze with the meaning of typhoid" and fell too often into the cadence of "O grasses and fence wire of glory / That have been burned like a coral with depth. . . ." Now, such cadences are modulated by carefully indicated pauses within the line: "He has only to pass by a tree   moodily walking head down. . . ." and his familiar elegiac and meditative vocabulary includes new tones, like the impeccable gaucherie of "Homeowners unite. / All families lie together, though some are burned alive. / The others try to feel / For them. Some can, it is often said." Still, these are not the clearest measure of Dickey's growth or of his achievement in this new book. Poems of real substance may be recognized by what they do to our commonplaces about poetry, not canceling them out but making them more true than they were before. We have known for a long time that the modern poet seeks in "la plénitude du grand songe" for "memorable speech." The virtue of *Buckdancer's Choice* is to insist that the deepest dreams belong to languages, not to men, and that the best poetry is speech remembering.

The Suspect in Criticism

A review of *The Suspect in Poetry* and *Helmets* by James Dickey

LEWIS TURCO

"Mr. Dickey may be a fuzzy-headed philosopher, but he is no critic at all."

I opened the door of the gallery and beheld the shattered idols lying fallen in their legions. There, in frosty ruins, lay the Winters of our discontent: Donald Drummond, an icicle piercing his snowy breast; Ellen Kay, her remains caught in a gigantic snowball. In one corner, trampled into a mob of howling shards, was Allen Ginsberg, beyond the aid of any gluepot. Thom Gunn's bust, clad in the rags of what had once been an impeccably tailored black leather jacket, took up another corner. And about the room lay scattered the many-splendored beads and gewgaws that had once encrusted the Aztec statue of Ned O'Gorman. There were others: Robert Mezey, Charles Olson, Anne Sexton, Philip Booth . . .

The choices of broken statues, it seemed to me, were often fairly good ones. But why, *why* these? What sensibility or system had informed this destruction? Baffled, I read on. And then, as though I had opened a secret door . . . Mr. Dickey *did* have a system.

In the section entitled "The Grove Press New American Poets (1960)" Mr. Dickey sets up his criteria:

> There are four or five main ways of reacting to poems, and they all matter. In ascending order of importance they are (a) "This probably isn't so, and even if it were I couldn't care less," (b) "This may be true enough as far as it goes, but, well . . . so what?" (c) "This is true, or at least convincing, and therefore I respond to it differently than I do to poems in the first two categories," and (d) "This is true with a kind of truth at which I could never have arrived by myself, but its truth is better than the one I had believed." The first two classifications are useful because they are what we feel about bad poems, very bad ones in (a) and half-bad or unsuccessfully realized ones in (b). In (c) are most of the poems

Originally published in the *Mad River Review* I (Spring–Summer 1965): 81–85. Reprinted by permission of the author and Mathom Press Enterprises, Oswego, NY 13126. All rights reserved.

we like well enough to call "good" in reviews and to which we may want to return occasionally, and in (d) are those we continue to call great when conversing only with ourselves, and which we would hope to die hearing or remembering. Almost all writers of verse aspire simply to reside in (c), and many a solid reputation— such as that of Robert Graves—has been founded on just such a semi-permanent residence, which is by no means as easy of attainment as I may make it seem. Even those whom we call "major" poets catch only a few glimpses of the world I have designated (d), or at most stand for a handful of moments in that bewildering light, in the certainty that they are bringing about an entirely new kind of human communication compounded of about equal parts of the commonality of all mankind and the unique particularity of the poet's vision and his language. The achievement of even a small but steadily authentic flame is immensely difficult, as we all know, and requires, as well as a great deal of luck, a lifelong attention to those means by which we might best hope to feed it.

It seems, on first glance, that these are reasonable assumptions. But we who live in a romantic age tend often to accept a seemingly reasonable statement as *in fact* reasonable. Let us, then, pretend that we suspect Mr. Dickey's reasoning and question his statements and their implications.

Let us take, first, the "reaction" which Mr. Dickey maintains is the best reaction we can have to a poem: "(d) 'This is true with a kind of truth at which I could never have arrived by myself, but its truth is better than the one I had believed.' "

I propose to begin our examination with a definition of the word *reaction* which, according to Merriam-Webster, means "the act or process or an instance of reacting." Since the dictionary uses the verbal in its definition of the noun, we shall have to refer to the verb *react,* which means, "1. to exert a reciprocal or counteracting force or influence—often used with *on* or *upon;* 2: to respond to a stimulus; 3: to act in opposition to a force or influence— usually used with *against;* 4: to move or tend in a reverse direction; 5: to undergo chemical reaction."

Since the only one of these definitions which makes any sense if applied to Mr. Dickey's statement is "2: to respond (response) to a stimulus," let us assume that that is what he meant.

We now have another word to define—*stimulus:* "1: something that rouses or incites to activity." We are thus, I take it, if we are to react to a poem, to *respond to . . . something that rouses or incites to activity.* If we can agree with these definitions, it follows that what Mr. Dickey describes as a "reaction" is not a reaction at all. Rather, I would suggest, it is a mental process of some kind, a process which in some way evaluates something that Mr. Dickey calls "truth."

Now, this "truth"—what is it? Again, looking at Mr. Dickey's statements about poetry, we discover that this is another indefinite word. In his description (a) of a "reaction," the implicit relationship of "truth" is with "This probably isn't so, but I couldn't care less." Unless I am confused, "This probably isn't so" is a reference to a fact of some kind: "A thing is *so*, or it isn't *so*" might be a reasonable, if fuzzy, synonym for "fact and non-fact."

Therefore, as nearly as it is possible to determine, in Mr. Dickey's equation truth *equals* fact.

If we have this much settled, we can go on to step (b) in Mr. Dickey's ascending hierarchy of "reactions" to poems: "This may be true enough as far as it goes, but, well . . . so what?"

Here the relationship of "truth" is again with fact ("true enough," i.e., you've got the facts straight, maybe), but there is something further: ". . . so what?" This last pseudorhetorical sarcasm also has a relationship with the second half of (a): ". . . I couldn't care less." Both imply a value judgment of some kind, dependent on the "facts." The implication is that the "facts" in both cases are trivial.

In "reaction" (c) we are to assume we may "respond" in this way: "This is true, or at least convincing. . . ." Here the implication is that *maybe* the poet has his facts straight, but even if he hasn't, at least he's made us believe he has. This "reaction," it appears to me, is suspect. In (b) the poet as a minimum had his data in order, trivial though they may have been. Thus, he had at least been "truthful." Now, in (d), he may or may not be truthful (Mr. Dickey evidently can't tell which), but at least Mr. Dickey is "convinced," and that apparently counts for something (". . . I will respond differently . . ."), even though Mr. Dickey's "response" may be to a clever lie.

We at last arrive back at (d), the top rung in the ladder of Mr. Dickey's "responses." And we are to "respond" by evaluating the "truth" of what the poet has said. Furthermore, this "truth" is "a better one than the one [he] had believed." The first question that comes to mind is, *how can one "truth" be "better" than another?* Is the implication here that it makes no difference, as long as Mr. Dickey is "convinced" that one is better than the other? Does one "truth" supplant another? i.e., is one set of "facts" less trivial than another set? If so, how so? If the facts of the lesser "truth" are straight, may they be supplanted by a more "convincing" set of non-facts?

However, to get back to our point: we are to "respond," but our "responses" have been called into question by (c). If we cannot be sure that the poet has his "facts" straight, even though he has "convinced" us that he had; and if, as it would seem, "facts" *equal* "truth,"

1. How is it possible for us to evaluate the "truth," uncertain as we are that the "truth" is the "truth"?

2. How can we "react" by "evaluating" to begin with, since an evaluation is not a "reaction"?

To proceed, now that we have called Mr. Dickey's premises into question:

is there any further enlightenment for his argument to be found in the remainder of his statements? Perhaps so. The next major statement Mr. Dickey makes is this: "Even those whom we call "major" poets catch only a few glimpses of the world I have designated (d), or at most stand for a handful of moments in that bewildering light, in the certainty that they are bringing about an entirely new kind of human communication compounded of about [*sic*] equal parts of the commonality of all mankind and the unique particularity of the poet's vision and his language."

But, is my "response," *what bewildering light?* Furthermore, you mentioned no "world" in (d); what you mentioned was "truth." Is "truth" to equal "facts" to equal "world" to equal "bewildering light"? Or, since the authenticity of the facts has been called into question, is "truth" to equal "facts" possibly, but perhaps non-facts (depending upon the poet's ability to "convince" us) to equal a "world" based either upon facts or non-facts? And is this tantamount to "bewildering light"?

And how about that "communication" which, I suppose, is the poem itself? Can we agree that, according to Mr. Dickey's hints and glimmers of what he's talking about, a *poem* may be defined as "The communication of a world of facts or convincing non-facts"? And, since he has kindly defined "communication" for us, can we say that "A poem is a bewildering compound of *about equal parts* of the commonality of all mankind and the unique particularity of the poet's vision and his language with respect to a world of facts or convincing non-facts"?

We could, if we wished, carry this analysis through many more pages of Mr. Dickey's criticism and arrive eventually at a much more complicated, but equally absurd conclusion.

Mr. Dickey may be a fuzzy headed philosopher, but he is no critic at all. He is evidently interested in language only tangentially but with "facts," or (let's be kind) "truths," specifically. The distinct possibility exists, therefore, that he is no poet as well as no critic, for empirical observation will show that most poets' first concern is with language, as Auden has indicated, and not with "truth," which is relative and not necessarily dependent upon facts of any kind.

This seems to be something that Mr. Dickey ignores, or is unaware of—that there are many purposes which poetry may serve other than the revelation of a particular "truth."

What kind of poem might a poet write if its structure is dependent upon a theory as tortured as this one is? And do Mr. Dickey's evident limitations as a critic call into question his ability to recognize a "true" poem when he sees one? If so, ought we to listen to him at all? Ought we to let him "convince" us of anything? It just might turn out to be a world of lies.

And, sure enough, I pick up his latest book of poems. I turn page after page of darkly mysterious subterranean murmurings, of snakes and frogs and flowers bogging along mumbling runic legends into Mr. Dickey's monotonous ear: Mr. Dickey is Theodore Roethke reborn as a tame black swan. I react: I shake my head sadly.

I "react" to poetry in none of The Four Ways of Mr. Dickey, and I suspect that very few others do either. And if, because of this examination of his theories, I am accused of quibbling with words, I admit it. Mr. Dickey should learn to quibble too. That's a thing the poet does: he quibbles with words.

A Way of Seeing and Saying

A review of *Poems, 1957–1967,* by James Dickey

LOUIS UNTERMEYER

"[T]his is the poetry book of the year . . . it will prove to be the outstanding collection of one man's poems to appear in this decade."

This volume, which includes the best of four previous books and twenty-three new poems, is a most exciting collection. It presents the work of a still young, affirmative, and—why boggle at a usually misused adjective?—major poet.

James Dickey's debut was not spectacular; it was accompanied by that of two other poets in the seventh volume of *Poets of Today.* His development has been so recent and his fecundity so rapid that the appraisers and compilers have not caught up with him. Practically everything he has written has been accomplished in a ten-year span. *Into the Stone* appeared in 1960; *Drowning with Others* was published in 1962; *Helmets* in 1964; *Buckdancer's Choice* won the National Book Award in 1965. Yet he is not to be found in the voluminous *Poet's Choice* (which includes William Dickey but not James), published in 1962, or in Brinnin and Read's *The Modern Poets,* which runs to more than four hundred pages and came out in 1963, or in *Contemporary American Poetry,* issued only a few months ago.

Nevertheless, Dickey's welling power was there from the beginning. If his first book had contained nothing besides "Sleeping Out at Easter," with its assembly of terse, single declarative sentences ("All dark is now no more. / This forest is drawing a light. / All Presences change into trees. / One eye opens slowly without me. / My sight is the same as the sun's."); "The Underground Stream," with its blend of full rhymes and half-rhymes; "The Other," with its dream-compelled surrealist imagery; and "Near Darien," a strangely insinuating love poem, these pages would be sufficient evidence that a new and persuasive voice was declaring itself.

The subsequent poems revealed various advances: an almost total rejection of literary backgrounds, a scorn of poems distilled from poems, and a continual

Originally published in the *Saturday Review* 50 (6 May 1967): 31, 55. Reprinted from the *Saturday Review* 1967, SR Publications, Ltd.

remaking of firsthand happenings. The gamut of subject matter widened to include sensations roused by a son recovering in a hospital while another son waits to be born, a brother making string constructions as he lies dying of fever, a dog sleeping on the poet's feet, the sexual paintings in the ruins of a brothel in Pompeii, an invalid mother gasping for breath but recalling snatches of a minstrel song, a fantastic heaven for animals where the creatures fulfill themselves everlastingly hunting and being hunted. These subjects are vivified in a unique utterance that combines the clarity of the thing keenly observed and the shifting images of the thing remembered, a union of directness and dream. What in a clever craftsman would have been merely a device becomes a natural, compelling way of seeing and saying.

There is, for example, Dickey's use of the flashback, his simple yet subtle juxtaposition of past and present. "The Firebombing" does this incomparably. The poet, "twenty years overweight," is eating a snack in his half-paid-for pantry in the suburbs

> Where the lawn mower rests on its laurels
> Where the diet exists
> For my own good . . .
>   where the children
> Get off the bus   where the new
> Scoutmaster lives

and he remembers that twenty years ago he was a pilot, a "technical-minded stranger with my hands" dropping 300-gallon tanks filled with napalm and gasoline, destroying neighborhoods much like his own.

"The Fiend" is another remarkable accomplishment. It starts out to be a study of a voyeur, an ordinary man who is not only a Peeping Tom but a potential Jack the Ripper; beneath the surface, however, there is cumulative horror that, in its paradoxical delicacy, is devastating. At the mercy of his lust he peers at a girl beginning to undress

>   and rigor mortis
> Slithers into his pockets, making everything there—keys, pen,
> and secret love—stand up.

Detail by detail the interior drama mounts until a commonplace worried accountant, invisible and omniscient, becomes a murderous monster.

> It will be something small that sets him off:
> Perhaps a pair of lace pants on a clothesline   gradually losing
> Water to the sun   filling out in the warm light with a well-rounded
> Feminine wind as he watches   having spent so many sleepless nights
> Because of her   because of her hand, on a shade always coming down . . .

The same gathering excitement intensifies "Slave Quarters." Here the speaker tries to exorcise the guilt of his mixed blood in a climax of intellectual agony:

What do you feel when passing

Your blood beyond death
To another in secret: into
Another who takes your features   and adds
A misplaced Africa to them . . .
What happens when the sun goes down

And the white man's loins still stir
In a house of air   still draw him toward
Slave quarters? . . .
                    When you think of what
It would be like   what it has   been
What it is to look once a day
Into an only
Son's brown, waiting, wholly possessed
Amazing eyes, and not
Acknowledge, but own?

"Falling" had its origin in a newspaper item about a young stewardess who was swept to her death when the plane's emergency door suddenly sprang open. Terror is in every line of the poem, but it is horror emphasized by a distant, almost detached, feeling as the girl plunges, seeming to float,

Still neat   lipsticked   stockinged girdled by regulation   her hat
Still on   her arms and legs in no world and yet spaced also strangely
With utter placid rightness on thin air

sensing, in a void of calm, and even appreciating the quiet aspects of earth as it rises to meet her,

                        . . . seeing mortal unreachable lights far down seeing
An ultimate highway with one late priceless car probing it   arriving
In a square   town   and off her starboard arm the glitter of water catches
The moon by its one shaken   side scaled, roaming silver   My God it is
good . . .

The impact of an event, personally experienced or experienced through others, acts upon Dickey like a welcome blow. He has an immediate response to violence as if he were glad to be challenged to equal vehemence, as if he believed that men were living more and more lifelessly, dependent on mechanical things to do their work, their entertaining, and what is left of their thinking. He echoes Synge's demand for a poetry fortified with the strong things of life "to show that what is exalted or tender is not made by feeble blood." At the same time, he is conservative in religion, ambivalent about war, and skeptical of social progress. He does not attempt to do anybody any good. He is no reformer concerning anything, not even poetry. His is a voice that is passionate in its own way, reverberating yet reserved, owing nothing to any predecessor except, here and there, to Roethke, one of Dickey's few admirations.

His is, in short, a moving poetry, a poetry utterly unlike the fashionable unemotional flatness of statement. Always there is a direct confrontation with the human as well as the inhuman condition, always a new slant on the familiar, a fresh idiom that makes the image no mere feat of phrase but a provocative insight.

This is writing at once tender and firm, warmhearted and free tongued; its exuberance is endearing and may well be enduring. For me this is the poetry book of the year, and I have little doubt that it will prove to be the outstanding collection of one man's poems to appear in this decade.

A Formal View of the Poetry of Dickey . . .

HARRY MORRIS

> "In Mr. Dickey's verse I find the observation myopic . . . ; form is adhered to but so meaninglessly or inexactly as to suggest casual concern only or incredibly inept management."

Traditionally we have expected poets to develop their powers of observation, to give form to their utterance; to be concise and precise, to seek a verbal music, and to enrich the texture of their verse with the devices of rhetoric. In Mr. Dickey's verse I find the observation myopic, sometimes filmed completely over; form is adhered to but so meaninglessly or inexactly as to suggest casual concern only or incredibly inept management. In addition to what seems a total inability to achieve conciseness within a single poem, Mr. Dickey appears unable also to conclude a poem in under thirty lines. Of the 108 pieces in this volume, only seven comprise fewer than thirty lines. The majority of the poems are close to fifty lines or over. Precision in diction is of so little concern to the poet that in many cases even prepositions are employed awkwardly or improperly. With the two foregoing misdeeds, music can be at best only a tiresome jangle, harsh and out of tune. Rhetoric in our fashionable age is out at heels and many will applaud Mr. Dickey's avoidance of all the old devices, but will they clap also for the resulting threadbare fabric of the verse?

Mr. Dickey is a poet of nature; he looks at a wide range of wildlife: shark, fox, wolverine, deer, cattle, big cat at the zoo, rabbit, sheep, dog, and mostly unidentified birds. But I wish to test Mr. Dickey's observation of snakes, reptiles being among the few creatures I know anything about.

"Reincarnation (I)" presents a former county judge reborn as a rattlesnake. Mr. Dickey does not know that the rattlesnake, like all pit vipers, is viviparous, not oviparous.

> . . . disappearing into the egg buried under the sand

> And wakened to the low world being born . . .

Mr. Dickey has heard that snakes employ their tongues in sensory perception, in some manner other than to taste. The scientists, much at odds about the

---

Originally published in the *Sewanee Review* 77 (Spring 1969): 318–25. Copyright 1969 by the University of the South. Reprinted with the permission of the editor.

matter, say that snakes smell through their tongues or feel through them or do indeed, like other creatures, taste through them. None that I have ever heard or read has suggested that snakes hear through their tongues:

> With his tongue he can hear them in their concerted effort. . . .

Mr. Dickey believes that snakes can pass through the grass without a telltale wavering of blades:

> he moves through, moving nothing,
> And the grass stands as never entered.

Such skill is rarely, if ever, true of the rattlesnake. Add to this recital his error in believing that rattlesnakes rattle as a warning and that they will attack a man unprovoked.

Perhaps more a failure in logic or in preciseness than in observation is the age of Mr. Dickey's snake. Observation would come into play, however, in a person's having noted that a newborn rattlesnake is rarely twelve inches long, whereas the snake in the poem would have to be several feet:

> Still, passed through the spokes of an old wheel, on and
>   around
> The hub's furry rust in the weeds and shadows of the riverbank.

Logic fails the writer when he presents us with a mature snake, one who has already "drawn from bird eggs and thunderstruck rodents," and yet tells us that the reincarnated judge is in the "new / Life of resurrection." Would not reincarnation be as a newborn creature rather than as something already existing, already full-grown?

I know very little about other animals of which Mr. Dickey writes, but when he makes six errors of considerable magnitude on a creature I know something about, I am reluctant to accept his teachings on others.

I have condemned the writer's casual nod to the conventions of form. In his earlier work, most of his pieces may be said to be stanzaic: pattern is observed in the number of lines to the stanza. Favored stanza lengths are five and six lines per unit, although couplets, tercets, quatrains, septenaries, and octets are frequently used. But why Mr. Dickey has observed such regularity in this one matter is beyond me. Since he employs no rhyme pattern, it is not rhyme that determines the length of a stanza. Since stanza units are not thought units, image units, or sound units, these factors do not dictate the length of a stanza. In fact, there is no justification for any of his groupings. Line length, at first glance, appears regular; but on scanning we find that Mr. Dickey ignores the number of feet in any given line whenever he pleases.

In his later work, Mr. Dickey is apparently experimenting with very long lines, broken on the printed page by extra spacing to indicate pauses or rhythm groupings. He is not attempting an alliterative revival as some reviewers have suggested, for no convention of Anglo-Saxon or Middle English verse with which we are familiar is observed.

I suppose he is writing by phrases—wanting cadences that to him must be attractive—but to get cadences he employs a good many loose constructions, a weakness that leads to my next objection.

Mr. Dickey writes verse so loosely that he may do anything in it, commit any dispersal, admit any discourse, follow any digression. In "The Escape," the title of which refers to arranging burial in a plot other than the family mausoleum in Fairmount, Mr. Dickey employs twenty-one lines to describe some of the surroundings the corpse will "escape." Mr. Dickey or the "over-witty in other mens Writings" will justify these excursions as scenes of life and death not to be encountered in the county graveyard in Alabama to which the corpse escapes; even as such the tableaux are loosely written, with much unnecessary verbiage. But they do not belong in the poem at all; a finer poet would achieve a greater poignancy through symbolic correlatives, delivered in the focused materials themselves.

Illustrations of Mr. Dickey's lack of verbal precision may be taken from almost any poem (my italics):

> *Bleary* with ointments ("Sun")
>
> With a ring of *convulsive* rubber ("Adultery")
>
> With dew our *porous* home
> Is *dense,* wound up like a spring,
>
> *Which* is solid as motherlode
> At night. ("Hedge Life")

Especially are his pronouns difficult. As in the last quotation above, where the antecedent for the relative pronoun *which* is impossibly ambiguous, poem after poem employs all the different classes of pronouns—personal, possessive, demonstrative, and relative—in bewildering uncertainty; see for instance "The Wedding." So often is dedicated search a necessary labor that a reader wearies and concludes the pains have outcost the truffles. Especially distasteful is the repeated use of *you* as an indefinite pronoun.

And, finally, Mr. Dickey's avoidance of all but a few of the devices of rhetoric, his eschewal of most of those things that would give density to his verse—and herein most especially symbolic action—leave his work so thin that a reader is left unsatisfied, and one who endures the full three hundred pages of *Poems 1957–1967* suffers a dulling tedium through which poetry should never put its faithful.

Unfortunately, I find little or no growth in this collection of the work of ten years; the only change is in the direction of greater dispersal, to be found both in the author's self-permissiveness in greater rambling and in his adoption of the long line. And, although no single poem satisfies altogether, here are the pieces that are least discomforting: "The Performance," "The Lifeguard," "Chenille," "Cherrylog Road," "Pursuit from Under," "Gamecock," "Mangham," "Angina," "The Sheep Child," and "Bread."

The Phenomenon of
James Dickey, Currently

A review of *The Strength of Fields* by James Dickey

ROBERT PETERS

"Most of these new poems, . . . instead of soaring . . . , skim the
tops of trees and occasionally crash."

James Dickey is a much decorated ace among American poets. He has re-
tracted his poem-wheels sufficiently often and gone winging off into the blue
to earn his place in that Poetry-Pilot Sky Hall-of-Fame. And, if he never decides to publish another line, or to rev up another poem/engine, his reputation
is secure. But he does keep writing. *The Strength of Fields,* out from Doubleday,
contains about fifty pages of new poems and about forty pages of what Dickey
calls "Free-Flight Improvisations from the Un-English," which are poems
based very loosely on a series of foreigners: Montale, Jarry, Po Chu-yi, Lautréa-
mont, Aleixandre, and Yevtushenko, among others. Since these "improvisations" are special, the result of a mixed engineering, so to speak, I shall simply
recommend them and in my remarks concentrate on those poems that are
entirely Dickey's own.

Nowadays, the public that notices poetry at all assumes that Dickey has
succeeded Robert Frost as Poet Laureate of America. This is at best a tacitly
bestowed accolade, since there is no formal office as such; the fame transpires
when either *Time* magazine features some poet on its cover, or the President
invites a poet to read a poem aloud at his inauguration. As everyone knows,
Dickey read a poem at Carter's inauguration, and that poem is the title poem
of this new volume. Well, the English have appointed Laureates for years, nay
for centuries, and until recently have awarded a butt of good sack as a prize.
(Did Carter present Dickey with a fifth of good Bourbon?) Moreover, these
English Laureates, apart from Wordsworth and Tennyson, are renowned for
their mediocrity. So it is probably just as well that we have no official Poet
Laureate of America.

Originally published in *Western Humanities Review* 34 (Spring 1980): 159–66. Reprinted by permission.

Which brings me to *The Strength of Fields,* published now, some three years after Dickey read the poem for Carter. Just how good a poet is Dickey today—assuming that this volume reflects the best that he is capable of now? I hope to explore this matter in some detail, realizing that to fuss about Dickey at all will undoubtly resurrect a host of confederate troops, supported by University of South Carolina cheerleaders, to march out here and lay waste my Southern California gardens, fields, domicile, books, and life. But I am sufficiently perplexed by what happens to our immensely successful poets to brave the dangers of strafing and mayhem. I mean to be entirely constructive in what is about to follow.

I

Poems may be seen as either tortoises or hares. Their Aesopian progress toward a goal (the end of the poem) may wreak strange transformations: the tortoise may metamorphose into a hare along the way, or vice versa. Projective verse apologists have sufficiently explained how useful the hare is as an image for the poem racing helter-skelter through the open field toward its burrow, and to safety. The hare is energy, madness, quick-spinning poem-life. The tortoise, on the other hand, is slow, plodding, apt to take his sweet time in a straight path along some sandy road. He may even stop to rest within the spaces of a single line of verse. More of this later, for it helps, I think, to describe James Dickey's new work.

II

Most of these new poems, with a pair of exceptions, instead of soaring off easily into the empyrean, skim the tops of trees and occasionally crash. They generate weakly, and, to shift metaphors, they are like tortoises plodding along, testing their way, being maddeningly self-indulgent, as they rest after every three or four words. Also, Dickey now reflects what I call *Momentosity,* an easy metaphysics, a yanking of the poem into *Significance,* which doesn't always work. It's as if Dickey feels that a poet as famous as he is is obligated to say Big Things—the poet as a Shelleyan universal Sky-Pilot for Mankind. Further, he frequently has trouble moving his poems, in their casual dispositions across the page, past the middle; by grabbing onto some vague concept, he tries to propel the poem on to its landing (hand-thrown rather than jet-flown projectiles). Finally, there's a sentimentality based in part on his affection for the male world of *men's* feelings (the only women in the book are either dead or are memories), recollections of military service, guitar-strummings, jogging, and football. The fact that he still manages some good poems containing the old high-octane revved magic makes us regret there aren't more such poems. As a poet who himself owes a good deal to Dickey, I sincerely hope that this book is merely a hiatus in his career; obviously, there is evidence in *The Strength of Fields* that there are good things still to come, possibly.

III

The title poem, read at Carter's inauguration, has trouble launching itself. Language is a problem; the first line informs us that a small town "always" has a "moth-force," once we are "given the night." I'm confused. Does a moth's force drive the moth to fling itself suicidally into light? I thought that small towns earth-anchored were incapable of leaving their earth-moorings and wafting towards glimmering bulbs. Perhaps, though, if you are a lonely man walking the fields outside town, the street lamps seen from across the fields are like moths—but doesn't a firefly rather than a moth cast a winking light? *Moth-force* is a phrase that sounds good rather than means much. Dickey separates these lines with white turtle space, indenting freely, forcing us to assemble his lines as a meditational act of sorts—we linger over *moth-force*; we linger over *night* (pretty frayed sentimental image); we linger over *field-forms;* and we linger over a "solar system" floating on above this walking/thinking man as "town moths." Stars as moths? Stars as fireflies? I'm lost. The tortoise underpaces me.

Dickey's attempt to develop an *Idea* also seems enervated. All men are around his walking man, including dead ones, he says—although they are "not where he is exactly now." But they are nevertheless still with him, just as "the strength of fields" is with him. Race consciousness? A kind of cosmic significance labors to be born, as this *Ur-Mensch* type, symbolizing the poet perhaps, in his night wanderings, quests after the metaphysical. A passing train, one of the sentimental motifs in the poem, appears, shedding its melancholy, hunger, loneliness, and "long-lost grief."

Dickey's conundrum, posed on behalf of his walker (and us) is—what should we do with our lives? A good Laureate-esque conundrum. He prays to "Dear Lord of all the fields" for an answer. In another inflated, sentimental turn, he hopes his good ambulating man will find his "secret blooming" by taking help from the dead who lie under the pastures. How did these dead get there? I thought people were buried in cemeteries, even in small towns. And who says the dead have nothing better to do than worry about our individual destinies, taking time out from their Eternity-Canasta games to prod us and guide us? Does Dickey have in mind a general image of rot, as Walt Whitman does in "Earth's Compost"?

Dickey next imagines the ocean as a possible answer-giver (thanks again to Whitman). Hundreds of miles off, ocean fumbles in its "deep-structured roar," a roar like that of nations in struggle with a "profound, unstoppable craving . . . for their wish." Well, what is this *wish?* Some variety of manifest destiny? And aren't *profound* and *unstoppable* hollow attempts to jerk the poems towards meanings only vaguely felt by the poet? "Hunger, time and the moon," after triad of frayed abstractions, indented way over to the right, don't provide an answer either. The repetitions of the three prepositional phrases beginning with *on* are like running a dull bit of film over again, hoping that to re-create the scene all over may ignite the fuel to blast the poetry-ship off into space. It doesn't happen, alas, and Dickey's observation that "it" has to begin "with the simplest things" recalls some of Robert Frost's shibboleths (see "Directive"), but lacking Frost's sense of the specific and the graphic. The poem concludes with our wandering *mensch* aware—as if there were any other choice—that his life belongs to the world. Knowing this now, he promises "to do what he can." The poem flakes off into the ether.

"Remnant Water," an ecology poem, is another piece with generator trouble. It too begins with pretty quiescent, tortoise-phrases slabbed out on the page. Variations on *thin, again,* and *water* seem to be the sparks meant to ignite the fuel. But it's a weary tortoise. Halfway through there are some effective touches, as dead fish emerge through the "scum-gruel" of the dying lake. Unfortunately, the presence of what seems to be a lone Indian lamenting the death of his tribe and his fish dying doesn't quite make it as either an image of then or now.

A pair of poems, fairly ripping with energy, are among the best of Dickey's poems. The first, "The Voyage of the Needle," has much of Dickey's old magic. The main metaphor really works. A child, carrying one of his mother's sewing needles, draws bath-water, and climbs in. As he lies there with the needle floating, attached to its paper, the paper soaks up, separates from the needle which remains floating on the skin of the water. The image turns towards Dickey's adult life and his memories of his mother. If, by some simple miracle from beyond the grave, she can drive her needle through the skin of the magical water to its *death,* to prick her son with pain, his love for his family will restore itself, and be as weightless as the needle floating on the water. In a superb turn, he craves for the needle to pierce his lips, as he lies (now a fifty-year-old man) lip-level in the bath. He imagines thorns bursting into rain on his mother's grave.

"False Youth: Autumn: Clothes of the Age" is another successful piece. It opens with precise, interesting detail: the poet enters a barbershop in Georgia, wearing a cap made of three red foxes. His hair is long, and he wears a denim jacket with a huge eagle embroidered on the back of it by his son's old lady. He strikes the barbers as a middle-aged hippy. As a matter of fact, the barber at the last chair says that he hates "middle-aged hippies." Dickey plays coward and replies that he does too, hoping, I gather, in a very human way, to deflect criticism. As he leaves, dressed in his "false youth," he turns so that they will be sure to have a good look, "a lifetime look," at his eagle's single word: *poetry.* There's no shallow writing here, no pushing towards pompous metaphysical abstractions, no forcing of feelings that aren't earned.

IV

The difficulties Dickey has beginning poems (one of the worst starts is this obfuscated opening for the very first poem: "That any just to long for / The rest of my life, would come . . .") is symptomatic of an underlying problem I find in many of these poems—a problem I call *Momentosity*. As I have already suggested, the title poem, read at Carter's inauguration, suffers from this malady. In an ambitious "Two Poems of the Military," the first poem is particularly instructive, since it contains evidence that Dickey can still yank up that old jock-strap and chase the hare through the fields. But, alas, he goes slack when he tries to net that Big Statement. He reminds me of Matthew Arnold, who in early middle age quit writing poetry for essays—he could no longer, apparently, sustain his special melancholy without puffing out abstractions he didn't feel. In one of Arnold's poems, "A Summer Night," he begins to conclude an otherwise nicely detailed, felt poem with this hollow ejaculation: "Plainness and clearness without shadow of stain! / Clearness divine! / Ye heavens. . . ." Instead of blowing our socks off and addling our brains, Arnold soporifically and tepidly lets us down. The metaphysics is shallow stuff rubbed between the muses' fingers into syllable ash.

Dickey's "Haunting the Maneuvers," the first of these paired poems, begins tautly and originally. He's declared "dead" during maneuvers. He lies dead on a spread of pine-needles, observing the needles as they point up compass-like into the night. They are whiter than his own skin. Great. But then Dickey gets into trouble: this luminosity dissolves into:

> O those who are in this
> With me, I can see nothing
> But what is coming   can say
> Nothing but what the first-killed
> Working hard all day for his vision
> Of war says best: the age-old Why
> In God's name Why
> In Louisiana, Boys   O Why
> In Hell are we doing this?

The rhetoric is sentimental, stagey, and turtle-slow. Instead of shedding its clothes, as a good poem should, revealing itself specific and bare, this one hides itself in the swaddling of a stuffed military uniform. The poem comes off as an attitude.

Another seemingly ambitious poem, this one too for a public occasion, the Phi Beta Kappa Poem, Harvard, 1970, creaks and groans towards Momentosity. Dickey does, however, makes intriguing use of lines and phrases by the poet Joseph Trumbull Stickney (1874–1904). Dickey calls his form a "dead-living dialogue." There are also several specific echoes of Whitman's poems. The piece is an odic lament over our polluted environment. The speaker, at Zuma Beach, California, with guitar (that sentimental image of Appalachian love, male tenderness, poverty, and healthy ecologies), laments the Los Angeles smog and the off-shore drilling threatening the beaches. The sun seems about to die. As Dickey sings and strums, thanks to Whitman, he becomes a child again (Whitman sang sans guitar on Paumanok Beach): "I playing from child-hood also / Like the Georgia mountains   the wind out of Malibu whipped her / Long hair into 'Wildwood Flower'. . . ."

His singing-meditation seems to alleviate his pain that California by to-morrow may be the deadest world of all. He is a bit comforted by knowing that there is a celestial universe towards which his thoughts now leap easily, as if they are mullet leaping in a dying stream. In a Dylan Thomasesque "country of death," things, I gather, are somehow righted and Dickey can jangle his guitar-strings and vocalize with his dead ancestors and lost poet-pilot predeces-sors. An Existentialist Abyss all by itself doesn't necessarily make for good poetry, and despite the skillful interplay Dickey manages between Stickney's lines and his own, when Stickney's "mysterious truth" turns Dickey's own thoughts *wild,* he hymns pretty warmed-over abstractions, calling on "the shapeless and very / Music of the universal / Abyss." One wonders: if Stickney's poems were better would they have generated a better poem from Dickey? Phrases like "solitude," "the quality of life," "better or worse," and "death changed forever" plod along like dull tortoises. The poem concludes as the poet wanders the beach "mumbling" to the dead Stickney in the musical "key of A," seeking rainbows in the oil on the beach. A good dab of kerosene would wipe the tar-oil from our heels and perhaps dissolve the poem.

V

One of Dickey's great gifts, both in his fiction and his poetry, is an un-canny ability to convey feelings occurring beneath the skin—withdrawing a barbed arrow-head from one's chest; brain ache; the slowly engulfing misery of lungs filling with water; the physicality of another person's self entering yours. In "The Rain Guitar," one of the best of these new poems, these qualities exist. He's in England, sitting by a weir in the rain, with his guitar, watching the water-grass wave. His own life, as he sits there in the wet and cold, is like eel-grass which tries to move downstream, but has all the necessary motions but one, the one that will move it with the current's flow. A peg-legged fish-erman approaches. Dickey begins to play his guitar. The Englishman is pleased. Dickey plays faster, as he soaks with rain. The guitar showers its sound as the fisherman casts his line and taps his wooden-leg on the cobbles, in time with Dickey's strumming and singing. He's playing Australian renditions of British marching songs. Both men are air force—and, hence, are buddies of sorts. So far, so good. The male world is neatly intact, as a sharing. The poem, though, comes apart in the middle. The guitar seems to represent a kind of plain-folks music-making, a charmer uniting men on some basic male level. One imagines the mountain-women in the background frying chicken, making crazy quilts, minding their bare-footed siblings. Now, in England, a buck dance settles over the weir. It's Epiphany-Time! *Momentosity* pulls its head out of its shell! There's an old Cathedral in the background, out of view, hidden in the English town. Whole worlds of tradition and metaphysical meanings waft through as the men reminisce over their war adventures. Dickey is now singing so well he has "mouths" all over him. The Englishman pounds his wooden-leg, keeping time. Memories of Burma, the Southwest Pacific, and North Georgia all chime together, drawing down "Cathedral water." The rain itself, thus, is mystical, falling as it does from some Cathedral in the sky. For me, the poem works well without the Cathedral; it's a bit like having the Mormon Tabernacle Choir on cue.

Dickey's male world, as a dominant motif, appears again in "For the Death of Lombardi" which celebrates the tough, famous sports figure dead of cancer. Football heroes keep us "men," Dickey informs us, much as General George Patton kept us "men" by creating his armies and driving them forward. Lombardi hypnotized us, so that we never knew for sure, and we know even less now, as we sit watching sports events on the tube, whether he freed us to be men or not. Yes, J. D., what of another side of the impact of sports heroes? their fostering of easy angers, cry-babyhood, bribery and shucked false grades at colleges and universities? But Dickey's poem isn't meant to go deep: he provides the easy sentiment to go with our Budweisers and Coors: "We're with you all the way / You're going forever, Vince."

Finally, "For the Running of the New York City Marathon" should please both hare and tortoise, since it is a natural for some jogging magazine. Again, Dickey delays the poem by re-running the first scene of a poem-movie: "If you would run / If you would quicken. . . ." It's as if he can't generate the poem. And the dependence on Whitman ejaculations ("O my multitudes") doesn't work. Dickey is best, as always, when he's detailing experience: he sees jogging suits plastered with bright emblems, parkas and hoods worn in hot weather, odd hairpieces, Zulu plumes. Once the marathon starts, Dickey conveys a sharp sense of the race; but he can't resist an easy sentimental mysticism: we are all runners, he seems to say; and as we move "farther into the dark" we cast shadows. A trite Existentialism? The poetry-darkness trap? An empty concept? As the runners stumble to their goal, Dickey stumbles over crippled language: we "breast our own breathless arrival. . . ." Repetitions of *me* are little more than tortoise breaths. And, almost as a sop to jogger-readers, he concludes that we are all winners—in the race of life?

VI

It is indeed difficult to render so negative an assessment of a poet who has as greatly enriched American poetry as has Dickey. He has inspired by being the rare iconoclastic writer who writes, publishes, and finds his audience without the blessings of Establishment (read "Eastern") poetry enclaves. Dickey is where he is pretty much on his own, which makes witnessing what seems a deterioration in his work particularly painful.

Momentosity will probably always be with us, as long as our poets feel obliged to see themselves as *legislators for mankind* and believe that success in the mass market obligates them to serve as wisdom-platitude figures. And there are other traps, given such renown. Certainly, the need to keep writing and publishing, even if one has nothing much to say, is real. And success in the mass markets and on the movie screens leads the writer to believe that he must not stir from the themes he's known for—in Dickey's case, the southern roots, the macho interests, the World War II experiences, the feelings of once-vigorous males now aging. When experiences seem to have written themselves out, it's time to move on. His publisher, obviously, deserves a good wrist slap: if a poet will bring in some bucks, publish whatever he writes. His avid public will buy, the investor will be pleased—so we'll publish, publish, publish, abrogating our editorial responsibilities. Just charge plenty for the book and make it pretty. Well, I for one, as an avid Dickey fan, will be cautious from here on.

Herself as the Environment

A review of *Puella* by James Dickey

WILLIAM HARMON

"Deborah . . . 'the poet's young wife. . . .' undergoes a metamorphic elevation
. . . her lineaments . . . heraldic, totemic, mythic, atavistic, primal."

Vicissitudes of reputation notwithstanding, James Dickey remains an extraordinarily talented poet.

True, his talent in other callings may be less than extraordinary. At one period, twenty and more years ago, he was an acute, provocative, and occasionally pugnacious reviewer: never much of a critic with abstract theoretical principles, but a dutifully solid reviewer. He has been something of a performer, "barnstorming" for poetry—and, practically from habit, lifting a metaphor from aviation. When, in 1969, aviation reached its extreme terminus, Dickey was *Life*'s Lunar Landing Laureate. Later, in the undistinguished movie made from his one novel, he played a small role very creditably indeed. Thereafter, in a sense, Dickey's personal and professional fortunes soared and sank along with those of another toothy James (well, all right: *Jimmy*) from Georgia. The 1977 inauguration may be likened to a sort of solstice for Dickey, and since then he seems to have become a less public celebrity.

Which brings us to Yeats's forced zero-sum choice between perfection of the life or perfection of the work. For a while, Dickey seemed to have chosen a gaudy perfection of the life, whereupon the work drifted ever further from perfection, reaching one nadir in *The Strength of Fields* then bouncing along to another in *The Zodiac*. But now—and I am delighted to say so—Dickey's new book, *Puella,* impresses me as his best work since *Buckdancer's Choice.*

The poet has kept some of his now-familiar idiosyncrasies. With the exception of the final poem, "Summons," *Puella* consists of rather modest poems in which every line begins with a capital letter and is centered on the page, with some portentous liberties taken with the spacing and line-feed. Apart from that typographical continuity, *Puella* differs substantially from most of Dickey's earlier work. The book presents, in eighteen poems, a complex persona named

Originally published in *Carolina Quarterly* 35 (Fall 1982): 91–94. Copyright William Harmon. Reprinted courtesy of the author and *Carolina Quarterly*.

Deborah whom the dust-jacket identifies as the poet's "young wife." The dedication of the book reads, "To Deborah— / *her girlhood, male-imagined.*" The
epigraph, a reminder that Dickey is good at remembering poets of somewhat
less than the first rank, comes from T. Sturge Moore: "I lived in thee, and
dreamed, and waked / Twice what I had been."

(Let me interpolate here another quotation that, by what I suppose is a
species of reviewer's serendipity, I just happened to come across on the day
that I began reading *Puella.* From Julia Kristeva's essay, "The Novel as Po-
lylogue," in *Desire in Language:* "There are men, enthralled by archaic mothers,
who dream of being women or some unapproachable master; exasperated and
frigid young women, confined within groups where what they take for lesbian-
ism leads them into seclusion from society; others, classic hystericals, search
for that impossible maternal fusion and are exalted in their frustration." Inevitably, I suppose, somebody will soon be applying this sort of Franco-Freudian
analysis to Dickey and to any number of other writers—Goethe, Yeats, Law-
rence, Graves, Bly, Mailer—for whom *the* central human act belongs to Girl-
Woman-Mother, and for whom any male writer is a mere nostalgic vestigial
appendage with a faint tissue-memory of what *real* creation amounts to. "After
the saccharine whirlwind of Jocastas and Antigones, next to a quietude fascinated with the self-indulgent whims of hysterics," Kristeva says, "the negative
awakens within the body and language of the other so as to weave a fabric in
which your role is tolerated only if it resembles that of women in Sade, Joyce,
and Bataille. But you most certainly must not consider yourself either as the
weaving or as the character against whom it is woven. What is important is to
listen to it, in your own way, indefinitely, and to disappear within the movement of this attentiveness." Here Kristeva adds a sentence that applies directly
to the phenomenal matrix of *Puella:* "This means that the wife of a 'poet,' of
this particular poet, no longer exists. Neither Mme Mallarmé's knitting, nor
Lou Salomé's subtle curiosity, nor Nora Joyce's proud and obedient excitement, nor Maria van Rysselbergh's asexual mythology, anymore than the grati-
fying coupling that 'virilized' the women of postwar existentialism or romantic-
communism—henceforth, all that is impossible, antiquated, a dismal relic.")

Dickey's *Puella* works as both a rare encomiastic tribute and a courageous
dispatching of the imagination. A notoriously macho poet, for whom 1982 will
be his sixtieth year to heaven, fancies himself privy to the sensibility of a character nearly the opposite of himself: a woman who seems to be quite young, no
more than twenty-five. The title suggests outright girlhood, but no one has
exactly surveyed the boundary between *puella* and *mulier,* "girl" and "woman."
The heroine of Cummings's *Puella Mea* is certainly an adult.

Although the title of the volume seems rather feeble (and *puella* is, for my
money, an ugly word), the titles of most of the constituent poems are vivid.
They trace a graph with uncommon eloquence: "Deborah Burning a Doll Made
of House-Wood" (and recalling Dickey's earlier fire sermons as well as Rilke's
Orphic transmutation of the dolls of childhood into terrible Angels of Other-

ness); "Deborah, Moon, Mirror, Right Hand Rising"; "Deborah and Deirdre as Drunk Bridesmaids Foot-Racing at Daybreak"; "Springhouse, Menses, Held Apple, House and Beyond"; "Deborah in Mountain Sound: Bell, Glacier, Rose"; and so forth, gorgeously and informatively.

One gets no sense of Deborah as a housewife or a citizen outfitted with a local habitation, a family name, a Social Security number. (She does sound pregnant at the end.) With only a first name, and with a book called something as abstract and general as *Puella,* the character undergoes a metamorphic elevation into pure Girl, her lineaments mostly symbolic, heraldic, totemic, mythic, atavistic, primal. Even the details of her self-portrait ("Bull-headed, big-busted, / Distrustful and mystical") that tracks her features back "from mother to mother" ("I am totally them in the eyebrows, / Breasts, breath and butt") recall the Coarse Old Party evoked in Auden's "Dame Kind" ("Steatopygous, sow-dugged / and owl-headed"). Deborah's voice, powerful and occasionally obscure, comes through as poetry from a Delphic doorstep, echoically poised between Girl and Woman, *farouche* and much-hyphenated. Over the language of such poems, a number of familiar spirits brood. Hopkins and Rilke, sophisticated poets of naive "betweenpie" states of becoming, are honored by epigraphs. Hart Crane's hyperactive syntax is here, as is the metamorphic spondaic rhythm of Pound's Canto II. Everything is exaggerated, but most of the time Dickey's invention is rugged enough to take the strain.

Now and again, the vocabulary of these poems seems to belong outside the persona's native precinct. Some expressions are writerly conceits ("End-stopping a creek," "off-prints / of lightning"); others suggest the warfare and aviation of Dickey's earlier verse ("flame-outs," "search-and-destroy"); still others come out of current popular science ("black-hole," "anti-matter," "steady-state," "light-sensitive" twice, and "flash point" twice). None of this diction is necessarily alien to Dickey's *puella*-persona, and the book provides many moments of intense somatic realization for which Germanically compounded adjectives and nouns seem entirely appropriate ("heat-shadow," "time-sparks," "thumb-echo of the harp," "Mortality-haze," "the worked, lopped glory-call of crows," "the psychic mob-sound of bees," "Reprisal-furies," "Hope-surfeited cedar," "ghost-smell," "Myth-chill," "void-sweat," "the overleaf and memory-make of tedium," "glory-touched steel-wool," "grit-smell," "lamp-rust," "the ice-dreams of sunstroke"). Some of those yokings may seem too spooky or lurid, and *glory* may be overused, but I don't see anything wrong with the general practice. I did grow tired of two applications of this arc-welding by hyphens. We have to hear "high-tension," "high-energy," "high-risk," and (twice) "high-concentrate"—all of which adds up to just too much "high" for me. The other irritant does things too much by halves ("half-sway," "half-slaked, half-eaten," "half-eaten, half-stolen," "half-coming," "half-way," and "half-holy"). Although Dickey's "limbo-light" may encroach on the turf of Ammons's *The Snow Poems* ("Light falls shadow and beam through the limbo / limbboughs"), it remains an interesting figure. I, for one, am happy that Dickey exploits an increasingly common feature of the American language and his own distinctive idiom to create a sympathetic character with an answerable style. Usually, he manages not to run hyperbole into the ground.

As before, Dickey defines the human center of *Puella* by deeply inscribed vectors drawn from the worlds of wild beasts, vegetation, inanimate things, and raw elemental forces. The choices of totems and emblems in *Puella* seem, pretty consistently, apt and manageable. In sub-titles that recall Yeats's "A Woman Young and Old," Dickey connects his Deborah with her manifold phenomenal and mythical homes: "Deborah as Winged Seed, / Descending with Others" (a peculiar echo of Dickey's earlier book-title *Drowning with Others*); "Deborah's Rain-Longing"; "Imagining Herself as the Environment, She Speaks to James Wright at Sundown." At moments, Deborah employs a poetry that goes well with her moods of terrible sympathy—"the wasp's delaying / Uncontested spasm at the pane." Although, as far as I can tell, nothing of the Hebrew meaning of *Deborah* (bee) matters here, there is a pleasant-enough resonance, conceptual and acoustic, at the end of the "Springhouse" poem in an accounting of "what I require":

> A stone house, a father, a window,
> The wasp's holocaust of location,
> The bees' winnowed over-stressed time-zone,
> Far orchards blazing with slant.

(Speaking of names and resonances, the "Deborah and Deirdre" who seem to be sisters here happen, unfortunately, to have the same fashionable names as Rojack's wife and daughter in Mailer's *An American Dream*. I suppose it couldn't be helped. Mrs. Dickey's name really is Deborah, I understand.)

Poems whose torque comes from sex and myth are easy to begin; prosecuting a series of such poems seems to be an enterprise that comes to Dickey easily, naturally, leaves to a tree; but satisfactorily ending the series, or even one of its units, must be impossible. How should such poetry stop, end, terminate? This has been one of the difficulties besetting Dickey for a long time now. He has a good eye, his heart is somewhere near the right place, his ideas are original, he gives his poems those helpful titles (against the grain of the age, which seems to favor such nothing-title poets as Creeley and Ammons), he follows through both tenderly and robustly, he has a sense of humor. But he seems not to place enough trust in his reader, and he definitely cannot end a poem or a sequence without recourse to tacky platitude. The worst poem in *Puella*—and the only bad one, I judge—is the last, "Summons," and the very worst part of it comes at the end, where the four portentously spaced, portentously italicized lines are arranged in portentous echelon:

> *unending*
> *invention*
> *go for it*
> *unending*

I had just seen "Rocky III" when I read this part of *Puella,* but that experience may not explain all of my recoiling from the reverberating wrongness of that "go for it." Restraining the impulse to bad-mouth the sadomasochistic–birdbrained–Vince Lombardi–jock–ethic of Dickey at his worst, I'll just say that here the poet took quite a chance, ransacking the threadbare thesaurus of sport, and it didn't pay off. But the feeble dud of an ending is no total loss. This pathetic moment, even at the end, cannot ruin what is after all a very good book.

James Dickey: *The Whole Motion*

RICHARD TILLINGHAST

"By the mid-1970s Dickey had become so much of a legend that we tended to forget he was, before anything else, a superb and stunningly original poet."

The publication this summer of James Dickey's *The Whole Motion* finally makes available under one cover the poems he has published during a career that has spanned more than four decades. The extravagant imagination of the man who has given us such titles as *The Eye-Beaters, Blood, Victory, Madness, Buckhead and Mercy* couldn't be content with something as drab as "collected poems," though the book's subtitle identifies it as such. Dickey came of age during a cultural moment when poets' reputations were often founded as much on the excesses of their personal lives as on the quality of their work. When one surveys the lives of Robert Lowell, Sylvia Plath, John Berryman, Allen Ginsberg, Randall Jarrell, Elizabeth Bishop, Theodore Roethke, and Anne Sexton, one gets the impression that mid-century American poetry somehow, with great difficulty, managed to get written between gin-fueled one-night stands in motel rooms and recovery periods in mental hospitals and drying-out spas, in an atmosphere of extreme emotional and mental states and strikingly unconventional behavior.

In the lifestyle arena, James Dickey has not disappointed. Stories about the man have become a thriving perennial in the field of literary gossip. I could without straining my memory probably tell you a dozen of these stories—most of them really funny, and many of them bearing at least some relation to the truth—and so, I imagine, could many readers of this review. But his lifestyle is not the only reason Dickey has become the most visible southern writer of his day. His interests in the backcountry survivalist movement, in whitewater canoeing, and in bow hunting have dovetailed with regional and national redis-covery of the wilderness.

The enormously popular movie made from his novel *Deliverance* made Dickey visible to all sorts of people who don't read contemporary poetry—as well as to people who don't read much of anything other than *People* magazine, Stephen King, and *TV Guide*. When Jimmy Carter, a president who in retro-spect looks better and better all the time, chose his fellow Georgian to deliver

Originally published in *Southern Review* 28 (Autumn 1992): 971–80. Reprinted by permission.

a poem at his inauguration, Dickey took on the ceremonial role in Washington that Robert Frost played in John F. Kennedy's presidency. By the mid-1970s Dickey had become so much of a legend that we tended to forget he was, before anything else, a superb and stunningly original poet. Few poets who began writing in the 1960s—certainly few southern poets—can credibly claim not to have been influenced by James Dickey. I gladly include myself as someone who has read, loved, and probably unconsciously imitated his poetry ever since I came under its spell over thirty years ago.

A delightful and unexpected feature of *The Whole Motion* is the inclusion of almost fifty pages of uncollected poetry written before Dickey's first book, *Into the Stone.* Here we see a less flamboyant poet than the one we would come to know later, but the general outlines of his style and his ruling preoccupations are already recognizable. One of these early poems, "The Sprinter at Forty," introduces a figure Dickey would return to throughout his work: the over-the-hill athlete. Sports, competitive sports in particular, are emblematic of life and youth for this poet who has often spoken proudly of his college football days at Clemson University, and has written about them notably in "The Bee" from *Falling, May Day Sermon, and Other Poems.* In "The Sprinter at Forty," the speaker states, "I receive the wish to live more / Which nothing but motion can answer" (a formulation that resonates with the word *motion* in the title of the entire collection). In an intellectual climate where football has been thought of as a "proto-fascist" activity, Dickey's identification with the sport has allowed him to put his finger on the pulse of our culture, because the competitive athlete is the American male's favorite fantasy hero. Dickey turns the superannuated athlete into a quintessentially American figure of pathos.

Yet Dickey avoids glorifying the athlete, presenting him instead as put-upon, often injured, under attack, as in "In the Pocket," subtitled "NFL", from *Eye-Beaters:* "hit move scramble," goes the quarterback's interior monologue, "Before death and the ground / Come up   LEAP STAND KILL DIE STRIKE / Now." "For the Death of Lombardi," from *The Strength of Fields,* shows how fully—in contrast to other poets, some of whom have tended to detach themselves from commercialized American culture—Dickey has operated within that culture. He has provided a point of intersection for the hero and the victim, one whose voice often enough is the American football fan's. Speaking for them, "those who entered the bodies / of Bart Starr, Donny Anderson, Ray Nitschke, Jerry Kramer / Through the snowing tube on Sunday afternoon," Dickey mourns the Green Bay Packers' legendary coach:

> . . . We stand here among
> Discarded TV commercials:
> Among beer-cans and razor-blades and hair-tonic bottles,
> Stinking with male deodorants: we stand here
> Among teeth and filthy miles
> Of unwound tapes, novocaine needles, contracts, champagne
> Mixed with shower-water, unraveling elastic, bloody faceguards . . .

In *The Eagle's Mile,* Dickey's most recent book, the celebration of "False Youth" is replayed in an overblown Whitmanian romp called "The Olympian," where, after an afternoon spent drinking Olympia beer, Dickey spoofs his own fantasy, imagining a race between himself, in his "hilarious, pizza-fed fury," and an Olympic champion:

> . . . O hot, just hurdlable gates
> Of deck-chairs! Lounges! A measured universe
> Of exhilarating laws! Here I had come   there I'd gone
> Laying it down   confusing, staggering
> The fast lane and the slow, on and over
> And over recliners, sun-cots, cleaning-poles and beach-balls . . .

In his early poems Dickey did not throw himself into the seductive punch bowl of contemporary American culture. He lived and wrote at one remove from all that, in the world of his own vision. In the very first poem in the collection, "The Baggage King," where the pile of soldiers' luggage on an island in the Pacific rises "Like the hill of a dead king," Dickey's predisposition to see experience in terms of ritual announces itself. The mythic dimension in his poetry has always exercised a strong attraction for me, and it shows both his continuity with and his break from older poets such as T.S. Eliot and Allen Tate and even poets closer to his own age such as Robert Lowell. These poets were drawn explicitly to religious conversion, and tried to adumbrate their sense of larger significances behind everyday events by reference to classical mythology. Their evocations of the Greek and Roman myths could take the form, in Donald Hall's parodic account of the period, "of long poems in iambics called 'Herakles: A Double Sestina' "; or they could be subtle and exquisite, as in the last two quatrains of John Crowe Ransom's "Vision by Sweetwater":

> Let them alone, dear Aunt, just for one minute
> Till I go fishing in the dark of my mind:
> Where have I seen before, against the wind,
> These bright virgins, robed and bare of bonnet,
>
> Flowing with music of their strange quick tongue
> And adventuring with delicate paces by the stream,—
> Myself a child, old suddenly at the scream
> From one of the white throats it hid among?

The early Dickey has more in common with Ransom than meets the eye—especially since the similarities of vision are obscured by strong differences not only of diction and versification, but of intent. (Ransom was, by the way, a Cleveland Browns fan, but a poem by him on professional football is unthinkable.) Dickey has never wanted to write just for the highly educated elite whom Ransom appealed to, but for the mass American audience.

But the personal myths of which I was speaking came to Dickey, it would seem, either from reading about pantheistic religions and fertility cults or simply from an intuitive sense of how well their way of seeing things triggered his own imagination. Watching the movie *Black Robe* recently, I was reminded by a simplified description of the Algonquian version of the afterlife—"At night in the woods the souls of dead people hunt the souls of dead animals"—of Dickey's "Heaven of the Animals," where not human hunters but animals hunt other animals: "These hunt, as they have done, / But with claws and teeth grown perfect, // More deadly than they can believe." Dickey's treatment of the fate of the victims might suggest a certain callousness toward others' pain, but I think it is more accurately seen as a mystical view of the world wherein predation and suffering are subsumed within an all-inclusive unity, where:

> those that are hunted
> Know this as their life,
> Their reward: to walk
>
> Under such trees in full knowledge
> Of what is in glory above them,
> And to feel no fear,
> But acceptance, compliance.
> Fulfilling themselves without pain
>
> At the cycle's center . . .

"The Owl King," one of the first Dickey poems I read, sublimates the predatory instinct in a similar way: "I felt the hooked tufts on my head / Enlarge, and dream like a crown." Here Dickey may be very close to intuiting how the raw power of feudal overlords became ritualized into the institution of kingship.

The Owl King must have represented at the same time a version of himself. I first met Dickey at the home of Monroe and Betty Spears in Sewanee, Tennessee, in about 1960, roughly the time this poem would have been written. Spears, who introduced me to modern poetry at Sewanee, was the professor at Vanderbilt whom Dickey credits with firing his enthusiasm for poetry when he entered graduate school after being discharged from the Air Force after World War II. In 1960 Dickey was still writing advertising copy in Atlanta for Coca-Cola—selling his soul to the devil by day, as he liked to put it, and buying it back at night by writing at the kitchen table of his suburban house, inventing himself as a poet. I can picture him there: "I in the innermost shining / Of my blazing, invented eyes." In "The Vegetable King," from *Into the Stone,* the poet explicitly becomes a king—the king of fertility cults, who dies with the dying year to be reborn with the spring. Here, "From my house and my silent folk / I step, and lay me in ritual down," the poet writes, "One night each April." He wills himself into ritual death and renewal, "And begin to believe a dream /

I never once have had / Of being part of the acclaimed rebirth / Of the ruined, calm world, in spring . . .''

Many of the poems from this period celebrate the act of willed possession, wherein the self is overtaken by the dream of kingship seen in ''The Vegetable King,'' or where the blind child in ''The Owl King'' from *Drowning with Others* receives his summons, delivered in the incantatory three- and four-beat anapestic line that Dickey wrote so beautifully in his early books:

> Through the trees, with the moon underfoot,
> More soft than I can, I call.
> I hear the king of the owls sing
> Where he moves with my son in the gloom.
> My tongue floats off in the darkness . . .

This call, this summons to a transformed reality, is always, in addition to whatever else it might be, the poem's summons, the siren song of the Muse or White Goddess. Dickey makes it quite clear that the call to poetic ecstasy, like the annunciation of kingship in the fertility rite, brings with it the threat of extinction, just as the Vegetable King, returning to his wife and family, ''bears you home / Magnificent pardon'' but also ''dread, impending crime.'' ''A Dog Sleeping on My Feet,' from *Drowning with Others,* recounts the summons specifically in terms of possession by the poem, and in an image of the crucifixion and a glancing echo of the rhetoric of the King James Bible (''Marvelous is the pursuit''), evokes the psychic peril of inspiration:

> The poem is beginning to move
> Up through my pine-prickling legs
> Out of the night wood,
>
> Taking hold of the pen by my fingers.
> Before me the fox floats lightly,
> On fire with his holy scent.
> All, all are running.
> Marvelous is the pursuit,
> Like a dazzle of nails through the ankles . . .

It may be that Dickey's greatest work still lays ahead of him at this point, but I wonder if he ever again achieved the exquisite purity, the Botticelli-like sense of sanctity, of the poems he wrote in the late-night isolation of the Atlanta suburbs.

The inclusion of the uncollected early poems makes clear how essential this kind of psychic self-immolation (I feel uncomfortable with my own ponderous language here, but it's hard to put it more simply) was to Dickey in the early days. ''Drifting,'' a marvelous poem I had never seen before, dramatizes the process of leaving the self behind—using a metaphor perhaps borrowed from Rimbaud's ''Le Bateau Ivre'':

> It is worth it to get
> Down there under the seats, stretched believingly out
> With your feet together,
> Thinking of nothing but the smell of bait and the sky
> And the bow coming
> To a point and the stern squared off until doomsday.

The metaphor may be Rimbaud's, but the details are very southern, with the idiomatic overkill of prepositions in "get / Down there under the seats" and the grandeur of the viewed sky undermined by the "smell of bait." Rimbaud in a bass boat!

If you can imagine this poem in the oeuvre of one of his contemporaries—Sylvia Plath, John Berryman, or Anne Sexton, to construct an implausible "for instance"—then this voyage would suggest suicide:

> Once in a lifetime a man must empty his pockets
> On the bank of a river,
> Take out two monogrammed handkerchiefs and tie them
>
> To the oars stuck in the sand:
> These mark the edge of the known . . .

This represents no death wish, however, but rather the poet's wish to leave his personality behind, and to float as Keats does—"Not charioted by Bacchus and his pards, / But on the viewless wings of Poesy."

If one thinks of Dickey's suburban pastoral as an idyll he entered gladly, gratefully, after the war, still the war continued to haunt him—a process that is especially clear in *Helmets* (1964). In the poem "Drinking from a Helmet," the GI poet, by drinking from the helmet of a man he imagines to have been killed, takes on that man's identity: "I stood as though I possessed / A cool, trembling man / Exactly my size, swallowed whole." This is an image of the warrior who must go back to his peacetime world and live the life of the civilian, all the time carrying within him the man who has fought, has managed to avoid being killed, has himself perhaps killed.

In *Buckdancer's Choice,* winner of the National Book Award in 1965 and the third of the astonishing trio of books that began in 1962 with *Drowning with Others,* Dickey addressed the dilemma of the returned warrior in one of his most controversial poems, eight pages long, "The Firebombing." The speaker in the poem, a comfortable yet uneasy suburbanite, tries in the midst of a typical middle-class life spent paying bills, mowing the lawn, and fretting about his receding hairline to come to terms with his experiences as a fighter pilot who carried out "anti-morale" napalm bombing runs against Japanese civilian targets. Memories of the firebombings intrude themselves just at the edges of quotidian concerns, cropping up as *fire* in the word *firewood* does in a broken line in this passage that describes his suburban home: "Where the lawn mower rests on its laurels"—the clichéd wording hinting at its owner's less than acute state of mind:

> Where the diet exists
> For my own good   where I try to drop
> Twenty years, eating figs in the pantry
> Blinded by each and all
> Of the eye-catching cans that gladly have caught my wife's eye
> Until I cannot say
> Where the screwdriver is   where the children
> Get off the bus   where the fly
> Hones his front legs   where the hammock folds
> Its erotic daydreams   where the Sunday
> School text for the day has been put   where the fire
> Wood is   where the payments
> For everything under the sun
> Pile peacefully up . . .

In 1967 Robert Bly, speaking from the pulpit of his influential magazine, *The Sixties,* castigated the poem in a vitriolic essay called "The Collapse of James Dickey." His main contention was that " 'Firebombing' " (note how leaving *The* out of the title changes its meaning) "makes no real criticism of the American habit of firebombing Asians." Bly was demanding that the poem's subject should be not the ambivalence felt by one particular pilot toward his own actions, but rather that the poem should become a kind of editorial against all American military action in Asia, with the premise that the war in the South Pacific against the Japanese was identical to the war against North Vietnam. Dickey once wrote that we live "in the age of the moral put-down," and, after attacks like Bly's, he was in a position to know. In abandoning any notion of aesthetic evaluation of poetry and insisting it become propaganda for the critic's political beliefs, Bly was ahead of his time—since his approach has become dogma among the Politically Correct theorists who now dominate academia. Bly condemns the poem because it displays "no real anguish. If the anguish were real, we would feel terrible remorse as we read, we would stop what we were doing, we would break the television set with an ax, we would throw ourselves on the ground sobbing."

I have addressed myself mainly to poems from the first part of Dickey's *Whole Motion*—the first 240 pages of a 475-page collection—because these are the poems that speak to me most strongly. While writing this piece I have reached for my original Wesleyan Poetry Series paperbacks of *Drowning with Others, Helmets,* and *Buckdancer's Choice* to remind me of the sense of discovery I got reading these books almost thirty years ago. Even the atrocious cover art of these books bespeaks an awkward sincerity, reminiscent of Baptist Sunday School teachers' instruction manuals. I have never been as enthusiastic about Dickey's work from *Falling, May Day Sermon, and Other Poems* on. In his introduction to *Falling, May Day Sermon, and Other Poems,* Dickey writes of designing "an on-end block or wall of words, solid or almost solid, black with massed ink, through which a little light from behind would come at intermittent places." And that for me is part of the problem. The wall of words, like the famous "wall of sound" introduced into Top 40 music by Phil Spector, seems to sacrifice some of the quieter, more subtle effects Dickey achieved in his earlier writings.

In poems like "Falling" Dickey tries to imitate a motion whose sweep outruns the ability of his language to keep up with it. "The Sheep Child," one of his most notorious (I use the word in its original, not its *People* magazine sense) poems, narrated by a dead half-human, half-sheep fetus pickled in alcohol in a museum in Atlanta, strikes me as southern grotesquerie gone over the limit. "Adultery," on the other hand, dares to treat the same fine line between originality and questionable taste (or am I sounding like Robert Bly?); yet it succeeds, because one thing that Dickey is not is a hypocrite. "Encounter in the Cage Country" continues this remarkable poet's intuitive interaction with the natural world, but I prefer the poems where Dickey goes out to meet the animals on their own turf, not in the London Zoo. Maybe I heard too many sermons when I was a boy, but I flip the pages of "May Day Sermon to the Women of Gilmer County, Georgia, by a Woman Preacher Leaving the Baptist Church" just as I flip my car radio dial past the Sunday morning sermons. "The Zodiac" may capture with perfect verisimilitude the drunken ravings of a poet with an unusual imagination; but I've been there myself sufficiently often to know that a little drunken raving goes a long way.

Having said that, and not having even ventured a glance in the direction of Dickey's achievements as a literary critic and novelist, I think there are many fine things in the later parts of *The Whole Motion.* Dickey's elegy for Vince Lombardi I have already cited. "The Rain Guitar" from *The Strength of Fields,* where Dickey sits in the rain by an English stream near Winchester Cathedral playing the guitar (he is of course a virtuoso picker) while an Englishman with a wooden leg casts for trout, is as tight, as inspired, as jaunty as anything he has ever written. The poem ends:

> I was Air Force,
> I said. So was I; I picked
> This up in Burma, he said, tapping his gone leg
> With his fly rod, as Burma and the South
> west Pacific and North Georgia reeled,
> Rapped, cast, chimed, darkened and drew down
> Cathedral water, and improved.

The reeling (of the fly reel, and the reel Dickey is playing on the guitar), the rapping (on the wooden leg, as well as the word in its 1960s sense), the chiming (of the two men's war experiences, along with the Cathedral bells) synchronize magically.

"A good poet," Randall Jarrell wrote in a much-quoted passage on Wallace Stevens from *Poetry and the Age,* "is someone who manages, in a lifetime of standing out in thunderstorms, to be struck by lightning five or six times; a dozen or two dozen times and he is a great." Less often quoted is the way the paragraph begins: "Some of my readers may feel about all this [Jarrell's remarks on Stevens's *Auroras of Autumn*] . . . 'Shouldn't the Mature poet be producing late masterpieces even better than the early ones?' . . . All such questions show how necessary it is to think of the poet as somebody who has prepared himself to be visited by a daemon, as a sort of accident-prone worker to whom poems happen. . . ." Dickey is, in this sense, surpassingly, sublimely accident-prone. May he continue to stand out in thunderstorms, wearing his famous denim jacket with the eagle embroidered on it, so that we, like the barbershop rednecks in "False Youth: Autumn: Clothes of the Age," can:

> get a lifetime look at my bird's
> One word, raggedly blazing with extinction and soaring loose
> In red threads burning up white until I am shot in the back
> Through my wings   or ripped apart
> For rags:
>
> *Poetry*

"Sermon" Packs a Wallop of Feminist Messages

A review of the performances of "Sermon," based on "May Day Sermon
to the Women of Gilmer County, Georgia, by a Woman Preacher
Leaving the Baptist Church," a poem by James Dickey

CLIFFORD GALLO

"Southern-born poet . . . James Dickey must be a born-again feminist."

S outhern-born poet and novelist James Dickey must be a born-again feminist. Having spent the bulk of his career charting masculine, often violent
adventures in most of his works—the 69-year-old writer is best known as the
author of *Deliverance*—Dickey shifted gears in 1982 with "Puella," a long
poem about a young girl blossoming into womanhood. Dickey makes the transition complete in "Sermon," a new poem premiering at Theatre West in Hollywood. Flawlessly staged and directed by John Gallogly and performed with
amazing grace by Bridget Hanley, "Sermon" is a trip to the promised land.

In "Sermon," Dickey uses a fiery woman's speech before a Baptist congregation in Georgia—the poem's complete title is "May day sermon to the
women of Gilmer County, Georgia, by a woman preacher leaving the Baptist
Church"—to celebrate the arcadian beauty of female sexuality while acknowledging how men, often God-fearing ones at that, use religion to control and
punish women for their erotic desires.

Dickey's poetry has been compared to the "liquid, billowy waves" of Walt
Whitman's verse. It's a telling comparison because "Sermon's" fluid power,
lush imagery and fecund beauty wash over us, creating a sensual experience
that is propelled by evangelical fervor and an elegiac current.

With the sound of rushing water, chirping birds and women's voices in
our ears, Hanley's Preacher, a solemn, sturdy woman in her Sunday best, walks
past a large, wood-stained Cross. She removes her sensible coat, then her hat,
revealing flame-red hair that has been pulled into a bun. She approaches the
lectern and its black-bound Bible, and with a deep, purposeful breath, she
begins.

Originally published in the *Los Angeles Daily News*, 27 November 1992, "L.A. Life Weekend," 21.

The intensity in her lilting Georgia accent grows as she tells of a girl on the brink of womanhood who was caught in a compromising situation with her motorcycle-riding boyfriend. As punishment, she was stripped and beaten by her willow-branch–wielding father, who shouted lines from the Scriptures, "using the tried-and-true rhythm of the Lord."

As "Sermon" continues, it takes on a mythic dimension that comes to fruition when the story takes a mystical twist near its end. Preacher goes on to tell how the young woman used an ice pick, "a long pine needle," to kill her father. "It's easier for a needle to pass through the eye of a man heading to heaven," she says with ironic satisfaction. Her vengeance complete, the young woman and her leather-jacketed lover zoom away without a trace.

Under Gallogly's lyrical direction, Hanley gives a passionate and heartfelt performance, preaching and ministering like a woman possessed. With silent eloquence, Hanley underscores everything Dickey has written with a deceptively simple act of rebellion that concentrates the play's intent in one telling gesture that symbolizes her loss of faith.

When a Predator Is the Prey

A review of *To the White Sea* by James Dickey

MALCOLM JONES JR.

"Dickey means to give you the creeps, and he succeeds
mightily in a great novel."

James Dickey collars you on the first page of *To the White Sea* and never lets
go. At the outset, a B-29 tailgunner named Muldrow is shot down over
Tokyo in the last days of World War II. The lone survivor of his crew, he
flees the city in the midst of a firebombing and strikes out for Hokkaido, the
northernmost Japanese island, where he aims to elude his pursuers in the
snowy wastes. It is hard to imagine a man in a worse fix. As Muldrow says, "I
was in the enemy's home territory. Everybody was my enemy."

To the White Sea, . . . the poet's third novel, is a first-rate adventure story,
as relentless and mesmerizing as *Deliverance*. Muldrow's laconic but earnest
narration ("I don't mind talking, I'll tell you anything I know") provides the
perfect deadpan accompaniment to his surreal adventures. Counting the plane
ride that begins his journey, he battles air, fire, earth, and water, countless
Japanese, and even a wild goatlike creature called a serow that gores him vi-
ciously. An Alaskan trapper and hunter in civilian life, Muldrow is a consum-
mate woodsman of almost mythic proportions. Describing his prowess, he even
talks like Mike Fink or Paul Bunyan ("I was as strong as a bear and could
climb like a squirrel"), but his boasting isn't empty: he can strike fire from flint
and steer by the stars, and has a near-feral knack for camouflage.

He is also a killer with no more scruples than a wolverine. At first, he kills
for clothes and food, but after a while, you realize he's not killing out of need
or even panic. A pure predator, he's driven by instinct. "I had a taste for blood
in my mouth, in my whole body," he says in the middle of his journey. And
when he decapitates one of his victims and stuffs the severed head in a water
wheel, you know he's one sick puppy. But by the time you figure this out, it's
too late to turn on him. He's already engaged your sympathy as a man com-

pletely out of place in the world, trying with all his might to get somewhere that looks like home. You root for him even after you know he is a monster.

Few writers make you squirm as Dickey can. *To the White Sea* allows no easy assumptions about nature or violence or war. What makes it so haunting, though, what keeps you reading, is the beauty of the prose. Never straying from the confines of Muldrow's plain-spoken diction, Dickey works wonders with a near-perfect cadence and an ear for the apt phrase. When Muldrow rows across from Honshu to Hokkaido, he gets caught in the double wake of two huge ships: "The whole strait was swirling around me from both directions; it was like being sawed in two by water." *To the White Sea* is both entertainment and literature: easy to read, it is not easy reading. Dickey means to give you the creeps, and he succeeds mightily in a great novel.

INTERVIEWS

Interview with James Dickey

ROBERT KIRSCHTEN

This interview was conducted by Robert Kirschten on 16 December 1995 and 6 and 17 February 1996, by telephone with Mr. Dickey from his home in Columbia, South Carolina. Questions asked of him were submitted to the interviewer by distinguished poets and critics from around the United States, many of whom are contributors to this collection.

WILLIAM HARMON: What kinds of knowledge must poets have to teach themselves to write? What must they get from others? And what must they avoid?

JAMES DICKEY: Well, I don't think you should avoid any. I think the material that you need is just a human life. Your own and—what would you say?—a love of language, a liking for fooling around with words and seeing what you can make them do. Poetic knowledge is essentially an attitude, which can be encouraged. The main attitude is that you have to have a native liking of the mystery that exists between language and reality. Not only the reality as the world presents it, but through the reality that it can be made to seem by means of words—what you can do with reality in your own way. This is the knowledge that's got to fascinate you. It's got to be a lifelong fascination, and you can't fake it. You can encourage it by not impeding it, not getting in the way of it, but saying, you know: "I think this is a good idea. I think this is a good image. I think this is a good observation, and I'm going to use them. I'll put them down, put them down in a notebook, and I'll just let them accumulate." Then, I go back to these observations and add others to them—all the time—and things just build up naturally in sort of an organic way.

ROBERT KIRSCHTEN: When you are teaching poetry, are there kinds of poetic "knowledge"—principles or techniques or exercises—that you require of students?

DICKEY: I give a course in poetry writing that runs two semesters. The first half is a course in forms. We work with a form a week, which is pretty tough. We start out, simply, with prose and work up through tougher forms such as gravestone epitaphs and haiku of seventeen syllables. The following weeks I introduce rhyme with one rhymed couplet, an epigrammatic couplet, then full-scale satire, the quatrain, the sonnet, and on to more complicated forms. We end with a sestina, which is very tough. It's a progressive stepladder sort of a thing from simpler forms on up to the more difficult. The second term starts on an entirely different premise. We begin with the material of the mind, the unconscious, the dream life, and what comes from free associations. I work with that and try to get the students to become familiar with the parts of themselves that they didn't know were there. These parts are revealed in their dreams and the whole life of the unconscious. We spend several weeks on their dreams, their subconscious or subliminal or whatever you want to call it. We explore ways of association that take place unconsciously, yet it's happening. We work with that then try the whole rest of the semester to search for an particular poetic form, and we spend the whole semester writing one poem, trying it a lot of different ways.

HARMON: In what sense are you a southern poet? Could you be a midwestern poet or one from New England?
DICKEY: I don't think I would have the same emphasis on things: the landscape down here; where the people come from; the southern tip of the Appalachians, that country up there; the rivers and so on—I mean the landscape that's present in so many of our poems. The landscape is part of it, and it is very southern. Also, the ways of taking life are inherited by being born down here. There are certain attitudes, especially toward the family and toward keeping your word. These are the old virtues that the southerners have always had, or the best of them have always had. I like to encourage those in myself and in my children. Another thing is that southerners like rhetoric. My father was a lawyer, but what he really liked was forensic rhetoric—the summation and opening speeches in the cases in the law court. He liked the eloquence. The speeches of Clarence Darrow and Robert Ingersoll, who were two of my father's favorites, are very rhythmical. They're not southerners, but they partake of that element.

ROBERT HILL: Are you still interested in Appalachian culture?
DICKEY: Oh, yes. I don't get a chance to go up in there very much. I took my family up there a few years ago, rather my wife and child, and showed them around some of the places. They liked it. I still have some relatives there, and we went to see them. I have the utmost affection for Appalachia. There is great mystery there. The book where I really tried to get as much of that as I could is in the one called *Wayfarer*. My father's people come from north Georgia—Appalachia. I spent quite bit of time with him up there when I was a child. That mountain scenery is familiar to me, not from having lived there for great lengths of time but because of the way I do see it. That world always seemed a kind of vision to me. So I draw on that whenever I feel like I can.

HARMON: About language and nationality: Is English a particularly effective language for your poetry?
DICKEY: It's the best language for anybody's poetry. It's easily the best that has

ever been concocted or invented or developed. I'm not all that much of a linguist, but I know that English is extremely flexible. It doesn't have a rigid subject-verb-object relationship. It doesn't have rigid rules like French does— with the French negative, that sort of thing. French is very confusing to somebody who is used to speaking English. The sound of English is good because it's got a mixture of authority like the German has, and it has lightness, grace, like the French has. It's not as euphonious like Italian so as to take away from the subject and concentrate on just the sound as you tend to do when you read Italian. The only drawback to English is that it's rhyme poor. You have to have extra technical resources to get around that, even to take advantage of it. For someone like Auden it's no trouble for him to write rhyming verse because he's so resourceful, and this is a lesson for us all. It's no problem for him at all. For other people—say, for some of my students—they struggle with rhymes because there are comparatively few rhymes in English compared to Italian, where almost anything will rhyme with anything else because every word ends on a vowel. But English is harder. Aside from that one drawback, English is the best. It's got that combination of strength and lightness, and you can vary the tones all the way in between. It has marvelous metaphor-making capabilities and a very strong sound, a very forceful, driving kind of sound, plus that tremendous vocabulary so that you can suddenly change a meaning. All of these are great advantages for a poet who works in English.

R. W. B. LEWIS: Describe the difference between composing in prose narratives and poetic narratives. You've worked in both.
DICKEY: It's a question of the form, depending on, let's say, if you were writing a narrative in blank verse or in the ballad. The medium you use is the determining factor for how you are going to present the material. In prose all you need is sentences and paragraphs. Now, you should have good ones, naturally, as good as you can make them, but you don't have the recurring stresses that you do in poetry with the strong, rhythmical thrust that poetry gives. Prose has its own strength, or what I call "adagio," but it's not based on the recurrence of accent, as poetry is. So, if you were doing a narrative in verse, blank verse, say, or ballads, or something like a silent sequence, like Meredith's "Modern Love," for example, the fact that you were using that form would be a determining factor in presenting the material that you are working with. There is a narrative element in a good many of my poems, but it is an episode. It is over quickly. It takes place in a matter of minutes, sometimes seconds.

KIRSCHTEN: Do you believe in the classical principles of plot construction in both mediums? Let's say, Aristotle's?
DICKEY: Yes, I do. I swear by those; however, you can make all kinds of variations on beginnings, middles, and ends. You can break up the narrative, and you can splinter it in various ways, but it still has to come out somehow. It has to start somewhere, and it's got to move through material, events, and people,

and so on, and it's got to end somewhere. That's fundamental. Aristotle was quite right.

KIRSCHTEN: Do you diagram plots or outline stories before you write them?

DICKEY: No. I actually don't. A lot of times in poetry, I just start out with a very simple notion or an image usually, or maybe it could be a word.

KIRSCHTEN: Not a dramatic incident?

DICKEY: Sometimes, but it's more likely to be an image.

KIRSCHTEN: So, you think primarily in the elements of poetry rather than in the elements of drama?

DICKEY: Well, I always try to get it going on at the same time. I mean, you don't really compartmentalize them.

KIRSCHTEN: Critics do.

DICKEY: Yes, they do. When writing poetry, a lot of times, I start out with only a relatively vague notion of where I'm going, but it's not that way with prose or fiction. I need to know what's going to happen at every point before I start in to write it—a novel, say. I want to know the beginning, and I want to know the end. I want to know something about how I'm going to get from one to the other. When I began writing *To the White Sea,* I had a fresh image of a guy hung up on a parachute on a gantry on a loading dock. I wondered who the guy was, then the war came into it. Then I wondered about his personality and how he would survive. Was he just going down into Japan and trying to survive pillar to post? That wouldn't be interesting enough. So, I conceived that he was a cold-weather man. He understood snow, vast wastes, wind, desolation, hunting, trapping. He not only understood that; he loved it. He felt at home in it, and he felt that if he could get up to the northern part of the country—which is, roughly, like the part of Alaska where he grew up—then he could survive. But it's not merely a matter of survival but a sort of quest, a search. The hardest part of writing *To the White Sea* was to establish a tone or voice for Muldrow which would be convincing and yet completely distinctive to him. He's practically illiterate, but he has a highly developed personal mystique, which he states as a matter of course as though anybody would understand it. Actually, nobody but he understands it. All of this comes out in his attempt to reach the White Sea.

KIRSCHTEN: Do you use outlines or charts when writing fiction?

DICKEY: Not really. Scott Fitzgerald used to start out with graphs and things. No, I would get so interested in that, I probably wouldn't write the story. If I was writing a novel, my sentences would get written right on the typewriter usually. I would have a blank sheet to the right of the typewriter, just flat on the desk, and write down roughly the sequences that I want to deal with and refer to that then write the actual story on the typewriter.

KIRSCHTEN: So, you outline as you go?

DICKEY: Yes, that's right.

R. BARTON PALMER: Is *Deliverance* about regeneration through violence?

DICKEY: In this particular case it certainly is, but I wouldn't recommend it as a general remedy. It's just that sometimes these things happen that way. It is certainly not presented as a formula.

PALMER: In fiction do you consider yourself a realist?

DICKEY: No, I would not say so. Not realism in the sense of someone like James T. Farrow or Theodore Dreiser, who report the facts, are very close to journalism, research things, and get correct details about events and situations. I have no interest in that at all.

LEWIS: I am currently writing a critical biography of Robert Penn Warren, and I wonder if his poetic narratives have been of value to you?

DICKEY: Yes, he goes at it a little differently than the way I do. His orientation is a good deal different than mine, but it does share certain things. Both of us have a tendency to skirt melodrama; maybe we should put in a little more melodrama. I think we fairly well resisted getting into too much of that, but we are both drawn to it. I know I am.

ERNEST SUAREZ: In the preface to *Night Hurdling* you wrote that "the impress of a personality is the most important quality in poetry." In many of your poems, even though they are written from various perspectives (animals, a woman falling out of an airplane, a sex fiend, a woman preacher), the "impress" of your personality or, at least, a fictional self, is evident. Yet, in *Puella,* as well as other works of yours, the "impress of a personality" becomes almost covert. Could you comment on the difference between your use of personality in poems such as "Falling" and "May Day Sermon" and the *Puella* sequence?

DICKEY: That's a little hard to do, I think. "Falling" is sort of a tour de force type of poem. I tell it about the girl falling out of the airplane, but it's not told exactly from her point of view. Kind of, but not completely.

KIRSCHTEN: The narrator is really the central personality in "Falling," isn't he? It's essentially your poetic voice, not hers?

DICKEY: I think it's a matter of the tone of voice that you use. *Puella* was more of an experiment in language. I put more emphasis on the actual language I was using than on the events I was depicting. I wanted to do that. I had read through most of my earlier work, and it seemed to me that I had given maybe a little too much credence to the events and the situations that I wrote about and not enough to the language itself. Some writer who concentrates on the linguistic part of it—somebody like Gerard Hopkins or Hart Crane or Wallace Stevens—they are on the other side of things. They don't seem to have the same interest in the subject matter as they do in the language in which they write about the subject matter. I thought maybe I could use a little bit more of that attitude. I tried to put that to work in *Puella.* I enjoyed that very much. That was a completely new dimension for me. I don't like to repeat myself. *Puella* involves a strange, disturbing kind of self-awareness, not possible to a child. It partly comes from childhood and partly from some unknown region called, I suppose, adulthood. *Puella* is a rite of passage, a passage from childhood to womanhood. This new, disturbing life includes a sexual longing, which the narrator, a woman, is fascinated by and afraid of. The last part of the book, "The Summons," is an imagining of the different forms her first lover might take.

PATRICIA LAURENCE: Did you think of Deborah as a woman, a voice, or a force in *Puella*—all of these or something else?

DICKEY: Sometimes I use her voice or her body or her physical sensations. Sometimes I focus on her social status, sometimes her status as a brand-new woman with menstruation and sex coming into it. But everything is conditioned by the transitional period she undergoes.

KIRSCHTEN: Does your language reflect that change in her?

DICKEY: I don't think so, really. I don't think anyone ever talked that way. It's supposed to be an angle of insight into her situation. The language is supposed to convey that, not the way she talks. The thing about her is that she feels all this new energy, but it's too early in her life for her to find any way to direct it. This energy remains essentially at the status of a mystery, more than anything else. She feels the mystery as energy, and it's going to go somewhere. She doesn't know where.

KIRSCHTEN: She seems ready to burst forth or explode.

DICKEY: That's right. That's what I want. *Puella* will last longer than most of my other things. It didn't get much play or attention when it came out, but that's fine with me. *Puella* will find its readers. The critics want something like what I have already done. But I don't like to repeat myself. This book was a real turning point for me because, as I said, I gave more play to the language the poem was written in rather than on the situation that the poem is about. I was getting tired of the poetry of the versified anecdote.

KIRSCHTEN: Do the poems in *Puella* progress?

DICKEY: I don't think they do. They are just different aspects of the same condition. I don't think the book has an ending, except for the invocation where she speculates on what her first lover will be like when he comes. He'll be one of these fellows or creatures or maybe none of them or maybe all of them at the same time.

KIRSCHTEN: How do you end individual poems in *Puella*?

DICKEY: I try to end on the dominant note that the poem is concerned with and, like most poets, with as strong a line as I can, for instance, "far orchards blazing with slant."

LAURENCE: Could you talk about your experiment in *Puella* and other poems to give a voice to nature or the inanimate?

DICKEY: I don't think that I could say anything sweeping about a controlling metaphor for that except that Deborah feels herself much more part of those things, like when she says in "Springhouse": "I shall rise and walk out through all the walls / / Of my father's house   holding, but not at bay, / High-energy cloth where I scotched it / Like iron between my legs / and go / / Whole-hearted and undoctored toward the hillside / Beaming its distances, the fruit in my hand / Encompassing, crackling with vitality." She is with all living things, and the stone in her father's house is also living to her. Everything has a new life. Her new powers give life to everything around her.

LAURENCE: Has giving a voice to women or a woman preoccupied you in other poems than *Puella?*

DICKEY: Not as concentrated in the same way as it is in *Puella.* It's funny. I was for so long supposed to be a macho-type person. People who say that have to remember *Puella,* and they also have to remember that my two most famous poems are about women and are told from the standpoint of women, "Falling" and "May Day Sermon."

KIRSCHTEN: How did you arrive at the topography, the visual look, of the poems on the page in *The Eagle's Mile?*

DICKEY: I'm very much interested in painting a sort of graphic representation of things. That certainly entered into it and, maybe, in ways I myself don't even know about. But that's very much a part of it. What I wanted to do—generally, I know—is to get a kind of a strange sense of balance of the poem on the page. I tried various ways to do that, and I would run one line over then I would drop down a few lines and let the lines sort of hang. I don't know, it's not really all that clear in my mind. I can't really reason it out beyond that. I just felt that, at this point in the poem, it was right to do it this way—that this is what I should do right here. So, I did that. One of the working principles I have is to take any subject through a lot of drafts. I like to try different things and try different ways, because something is almost invariably bound to be better than another way. I want to give all the ways I can as much chance to be heard as I can figure out.

KIRSCHTEN: Are all your drafts still written on typewriters?

DICKEY: Yes.

KIRSCHTEN: You don't use a word processor or a more advanced technology?

DICKEY: No, I'm afraid of those things. I'm too old for that.

KIRSCHTEN: What do you do when you rewrite?

DICKEY: I look to see what is struggling to become clear. I try to implement that any way I can. If I have any adventures in writing, it's in revision. To take something and say, "Now this is what I seem to be meaning, right here. It would be clearer and it would make more of an impact if I did this right here—if I change this word or this rhythm or this metaphor or whatever it might be. It might be better if I did this, so let's put that down and look at it and see what happens." You have to have an extensive use of what Auden calls the "censor," which tells you what can come in and what can't come in.

KIRSCHTEN: You conclude *The Eagle's Mile* with an extremely strong section of lyrics that you call "Double-tongue: Collaborations and Rewrites." What are those?

DICKEY: That's an interesting idea, but I don't think it's original with me. Someone said of Robert Lowell's "imitations," when they were going to be published, that "We like these, but tell Mr. Lowell not to call them translations. He takes too many liberties." But that's good. Between the English language and a poet who writes in English who wants to translate some poem in another language, there exists an enormous limbo of possibility. One part of this is a literal translation: to get an equivalent in English as close as possible to what the original text says. I mean, word for word. You can never really get that because the shadings of meanings vary from language to language. You can never get the exact equivalent, but the attempt to do it is one thing that guides a certain kind of translator, one who tries to be as accurate as he can be. Then there is the other extreme: a writer who may not even know the other language that he's supposed to be translating from. He gets a pony or something like that from somebody else, and then he sits down, like Pound did with the Chinese, and he tries to get what he thinks is the spirit of the original poet into English, rather than the exact translation of the words. Now that produces stuff like Pound's Cathay poems, which are wonderful and among the best things he ever did. But they are not literal at all; or, he translates from the Latin, "Homage to Sextus Propertius." That's very far from what the poet said, but it's very good for what Ezra Pound said, that is, by using Propertius as a persona.

KIRSCHTEN: You sort of translated or "collaborated" from the Chinese?

DICKEY: Well, I did that. You could do any language you want. If you have some approximation of what the guy's trying to say, you can just take off with it, and ain't nothing says you can't.

KIRSCHTEN: You begin with a text by a poet?

DICKEY: Right, or somebody else's translation. And I say, Well, this would be pretty good, either the original poet said that or the translator said that, but this is what he should've said, what I would've said," and then you put that down. A "rewrite"—I suppose I get that term from journalism or advertising. But that's essentially what it amounts to. A "free translation"? I don't know. There are a lot of different words for it. Rendition from, or something of that sort. What it actually is, is a rewrite.

KIRSCHTEN: You figure there is another draft of a poem in their text?

DICKEY: Just to see what happens. Because the great thing, if I may interpolate this, the great thing about this whole endeavor is the sense of adventure and discovery and trafficking with the unknown. That's the exciting thing about it. That's the thing that makes us do it and keeps us at it until we die. Because we want to go into that unknown territory, which only we have access to. Because, if we are who we are, if our own personality and our dreams and biorhythms and so on are just exactly as they are, only we know where this place is. We don't know what's there, but we know something's there, and we want to go into it. We want to be out there at the periphery of what's been done before and push out further. We *don't* want to be where the thing has been done before. That's the fun of it. It's a perpetual excitement.

KIRSCHTEN: This is the adventure that is fundamental to you in writing?

DICKEY: Absolutely. There is nothing else. That's why a poet will sell his grandmother down the river, or she'll let her children starve, or he'll murder his wife. Anything to be able to keep on writing. It's worse than any addiction from substances, from alcohol or narcotics or anything else. This is worse than any of them and all of them put together. Worse and better.

RONALD BAUGHMAN: How do you arrive at a book of poems? Do you conceive of a book as a unit?

DICKEY: To answer the last question: no, except in the case of *Puella,* where the overall theme was the formidable adolescent years of a young girl. But, in general, there is no deliberate theme for my material. They all add up, though, in some way. Maybe the informing spirit of it is my own personality. There is no plan.

RICHARD TILLINGHAST: How has your poetry been influenced by your guitar playing?

DICKEY: If I had to choose what has influenced the rhythmical part of my work the most—the English prosodic tradition or the pulse of the folk guitar—I could not choose between them. Though, I would be inclined to choose the guitar.

STEPHEN ENNISS: Speaking from my experience as curator of the Dickey Papers at Emory University, I notice a duality in your career between romantic self-expression or exuberance and the minute detail and order (notebooks, daily work plans, notes) which mark your work. How do you explain these opposite impulses?

DICKEY: Well, part of my heritage is German, on my mother's side, and I suppose I get a lot of that from the orientation I was raised with. I try to be more systematic than I am, but I'm like a musician who plays a lot or practices a lot so that he doesn't have to practice. He gets his motor circuits so deeply bruised so that they just play the instrument for him. I try to clamp that super-discipline on myself as much as I can then take it off and try to fly.

ENNISS: Do you continue to believe that *Alnilam* is your best novel? Why?

DICKEY: Easily. It's charged with more. It's more interesting; it has more people in it and more mystery of a certain sort. It raises more questions that people will ponder, and I think the dramatic presentation of the blind man who by accident comes in contact with his son's personality through other people is a good plot device. The split page adds a bit to the capacities of prose fiction, adds another dimension. It adds the blind man's interpretation of the scene that he's participating in to those of the people he happens to be connected with at the time. The other side of the page is showing what's really there. I didn't want to overuse that. I used it in just a few key scenes. I think all that adds up to being the best I can do as a novelist.

HILL: What kinds of criticism are most valuable for examining your work and which least?
DICKEY: The overanalytical ones are the worst, the ones that yield least to me. I have never gotten much that I could use through those. The criticism that I like best are the interpretative ones, in which the critic seems to enter into the spirit of what I've written and write about it from the inside. There are few of those. Warren was one of those who could do that with my work. Stanley Burnshaw was another and Dick Lewis. Those are the critics who are serviceable to me. And that's really what you want critics to do. You don't mind if they praise you. You don't like it when they put you down, but what you really want is for them to give you something you can use.

HENRY HART: How did you get interested in myth?
DICKEY: I've always liked magic, and I've always liked ceremonials of various sorts, and I've always liked primitivism and primitive tribes, when things were both very basic and simple and revolved around staying alive and surviving. I have always been interested in cave paintings; that's essentially a form of ritual magic. One of the best long poems I've done is called "The Eye-Beaters," which is about that.

KIRSCHTEN: One of your best and most recent poems is "Last Hours," about your brother, dying of cancer. In his room, during his "last hours," his daughter is reading to him the story of the mass murderer Theodore Bundy. How did Bundy get in there?
DICKEY: Exactly as the poem has it: the daughter was reading to my dying brother, and that's what she was reading. It really happened. She wanted to read something, so she just read from that. He became fascinated by it. The Civil War that he had devoted his life to no longer held any interest to him on his deathbed, but he picked up on the chronicle of a mass murderer. Strange things happen in life.
KIRSCHTEN: Bundy becomes another of your mythological characters.
DICKEY: He does in the sense that he's a savior.
KIRSCHTEN: Charon, the ferry man who ferries the souls of the dead to Hades.
DICKEY: Yeah, right. Exactly.
KIRSCHTEN: Like most monsters, such figures are capable of great evil but, poetically, also of great good. They are Janus-faced.
DICKEY: Yes, but they themselves don't know it. And it takes place after they themselves have been executed for their crime. He shows up when I wanted to blindside the reader, right there. Have him follow, with whatever fascination he would follow, the murderer.

DAVE SMITH: The "knock" on the poetry of the last third of your publishing career has been that you are hermetic to a compromising degree, that poems so sealed in by a language that minimizes referential exchange are self-indulgently noncommunicative.

DICKEY: Let those who say that spend time on the material. I can guarantee that the stuff is there if they are up to it.

SMITH: How do you distinguish the poems of *The Eagle's Mile* from the widely known poems of your early and middle periods?

DICKEY: I come back to the fact that there is more emphasis on charging the language itself in *The Eagle's Mile* rather than depending on the situation that the poem is about. There are situations to some degree, but there's not nearly so much emphasis on that aspect as on the language in which the experience is rendered. There are few plots in what I would call the "vector," or the direction, in these poems. But this new emphasis on the language is quite conscious.

KIRSCHTEN: Are you looking for a new voice to come out of these energized word groups?

DICKEY: Yes, I think one does. These poems don't sound like they're spoken by the same person as the earlier ones. In the earlier poems I was after the quality of trying to be simple without being thin. Now, I don't mind trying to be complex and hope not to be thin in that. I like the later method very much. I'm not completely used to it, but it yields much, and it promises much. I still like a little bit of the narrative and the situation to be retained also. I'm not looking for a compromise but for an idiom that gets the best aspects of both together.

SMITH: People who have written about the poets of the South have tended to view your work as a descendant of the poetry of the Fugitives . . .

DICKEY: Not in the slightest.

SMITH: . . . especially from that of Robert Penn Warren. But a close comparison suggests that yours is a more positive vision of man in a threatened and threatening world.

DICKEY: I would say that, as far as diction, I am probably closer to Allen Tate than Warren, though I am closer to Warren in spirit.

KIRSCHTEN: You have written extensively on a great number of prominent poets. In a line or two, how do you feel about them now? Let's say, Roethke.

DICKEY: Roethke is one of the finest poets we've ever produced in this country. He has a fabulous rapport with the world of nature and also with the world of insanity, on the most creative possible level. If you hear wind blow, you have heard Roethke's wind.

KIRSCHTEN: Hart Crane.

DICKEY: He's a great master of language. A lot of times he did know exactly what he was saying, but he was intoxicated with words, especially with the connotations of words, and that yields an area to poetry that had never before been explored to the extent that he explored it. He's a remarkable innovator. Now this is an area I know something about. Any poet who can refer to "war's fiery kennel" is an original poet, sure enough. Fiery kennel, like dogs, the thing of dogs burning up!

KIRSCHTEN: Dylan Thomas.

DICKEY: Now, Dylan Thomas is a most original poet in English. The great thing about Dylan Thomas is that his originality is completely natural. Hart Crane's or Mallarmé's or Hopkins's is essentially arrived at. It's thought out in advance in some way. Crane, with his theories of connotation, say, and then Hopkins, with his theories of meter and strong rhythm and those things—those things are thought-out approaches. Dylan Thomas is natural. I mean he talks that way. All you have to do is read his letters. His letters are just as much Dylan Thomas's poetry as the actual poems are. They are just as much him and his imagination. The only difference is the poems have the advantage of being in lines and being able to concentrate the rhythms so much better because the poetry is the medium being used. But the same personality and the same imagination is in everything he wrote: in the letters, the stories, everything. It's all Dylan Thomas, and it's all perfectly natural to him. And that's the wonderful thing. That's what you call genius, being born a genius.

KIRSCHTEN: Robert Penn Warren.

DICKEY: He's one of these searching, uncompromising writers, who is given to images of anxiety and hysteria and violence and uncertainty. He's extremely powerful and primitive. It's strange, really, that, as much as he knew about the techniques of poetry, you don't think about those things at all in his best poems. His vision has such a tremendous capacity to impress itself on you that you don't think about those technicalities at all when you read him.

KIRSCHTEN: William Blake. You took the title of your most recent book of poems, *The Eagle's Mile,* from his "Auguries of Innocence" ("The Emmet's Inch & Eagle's Mile / Make Lame Philosophy to smile").

DICKEY: Blake is one of the great hit-or-miss poets. There's an awful lot of Blake that is extremely boring and self-indulgent. But he, in his way, is an original. The fact that he's a visionary—in the way that these other people are not and that he was, I suppose, technically insane in some ways—increases the interest in him. The fascination with Blake is that you don't know whether he is uttering immortal words or just some sort of mystical gobbledegook. But you like it both; you don't want to miss anything.

KIRSCHTEN: G. M. Hopkins.

DICKEY: He's a great writer, very narrow. He suffers from a lack of subject matter. All of the poems are combinations of nature, observations, religion, and the conversion of those into some sort of religious pronouncement. As original as he is and as good of an ear as he has and as unusual a technician as he was, you have a sense, in Hopkins, of a certain sameness and monotonous-ness. His work becomes almost the same as a formula. I think he's an example of a poet whose time has served very well because he didn't write any more. We've got enough of Hopkins, but a whole lot more would've shown up as this formalistic cast that his poetry does have.

KIRSCHTEN: Whitman.

DICKEY: Whitman is great because he takes in so much. What is it he says to the common prostitute: "Not so the sun excludes you, do I exclude you"? This is very noble, humanistic. Humanism almost to the point of vision or religious sanctity. I don't know what you would call it, but that attitude is worth a very great deal. Especially for an American. Especially for this place that is relatively new territory over here. We needed a voice like that, one that was all-embracing. Again, Whitman wrote too much, a lot of it tiresome and repetitive, but some of it is marvelous and couldn't have been written by anybody but him. The vision and the attitude is so important in Whitman. Some of it is kind of phony, but a lot of it isn't. And we need him.

KIRSCHTEN: Yeats.

DICKEY: I've been reading a lot of Yeats lately. There are a lot of poems by Yeats that I cannot for the life of me connect with. I like some of those mystical poems and the poems he writes about in connection with his book *Vision* and all those. They are as strange as they can be, but they don't really speak to me. The poems in which Yeats is best are the ones in which he is most human and speaking out of his own condition rather than trying to be a mystical prophet. Although he's not bad with a sort of a one-man religion, a good religion, an interesting religion, because it's antiscientific, and it's got its own laws and its own meaning, and it's perfectly self-consistent. Somebody asked Yeats whether he really believed it or not; he said that's irrelevant. And it is. It's fascinating in itself.

LAURENCE LIEBERMAN: Your poetry is filled with animals—eagles, horses, sharks, eagles. At this point in your life, how would you like to be reincarnated?

DICKEY: The wolverine for me is the ultimate wild animal, and I still like him a lot. In the air, the peregrine falcon. In the water, the barracuda!

Interview with John Gallogly and Bridget Hanley, director and actress for James Dickey's "May Day Sermon"

ROBERT KIRSCHTEN

James Dickey's eleven-page poem "May Day Sermon to the Women of Gilmer County, Georgia, by a Woman Preacher Leaving the Baptist Church" was produced under the shortened title "Sermon" at Theatre West In Los Angeles during the fall of 1992 and the winter of 1993. John Gallogly directed the production, which starred Bridget Hanley in the role of the Baptist woman preacher. This preacher is the poetic voice for Dickey's own retelling of "a local folk myth" from the hill farms of Georgia: a Bible-quoting father beats and abuses his daughter for taking a lover; the daughter kills the father with an ice pick then later dies with her lover when they crash into a backwoods river while riding away on his motorcycle. In an ecstatic, one-hour explosion of southern oratory, Bridget Hanley wove this simple country legend into a sermon for the poetic women of Gilmer County and for the real audiences of Los Angeles. Dickey's sermon reverses both the legend and the daughter's fate. For the power of the preacher's word gives the daughter eternal life as the poet's words and images enter the souls of the congregation of women. For instance, of the creek where the lovers die, the preacher tells her audience:

> Children, you know it: that place was where they took
> Off into the air   died   disappeared   entered my mouth   your mind
> Each year . . . (10)[1]

"Sermon" thus becomes an annual fertility rite. This rite is designed to restore all women and the entire earth to a natural state of fruitfulness through an ancient ritual of blood sacrifice, directed this time not against women but against the abusive, religious patriarchy that degrades them. Not only is sexual instinct revitalized on May Day, but nature itself—conceived by Dickey as sacred and feminine—becomes a universal festival of energy and renewal, all effected by the oratorical triad of energized women who constitute the speaker, audience, and homiletic text.

Critical reaction to this production was exceptional. In the Los Angeles *Reader* Kit Roane noted that "director John Gallogly presents a wondrous and raw interpretation of what is sure to become an American classic." In the *Los Angeles Times* T. H. McCulloh wrote that "Hanley, under John Gallogly's astute, bravado direction, never misses an intake of breath, a quick riveting glance at her audience or the violent crescendos and sudden confidences of the writing. . . . [Hanley presents] a remarkable re-creation of a Baptist preacher in the Deep South, as theatrical and transparent." And in *Drama-Logue* Richard Scaffidi claimed that "Hanley's unrelenting performance starts with firmness, rapidly advances to flamboyance, and fires itself up to near-frenzy. Yet there is control here, evidence by the precision blocking and attunement to rhythm. The impressive results bespeak harmony between a bold director and a trusting, talented actress. . . . Church was, alas, never like this—even on May Day."[2] Because of the extraordinary quality of this performance and because this collection of materials includes two other re-creations of Dickey's work in the mode of performance art, the editor thought that it would be interesting for the reader to see how one of Dickey's best poems—certainly his most powerful woman's poem—has been dramatized. What follows is a detailed account of director John Gallogly's and actress Bridget Hanley's process of producing Dickey's long lyric "May Day Sermon" for the theatre.

How Did You Find This Material?

JOHN GALLOGLY   In 1977, when I first discovered James Dickey's "Sermon," I was working on *Runaways* in the New York Shakespeare Festival at the Public Theatre in Manhattan. We were getting ready to take the show to Broadway, and I heard Dickey read on the "Dick Cavett Show." Dickey was reading a poem, and his voice stayed with me: the southernness of the voice, the accent, the baritone. I went to the Gotham Book Store on Forty-seventh Street in the diamond district and bought *Poems 1957–1967*. I read the first two pages of incredibly dense language and imagery and said: "My, God. What is this?" It was "Sermon."

It took me about six months to get past those two pages. I knew that as soon as I read the poem that it was a play. It was extraordinarily theatrical. It has everything that a stage play needs, which is an audience and a performer. The audience was built into the poem because the women of Gilmer County are present in the poem. When I read the poem, I knew that I was too young to do it. I wanted to perform it myself! I knew that I had to find a woman who could do this, and that I had to be old enough to understand it. To do this poem, you have to be at least in your mid-thirties. The closer you are to fifty, the better off you are. So, I put the poem down for ten years.

Fast-forward to 1987, and I'm working at the Mark Taper Forum, where Derek Walcott gave a lecture on verse in the theatre. He claimed that, because so many playwrights were currently working in a modern, naturalistic style, they had given up a tremendous tool [by omitting verse] because the logic of verse is not linear; that is to say, poetry fits awkwardly into a realistic plot. Though he didn't have Dickey in mind, I can see what he meant if, say, an actor reads a line from "Sermon" such as "Often a girl in the country will find herself / Dancing with God in a mule's eye." In a prose play—a realistic, naturalistic drama that is a slice of life—the line makes no literal sense. But in a play of verse it is a brilliant line that refers back at once to three or four different images. To be given credibility, the line does not demand a leap of faith by the audience. The audience allows you to use the line like a song in a musical or like a soliloquy in Shakespeare. The line offers a heightened emotion, a greater range of colorful image; so, you can combine God, a mule's eye, and a girl dancing in one highly focused, emotional picture. After Walcott's lecture I pulled Dickey's poem out of my trunk, reread it, and I knew that I could do "Sermon."

What Attracted You to Dickey's Poem When You First Read It?

GALLOGLY   It is the voice, again. A voice that is singular, rural in the sense that it lives in nature, one that is in touch with the life force (including life and death) that is in nature. I love that. I love the power. I like the sex. I like the retributive violence against abuse which is carried out in the name of religion. I like the spirituality. In conversation with me Dickey claimed that there is no such thing as spirit. "You show me spirit," he said. "I know nothing of it. I know only the physical. I know only the things of this world." But there is a great deal of spirit in his work, a spirit that comes from the real world. Not a world of dead, literary myths, but a real, living belief system of energy and spirit that draws you in and keeps you there. The first line of the poem stunned me: "Each year at this time I shall be telling you of the Lord / —Fog, gamecock, snake and neighbor—giving men all the help they need / To drag their daughters into barns" (3). The starkness, the brutality, the brilliance of being able to use a symphony-like coda—"Fog, gamecock, snake, and neighbor"—in the middle of a declarative sentence; all that pulled me right into the poem. I was there. That's what I meant by the voice, as well as the sound, of this man Dickey, reading in my head.

BRIDGET HANLEY   John Gallogly gave me a copy of "May Day Sermon" and suggested that we perform it. I then read the poem on an airplane. It was so dense and so full of images, and the images flew one upon the other upon the other upon the other, that I was devastated. I thought, "Oh, I don't get it." But I did get it because I wept. And I truly wept. I had to hide my face from the stewardess. I didn't know why, but it moved me in such a way that, when I got to New York, I called John and said: "I don't know what we're going to do with it, but I feel an extraordinary need to give it a try. Let's try the first five minutes and see what happens."

When Did You First Think of "May Day Sermon" in Performance Terms?

GALLOGLY   As soon as I read it, I knew it was a piece of theatre, but it took fifteen years to flesh out those terms. There was just no way that I understood it emotionally. Not until I had my own child. I could always see her—the daughter in "Sermon"—being beaten, and I could always hear the preacher.

HANLEY "May Day Sermon" is a perfect dramatic piece because it is this extraordinary event. It is this woman coming to give her final performance with extraordinary fervor, intensity, and devotion to her subject. She has so much information she wants to impart. Even though there are many different voices present in the poem, it is still one event. Whatever person the Woman Preacher becomes—whether she's herself, the daughter, the father, or the lover—all of these voices come alive within the framework of her final words.

Did You Alter the Poem for the Stage?

GALLOGLY I knew that the piece was whole and complete, but I didn't know how to make it work as a whole. I didn't want to fool with it; we didn't and it paid off. From the very beginning of the workshop process, people told us to cut this and that, especially sections about the fog, the river, and the motorcycle, which befuddled them. Also it's an hour long; it's emotionally intense, and people couldn't handle it at first—at least the way we were doing it in the beginning. We needed to develop it enough so that we could make it move as an entire whole. There's an art to a piece like this, which takes time to find. The performance begins when the preacher walks into the church at the beginning and ends when she walks out. Each paragraph and line needs to be strung together into an overall look that has an impact greater than all the parts. The art is in finding out how to fit together all the parts; that is the process I had to discover.

HANLEY I have fallen so in love with every word that I would miss desperately anything we were to change or cut. There are many repetitions. When we first started rehearsal, I felt many of them could be changed or shaved, but now I would miss any space, pause, or line left out.

Describe the Development Process for This Production

GALLOGLY I worked on the poem by myself for quite some time just to figure it out. Then Bridget and I sat down across a small wooden table in my office to identify major themes. I treated the poem as an opera or symphony and identified four different topics in the opening such as "fog, gamecock, snake, and neighbor." We asked, why are these terms in that first line? Where will they pay off later in the place? It is a dramatic story in which the end is somehow in the opening. We spent a month, three or four hours at a time, across that table, talking about the baby, the incest, the religion, the sound of Obidiah, the religion, the blood, and about how each element echoes throughout. What about the pole of the willow limb? Where does that pole show up? It shows up in the barn. It shows up smacking into the male lover's eye. We figured out all the cross-references: where each image began and where we wanted to go with it. Once we got to a certain saturation point, we got the piece up on its feet.

From the very beginning Bridget went full boar like that hog in the poem, roaring into May Day. We'd go flat out for a page and a half to see what she had then go back and work on that. The whole process took eight months before we put it on for the public, but in two or three months we were putting it on at the Theatre West Workshop on Monday evenings. We put up twenty minutes at a time. We separated it into three big sections and six smaller sections within those three. We worked on one section at a time then put them together. For example, we would go up to the line, "You can beat me to death, and I still will be glad," then work sections A and B together then work on C. We then put thirty minutes onstage and read another thirty at the podium to see how it played.

Because we wanted to present the poem authentically, we got books from the Depression: the 1930s, 1940s, 1950s—pictures of the South, WPA [Works Progress Administration] pictures. If the preacher was preaching in the 1950s (which is when we set the time), we thought the style of dress would be from the 1930s and 1940s, because this is a backwoods hollow. We thought that the preacher would have grown up in the 1920s and 1930s, so we had to find pictures to evoke that time and put those images into our own minds while we worked.

We needed a back story that we could play. A back story is very different from the actual story. A good actor works off of a subtext, a feeling underneath the text which says something different from the words. A back story is the same thing for a character; it may not be written into the piece, but it is the story that happens before the piece begins. We had to make it a story Bridget could play. Who was the girl? Who is the preacher? What is the relation between the girl, the preacher, and the father? Is the preacher the wife of the father and the mother of the daughter? Is the preacher the child herself, who kills her father? Those questions must be answered then strung into a coherent back story. We created a back story that filled in motivational holes not written directly into the poem. We needed to make the back story as close as possible to Bridget herself so it would play emotionally for her. Bridget has a real eighteen-year-old daughter going off to college. If the preacher is the mother of the daughter, the daughter's pain and tragedy are much stronger for Bridget, as they would be for any parent. This invented back story enables the actor to feed off herself emotionally in a way that echoes throughout when she performs the poet's script.

Another step in the workshop process is physical. We had to make this material into a performance rather than just a reading. We took the piece as a literal sermon and used a pulpit to anchor the story. We needed physical spaces for the actor to play in. So, we put the barn and the pole of light in one place, the father and the mother in another, so that Bridget had a consistent pattern of movement as she worked. Physical signs for the action surrounding different characters was also important. We had to create a physicality to match the preacher's account of them. For example, when the motorcycle passes through the trees in God's land, how do you create the trees? We used both of Bridget's hands in a stiff motion, moving from the top of the podium up past her ears in a very martial way. We then slowed down that motion as she got more and more into the land. The murder of the father, the beating of the daughter, the release of the animals, the fog—all those verbal images had to be signaled by something physical. In musicals there is a physical score that is separate from the subtext and from the lyric of the song. The physical score creates emotional images in the minds of the audience. It does not necessarily reflect the literal meaning of the words but gives a fuller emotional power to an image in the song. For example, when we hear Dickey's words, "she knows she was born to hang / In the middle of Gilmer County   to dance on May Day, with holy / Words all around her   with beasts and insects" (4), Bridget caressed her hair as if she were doing a television commercial for a shampoo. She then shot the caressing hand straight up above her head and went up on her toes as if she were being hung. Later on, when she says, "streams born to hang / In the pines of Nickajack Creek" (1), we repeated the gesture. The streams are not hanging from a rope or hanging from the trees, but we had to create a physicality that mirrors the image of hanging from the poem. Those "streams born to hang" are like "she has learned / / That home is to hang in   home is where your father cuts the baby / Fat from your flanks for the Lord" (8). It's the same hanging image, and we tried to find an effective voice and gesture that would reflect the action of the image.

There are sections in "May Day Sermon" in which Dickey writes long lines that are never interrupted by pauses. There are other places in which the writing is very staccato—two words, two words, two words—with three or four spaces between each unit. Dickey uses punctuation marks in different ways. He uses colons or spaces when he wants a strong separation between major sections. You have to find ways to make the preacher's voice and her gestures reflect both the literal meaning of Dickey's words and the rhythms indicated by his punctuation.

In any performance there is also something called a vocal score. For example, when the motorcycle of the girl's one-eyed lover drives through the back woods, you need to hear and see the sound of a dirt bike revving up, getting stuck, slowing down, revving again, then exploding along dirt roads. As Bridget acts out these events, they cast an emotional image on the audience. The audience does not say, "Oh, the actress is doing a motorcycle now." But her vocal scoring of the sound of a motorcycle nonetheless carries a powerful effect. The actress also paces her score vocally. Before the line "in the red-dust, Adam-colored clay / Whirling and leaping   creating   calling" (6), Bridget speaks slowly with several rest stops. At this point she begins to accelerate until she's almost unstoppable:

O on the dim, gray man-
track of cement flowing into his mouth   each year he turns the moon back

Around on his handlebars   her image going all over him like the wind
Blasting up his sleeves. He turns off the highway, and . . .

(6–7)

In this passage the intense rhythm of her voice reflects "this madness of engine" and the madness of the lovers (as they head "off the highway" to their
deaths) and the madness of the preacher as she narrates the ecstatic fusion of
all these elements. You want to make the audience live the same experience
that the poem makes you live.

HANLEY   We spent an enormous amount of time reading the poem, discussing
each and every image until we had such a strong "through [plot] line" that we
understood what each image meant. At the first rehearsal we were so grounded
that we could then follow the incredible flow of the poem. Theatre West is an
actor-run workshop, and, because actors understand the needs of actors, they
gave us all the preparation time we needed to allow this marvelous material to
find its own rhythm.

In the Workshop at Theatre West we started by doing the first five minutes. No one could speak afterward. They didn't know what it was. No one
could speak after the second five minutes, but they thought we were onto
something quite unique and quite wonderful. So did we, and, as we continued
with the next two and three pages, we became more convinced. The sermon
just kept unfolding. The process was long, hard, and scary. The board of directors at Theatre West was scared because "Sermon" is so nonmainstream; they
were very worried that we would not attract enough people to see it, but they
were still fascinated by the concept. We all wanted to see if it could hold an
audience.

We wanted to put it on in the final week of the Theatre West Festival, in
which new work gets one weekend for its presentation. John called Jim [Dickey]
and got more than his blessing. Jim was very excited, and we wanted him to
come to Los Angeles for the opening. Before he arrived we first did "Sermon"
at the end of the Theatre West Festival on a Friday, Saturday, and Sunday to
big houses, and you could have heard a pin drop. Some people were blown
away; some had to go out and sit in their cars to let the effect of the words
wash over them. Some walked out indignantly after it was over and asked,
"What was that all about?" But everyone had an experience that they wouldn't
let up. They were drawn strongly and deeply into it, even if they didn't get
each image—it's so convoluted; those who came knowing the poem were, of
course, that much further ahead. It was a fascinating weekend, and we knew
we were really onto something. We opened "Sermon" officially on 13 November 1992 to reviews that were wonderful. Jim was there; he participated in
whole opening weekend; it was a dream come true.

How Did You Develop the Character of the Woman Preacher?

GALLOGLY   As I said earlier about back story, we made the woman preacher
the mother of the abused daughter who died in the motorcycle crash with her

lover after she killed the abusing, Bible-reading father. This grieving mother returns from the grave site one year after the girl's death, on the anniversary of the death. This woman has buried her grief in her religion for one year, then she could no longer deny it, could no longer deny the beatings nor all the reasons for what had driven the child to kill her father. When she sees the mist rise off the creek, this mother has come to believe in the emotional resurrection of her daughter as firmly as she used to believe in Jesus' resurrection. We created a character who is partially "mad," but her madness to some extent was already present in her previous belief system. Her "madness" also lies in the transference of the passion of her previous beliefs into her new belief that her daughter somehow continues to live. The preacher is out of control. She is also mad—enraged—because she needs to fight against the pain she feels by creating a healing place in which the memory of the dead daughter can meaningfully live. She is a very powerful woman and a very powerful character who is going to spend her time—at least, this time—making sure that the women in her congregation do not fall into the same trap. She does not want them to follow a religion that allows them to be abused or refuses to accept the glory within them. Consequently, she changes everything: the religion, the congregation, their conception of woman, the season, and the very ground—the earth— where they worship.

HANLEY   I see her as a woman with an incredible purpose, an incredible mission, with a story to tell to women, to young women, to children; she has life force information to impart. She is telling a myth that will shatter the patriarchy and the malicious, religious misuse of man's power. She has a myth to share with other women. She is the protagonist; she is the leader; she is there to set women free. In some moments her zeal to tell this story borders on madness; she is in and out of her own reality. She is called away to other times and other selves. She is all women: she is a preacher; she is a mother; she lost a daughter; she is Mother Earth saying, "Come home." Her ultimate goal is to give the gift of new life.

John and I created a back story that gave me, as an actor, something to hold onto. This back story gives me the reason for preaching this evening: I have just come from the river where my daughter and her lover disappeared. I have decided that I can no longer live a lie. I can no longer preach the Bible's law when men have turned this law against nature and against what women deserve. Because today is May Day, this is the perfect time to enable women to find and live the life force of the season of spring. This is my last opportunity to let them know what I hope for them, what I expect for them, what I challenge them to do, and what I'm trying to lead them toward: the joy, the love, the power. I must see that their path is made clear.

To find out who this woman preacher is, I visited the Ebenezer Baptist Church in Atlanta, Georgia, for what I thought would be a thirty-minute observation. I stayed for the entire service, four and a half hours, and participated myself in an incredible church experience. When I first arrived for this service,

I sat in the back row. There was a stained glass window on my right. At the bottom there was the name Hanley. So, I thought I must be in the right place. I also prepared by listening to recordings of accents and by talking to people from the South. I developed my own accent from these combinations and came to realize that a preacher has absolute license to say "God" in any way he or she chooses. I guess I'm now thinking that God is a woman! Personal study and growth and research—the study to find this woman was all-consuming.

What Kinds of Technical Effects Did You Invent for "Sermon"?

GALLOGLY One important element is a ladies' choir: seven or eight ladies with a choirmaster, also a woman who played the piano, which sat outside the church, that is, in the lobby of the theatre. When the audience arrived, they heard classic spirituals in original arrangements. The ladies were dressed in an antique style because we wanted the audience to see the real women of Gilmer County. More important, we wanted to take a jaded Los Angeles audience, very sophisticated in its own mind, and play into these feelings of superiority. We wanted the audience to think that they were going to hear some simplistic Baptist reading of the Bible. We wanted to take them down one road, then up another. We wanted to remove the audience from Los Angeles, to get them to drop their systems of disbelief and get them back to the South and to get them back to going to meeting.

When the audience was seated, the lights went to dark for ten seconds, just long enough to make them anxious. Then we began the sound of a river. Then the sound of ladies, chattering, entering the church. A pin spot[light] came up on a Bible sitting on top of a podium, then another pin spot came up on a Cross. The Cross is seven feet tall by five and a half feet wide. It's made out of two-by-fours, screwed together, completely plain. I bought scrap lumber from the wood store because I didn't want the Cross to look new or milled. The light for the Cross was at an oblique angle from the side, and it threw the shadow of the Cross on the back wall. The stage was completely black: black floor, black back wall, and black curtains, simple and spare. Then the choir members sang: "Praise be to God who bids the earth rejoice, / Sends precious spring and earth's reviving voice." When they finished the first of three verses, an overhead light came up on a chair. The chair was from the 1800s, an old ladder-backed chair with a cane seat. Bridget entered from behind the Cross. She was dressed in an old woolen coat, with a little brown, straw hat. No makeup, her hair pulled back in a severe bun. The reason for all this is to continue to remove the audience from Los Angeles. When they see the Bible, the audience is completely in the place where the church ladies are going. They are "now"; they are present.

HANLEY We had minimal sets. We had a podium, a rough-hewn cross, a little Kentucky chair that was my mother-in-law's. She was born and raised in Ashland, Kentucky. A lot of the set evolved. I had a funny little hat that I got at a garage sale, a perfect, flat, pancake hat. I found a navy-blue dress from the

1940s. It was her Sunday preaching dress. We added a cameo, a handkerchief that we felt had been embroidered by her daughter, and a pair of waggy shoes that are sensible, like nun's shoes. Each piece was added out of love and in the spirit of the minimalism we felt was important for this piece. The Bible was my mother's, which meant a lot to me. It gives me another personal branch to hang onto. When the preacher first appears from backstage, all these elements—the Bible, the chair, the Cross—all shimmer as if the preacher appeared mysteriously out of the fog.

How Did Audiences Respond in Los Angeles?

GALLOGLY   Audience response was very good. Critical response was stunning. Different audiences, naturally, had different reactions. Some audiences would sit afterward for ten, fifteen, minutes. People would cry. Some would say that they didn't understand the words. After a while many stopped trying to figure out the words and just let the words wash over them, then the poem made sense. Just about everyone was moved. A few people walked out, not in a huff, but it just wasn't their cup of tea. "Sermon" struck people forcefully, depending where they were in their lives. It made a good deal more sense to women than men, but that's true of the poem in general, because it's designated for women. It's about things that women accept as a matter of course, like birthing, menstruating, things that men don't get, don't want to, and are afraid of. Never was the audience reaction flat.

HANLEY   Each audience was different. The reaction depended on the audience's makeup, whether they were young people, students, women, or men. Women made an immediate connection with the material even if they didn't follow all of it. At the first hearing this long, complex poem is mystifying. Women were moved. Men were challenged, sometimes got pissy, and felt threatened and uncomfortable. Men more than women made suggestions about reworking certain areas. Maybe men felt betrayed—as if they came expecting not exactly to see *Deliverance* but to see their vision of James Dickey's poetry. Some men were so moved that they had to go out and sit in their cars to let the words wash over them. One man said to me that I had found James Dickey's silences; this man was so thrilled. There were many men that got each and every nuance, but there were a number who felt Jim betrayed them, as if "How dare you not be on our side?" But it all made for extremely stimulating conversations after the performance.

How Did Women React to Dickey's Woman Preacher?

HANLEY   After one performance I came out front, and there was a row and a half of women just sitting there. I wondered: "Oh, my God. Do the tomatoes start flying or what?" A woman looked up at me and said: "Oh, you must forgive us for not leaving. We just need to sit here." They needed to sit there because they were so moved and had so many thoughts awakened in them. They needed to sit there and just process it all. There were other times when the piece would end, and women would just sit there and sigh. There were times when there was absolute silence. My daughter Megan and her friends, seventeen-year-olds, came to see "Sermon" a number of times and were knocked out. At first they were timid about their feelings. Many women were more aware of what they had seen than they were willing to talk about. They were frightened. They were intimidated that they weren't up to it or that they weren't literate enough or that their intuitions were incorrect. That's why John and I began to follow up performances with a question-and-answer period that would allow the audience to show how smart they are. My daughter and her young friends picked right up on it. They were up in their socks. They were thrilled. Young women react wonderfully to "Sermon."

Among men and women there was a wide variety of reactions, some funny, many moving. I wrote down several. One gentleman said: "Don't add anything. It is an incredible environmental piece. If you add anything, you would ruin the enchantment." A woman said, "It touches people in a mythic place." A Hollywood hairstylist said, "This is very now, and it makes you want to know her in real life." Another woman said, "The performance was very Martha Grahamesque," and she was thrilled with the understanding and the interpretation. Another woman felt that it was crucial for battered and abused women to see "Sermon." She said it would be an important part of their therapy. She got the sexual violation. She said: "You must get this on. It must go forward. It is so timely." Another woman wrote: "I loved your performance. I thought it was bold, raw, and actually a little scary in its daring." Teachers came back and brought their students. A lot of women would come up and say, "I got every gnat and every weasel."

Have You Modified the Production since It Opened?

GALLOGLY After a six-month hiatus between November 1992 and July 1993, I spoke to a friend who deals with abused children and who deals with loss. I spoke with him because, after the initial run of our production, Bridget had been so involved in the death of her dramatic daughter that she had actually gone through the grieving process: denial, anger, then resolution and peace. Her emotional reaction to her performance had changed because she had resolved the daughter's death and worked through all these issues. Therefore, we had to incorporate this new actor into the original production. This real change in a real human being playing an invented character turned out to be valuable, because the preacher in subsequent performances comes to an emotional peace, which was left out in earlier presentations.

Final Words

GALLOGLY I'm glad Jim Dickey was able to see "Sermon" and that we invited him out to LA. Because, in the final analysis, the poem worked; it worked onstage. I can't build an engine in terms of poetry, but I can make it run. I think that the dramatization fulfills the poem in a way that reading it from the page would not. This is a sermon and was meant to be presented between people. One more thing: I wouldn't try this poem without a great actress. Bridget is a stunning actress, physically, vocally, but, more important, emotionally. She is courageous. She has all the tools that an actor needs to say something difficult. She is a pitbull. She will not quit. It doesn't matter how scary or physical or sexual the part is.

HANLEY Performing this poem is the most extraordinary acting experience I've ever had. At this point in my career I was disappointed with my television work, and "May Day Sermon" reinvented my love for acting. I told this to Jim at lunch: "Your work has made me love my profession once more. I can't even go on my morning walks in the same way." After we began working on "Sermon" and as I found my own personal images within Dickey's poetic images, I refound nature, even the smallest things: a spiderweb with dew on it. I grew up in Seattle in the Northwest with the things of nature all around me. Between then and adulthood I forgot all that. I got used to the Los Angeles River, which is not a real river. It's rainwater in this huge cement gutter. "Sermon" changed the way I look at things, certainly at women and religion. More important, it changed the way I look at my work, at acting, at the thing I now really love.

NOTES

1. James Dickey, *Poems 1957–1967* (Middletown, Conn.: Wesleyan University Press, 1967), 10. All citations are from this text.

2. Kit Roane, *Reader* (Los Angeles), 27 November 1992. T. H. McCulloh, *Los Angeles Times,* 19 November 1992, "Calendar," F10. Richard Scaffidi, *Drama-Logue,* 19–25 November 1992, "Theatre Reviews," "Sermon."

ESSAYS

From Manuscript to Performance Script: The Evolution of a Poem

JANET LARSEN MCHUGHES
with an afterword by James Dickey

One of the legacies of literary research in the 1970s is a new understanding of the relationship between reader and text. Following the theoretical leads of Roland Barthes and the structuralists, critics began to see the silent reader as a fully active partner in the process of creating a literary text, rather than merely a receiver of already-formed cognitive "content" and image constructions. The news was met with some self-satisfaction by oral interpreters of literature. Interpreters have believed for a long time that the reader interacts personally with the poem on the page, so that the performance is somehow a new product, a melding of performer and poem. Yet interpretation theory has not always reflected what seemed to be empirical truth; even as late as the mid-1970s, interpreters called themselves "re-creative artists" and "auxiliary artists," as though the performer were far inferior to the original author in the hierarchical scheme of things.

With the impact of phenomenology on the field of interpretation, the score began to be evened out a little. In his phenomenologically based text, Wallace Bacon argued for a *matching* between reader and text, a genuine congruence of consciousnesses.[1] In so doing, Bacon suggested that the performed text was somehow importantly different from the text met on the page, a view that squarely placed interpretation theory with the new work on transactional reading theory by such critics as Norman Holland and Louise Rosenblatt.[2] In her latest book, *The Reader, the Text, the Poem,* Rosenblatt redefines two familiar terms to help explain the new relationship between silent reader and literature. The "text," she suggests, is what comes to the reader, in a medium such as the printed page, and stands only as a blueprint, a series of potential meanings. " 'The poem' comes into being in the five circuit set up between the reader and 'the text.' As with the elements of an electric circuit, each component of the reading process functions by virtue of the presence of the others."[3] The poem's very existence, then, depends as much on the reader's creation of it as it does on the poet's wording of it.

Originally published in *Literature in Performance* 2 (November 1981): 26–49. Reprinted by permission.

If the clarification of the fully creative role for the single reader is rather new, acceptance of such artistic creativity for the adapter/director of group interpretation seems almost commonplace, interpreters have long understood that *adaptation* of literature for Readers Theatre or Chamber Theatre places the interpreter in a clearly creative role. In fact, this active role in script creation has attracted many talented theatre directors to the Interpreters Theatre medium.[4] One of the happy consequences of the new evidence for the creative role of *single* performers is that it lends theoretical credence to the long-standing creative practice of *group* interpreters. In an address before the 1979 Kentucky Commonwealth Interpretation Festival, Phillis Rienstra Jeffrey, one of the authors of *Group Performance of Literature*,[5] suggested that Rosenblatt's definitions of *text* and *poem* be applied to group performance. Simultaneously the 1980 text *Theatres for Literature* offered three terms—*work, text,* and *script*—to clarify the creative relationship between the Interpreters Theatre director and the literature to be staged. The "work" is the literature as it is transmitted from the poet to the reader, usually (but not always) in writing. The "text" is the work made meaningful for the reader. "Transforming a work for Readers Theatre is an extremely creative act, in which you constitute meaning by engaging in a shared relationship between your world and the world of the literature. That shared relationship is your text of a work."[6] Finally, the "script" is the cocreated "poem" (to use Rosenblatt's term) ready for the performance. A compatible interference is that the "performance" is yet another step in the creative evolution of the poem, for both the adapter/director and the audience members who witness it.

All transactional theories of reading, adapting, directing, and performing are based on the notion of literature as a *process*. The roots of the process are in the poet's intuition and have matured, normally through several manuscript stages, to the moment of publicizing the status of the progress (i.e., publication). Whereas interpreters have theoretical and practical understanding of the process of adaptation once the literature is met in print, there have been few opportunities to trace the full process from the poet's inception through the manuscript stage, all the way to full performance. An investigation of the whole process cycle, particularly when the final presentation is witnessed by the initial poet (thereby taking literary experience full circle), might have considerable value for those interested in probing the practical relationship between poet, poem, and interpreter. By a series of fortunate occurrences, such an investigation is possible of the evolution of the poem "Sleeping Out at Easter" by James Dickey. The purpose of this article is to provide a practical examination of the actual process by which "Sleeping Out at Easter" evolved through its manuscript versions into a full-scale Interpreters Theatre production witnessed by the poet.

BACKGROUND OF THE INVESTIGATION

On 2 May 1980 the contemporary American poet James Dickey was an audience member of an Interpreters Theatre production staged at Southern

Illinois University's Calipre Theatre. The performance, "The Passionate Myth: Poetic Tales by James Dickey," was staged by this author in Dickey's honor and featured Readers Theatre and Chamber Theatre productions of eleven of his most famous works—"Sleeping Out at Easter," "May Day Sermon to the Women of Gilmer County, Georgia by a Woman Preacher Leaving the Baptist Church," "The Vegetable King," "The Sheep Child," "The Fiend," "Madness," "The Lifeguard," *Deliverance,* "For the Last Wolverine," "Looking for the Buckhead Boys," and "Falling." The focus of this study is the evolution of only one of the selections, "Sleeping Out at Easter," from its first manuscript stages to its full-scale performance more than twenty years later.

This investigation is made possible only because James Dickey has permitted access to his pre-*Deliverance* manuscripts by depositing them in the Special Collections Library at Washington University in St. Louis.[7] The collection is truly impressive. Over 1,500 pages of copiously edited manuscripts, as well as a massive private correspondence, are available for inspection. Since Dickey types his manuscripts and then enters most changes by hand, alterations are relatively easy to trace. Dickey's pattern is retype the same poem over and over again, each time incorporating new changes, until the poem achieves some kind of solidity. Through the Washington University collection, then, evidence is available of the stages of pre-publication development in the poem now known as "Sleeping Out at Easter."

Similarly, evidence is also available—again, by happy coincidence—of the stages of script development for the same poem. Currently, three scripts of "Sleeping Out at Easter" by the same adapter exist, each a refinement and elaboration of its predecessor. The scripts themselves, composed over an eleven-year period, seem to parallel the stages of manuscript development. Together, the phenomena of the available manuscripts and the long maturation process with script creation form a full creative process spanning more than twenty years. (It should be noted at the outset that the script adaptations were done prior to the interpreter's knowledge of any existing manuscripts of the same poem. Similarities between manuscript evolution and performance script evolution are, therefore, more genuine than they might be if the interpreter had been influenced by an examination of the manuscripts.)

BACKGROUND OF "SLEEPING OUT AT EASTER"

From 1956 to 1961 James Dickey worked in the advertising business, composing slogans for such accounts as Coca-Cola. Known as "Jingle Jim" during the day, Dickey worked to build a different kind of reputation at night and in his free time—a reputation as a serious poet. In *Self-Interviews,* Dickey recalls:

> I had no illusions about being full of integrity as far as the advertising business was concerned; I was in it for the money, to make a living. The integrity came at night, on weekends, at sales meetings, on holidays, or whenever I could get to write my "own thing."

After I had been trying to please different people—copy chiefs and assistant creative directors—all day, it was exciting to be able to sit down in front of a typewriter and write something I wanted to. . . . I was selling my soul to the devil all day and trying to buy it back at night.[8]

"Sleeping Out at Easter" was written under such an arrangement, during a period of about three weeks. The poem was conceived as an experiment in verse form, à la Thomas Hardy, with lines in a long-long-short pattern, culminating in refrains. Dickey's first "Hardyesque" lines were apparently overwrought with rhetorical effects. (No early manuscript exists of these false starts.) Dickey's recollection is:

It was more of a game than a poem. . . . I thought, "Now why the hell get so complicated with the line? Nobody wants to read something *that* busy! Why not try to say it starkly, making statements one after the other: this happens, that happens, this happens. And then if you want to become more complicated, use an interchangeable refrain technique invented for the occasion." I also told myself, "Make it immediate. Put the reader and yourself *in medias res,* in the middle of an action." So I just sat down and wrote:

> *All dark is now no more.*
> *This forest is drawing a light . . .*

I wrote several more lines and thought, "Hot dog! *That* sounds like something!"[9]

Dickey's recollections are not precisely supported by evidence from the first manuscript of "Sleeping Out at Easter," yet the spirit of his recall seems accurate enough. The second line Dickey remembered is five drafts away. The first manuscript of the poem, then called "Sleeping Out in June," is reprinted as figure 1.[10]

The poem is based on the poet's actual experience of camping out in his own backyard and waking to feel a kinship with nature and the force that creates it. From the first manuscript Dickey achieved a duality of everyday experience infused with mythical symbolism. A hand tingling from cut-off circulation contains "the secret of life," and a dark army blanket takes on the properties of a "magical shepherd's cloak." Furthermore, there is a mysterious doubleness of persona(e) in the poem. Although the poem commences in first person, as early as the third stanza a second person or presence is introduced with "Put down the seeds in your hand." Dickey seems conscious of the shift in person, as he deliberately alters two references to *your* in stanza 3 to *my.* If more than one persona or presence exists, the poem has not made the duality clear.

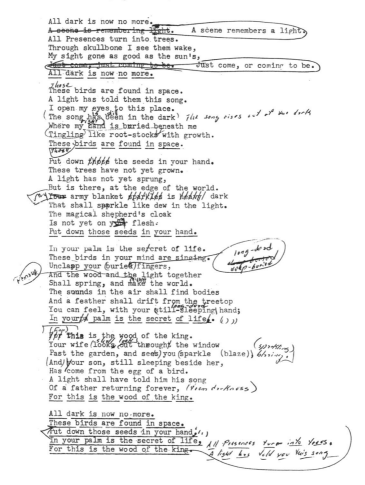

Figure 1: First Draft, "Sleeping Out at Easter"

There are a few vague religious references, particularly with such phrases as "magical shepherd's cloak" and "wood of the king," but the poem has yet to find its full expression both structurally and symbolically. Dickey's first manuscript effort is, however, surprisingly like the published form; the presence of at least thirty lines identical or very similar to those in the printed version indicates that Dickey may tend to compose many of his poems mentally before putting anything on paper.[11] It is entirely possible that whole lines of poetry danced in his head at the same time that he carried on conversations with copy directors and Coca-Cola clients.

The first important change in the second manuscript version (fig. 2) is the inserted line in stanza one: "The earth turns, waking a choir." With the men-

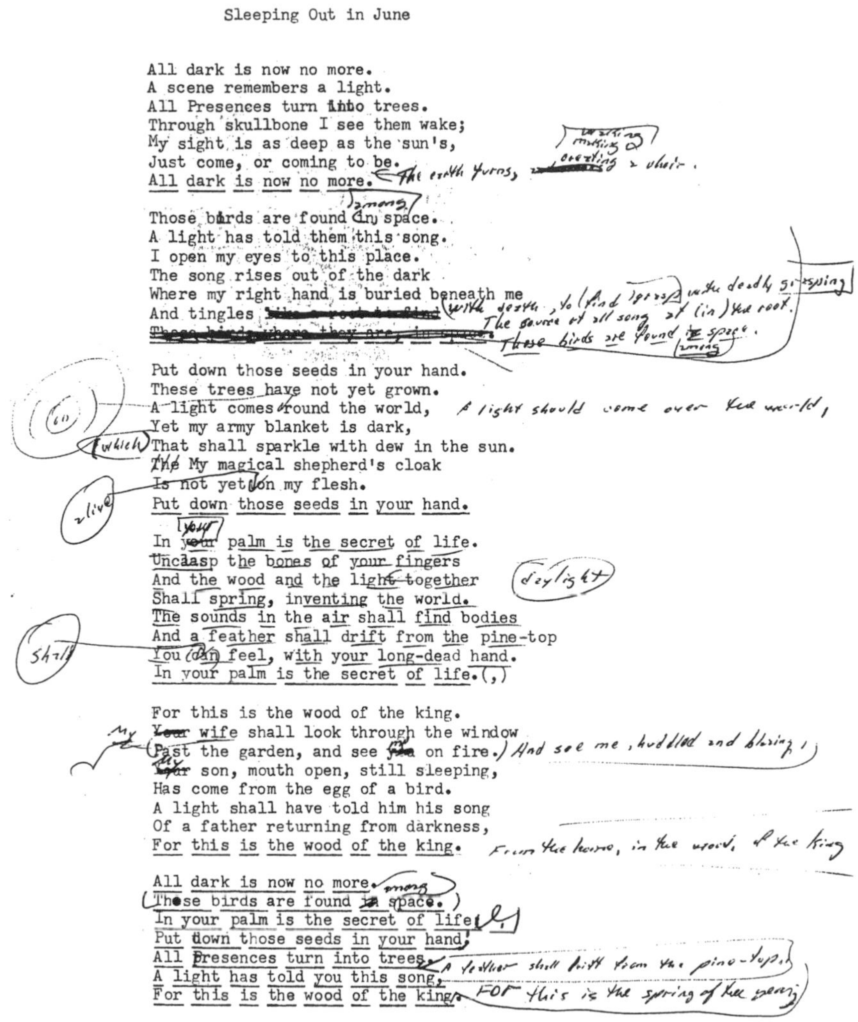

Sleeping Out in June

All dark is now no more.
A scene remembers a light.
All Presences turn into trees.
Through skullbone I see them wake;
My sight is as deep as the sun's,
Just come, or coming to be.
All dark is now no more.

Those birds are found in space.
A light has told them this song.
I open my eyes to this place.
The song rises out of the dark
Where my right hand is buried beneath me
And tingles

Put down those seeds in your hand.
These trees have not yet grown.
A light comes round the world,
Yet my army blanket is dark,
That shall sparkle with dew in the sun.
The My magical shepherd's cloak
Is not yet on my flesh.
Put down those seeds in your hand.

In your palm is the secret of life.
Unclasp the bones of your fingers
And the wood and the light together
Shall spring, inventing the world.
The sounds in the air shall find bodies
And a feather shall drift from the pine-top
You can feel, with your long-dead hand.
In your palm is the secret of life.

For this is the wood of the king.
Your wife shall look through the window
Past the garden, and see on fire.
Your son, mouth open, still sleeping,
Has come from the egg of a bird.
A light shall have told him his song
Of a father returning from darkness,
For this is the wood of the king.

All dark is now no more.
Those birds are found in space.
In your palm is the secret of life.
Put down those seeds in your hand.
All Presences turn into trees.
A light has told you this song.
For this is the wood of the king.

Figure 2: Second Draft, "Sleeping Out at Easter"

tion of a choir, the poet builds the role of sound in the poem beyond the hints of "song" and "bird." More importantly, the creation of a choir establishes a kind of presence or force which could account for the use of second person; the choir could speak the second-person lines, or the choir could represent a portion of the main persona's consciousness that is engaged in an inner dialogue. The third function of *choir* is that the word adds slightly to the growing religious context of the poem.

In the fifth stanza the addition of the line "And see me, huddled and blazing" intensifies the persona's emotional level considerably. More and more, the subject of the poem is being elevated from the mundane activity of sleeping in one's backyard to some kind of mystical experience.

Finally, the insertion of "For this is the spring of the year" is a crucial step in the evolution of the poem. This line will be dropped by the fourth manuscript, but the poet's thought behind the line—of spring and the regeneration of life—opens the door to the forthcoming title metamorphosis. The title revisions are keys to the maturation process of the poem's symbolic level. "Sleeping Out in *June*" (my italics) no doubt reflects the seasonal accuracy of Dickey's actual camping-out experience, but the title change in manuscript three (which is suggested by the "spring of the year" line in manuscript two) is a major evolutionary step in the growth of this poem.

With characteristic specificity the poet does not change the title in manuscript 3 (fig. 3) to "Sleeping Out in Spring" but to "Sleeping Out in April," with all the connotations that *April* brings to the theme of ritual regeneration. The "grove of the king" is added to the first stanza, but *grove* quickly gives way to *grave* in the fifth stanza. The single vowel change is masterful. Once the phrase "king's grave" is established, together with the new setting in April, the poem takes on new Christian connotations. A new refrain line, "For the king's grave turns him to life," introducing the notion that a person—a king—dies to be reborn, triggers the next phase in the poem's evolution: the final title change in the fourth draft (fig. 4).

Once the word *Easter* is introduced, the poem takes on a new symbolic dimension. Words and phrases such as *sun's* (*son's*), *grave of the king, choir, buried, light . . . round the world, magical shepherd's cloak, palm, nail-holding fingers,* and *father returning from darkness* have a distinctly Christian flavor. No longer is the poem merely a record of a suburban man's camping-out experience on a warm spring evening; it is a personal account of a religious experience on Easter morning in which an ordinary man feels an extraordinary oneness with Christ. With manuscript four, the poem seems to have found its own voice.

THE PUBLICATION OF "SLEEPING OUT AT EASTER"

"Sleeping Out at Easter" is the lead poem in James Dickey's first published collection of poems, *Into the Stone,* which was produced as part of the 1960 Scribner's *Poets of Today* series.[12] With minor exceptions, the printed version of "Sleeping Out at Easter" (fig. 5) is identical to the fourth manuscript version. (Note that the second line, as Dickey remembers it in *Self-Interviews,* does not appear until the published version.[13]

In his introductory essay to the 1960 *Poets of Today* publication, editor John Hall Wheelock writes, "James Dickey reveals himself as a poet concerned primarily with the direct impact of experience, the complex of sensations, feelings and responses involved when we are living something rather than thinking about it."[14] Wheelock's observations are more than enough to tantalize the adapter-director of Interpreters Theatre. If a poem such as "Sleeping Out at Easter" is indeed concerned with *living through* an experience, then it is a

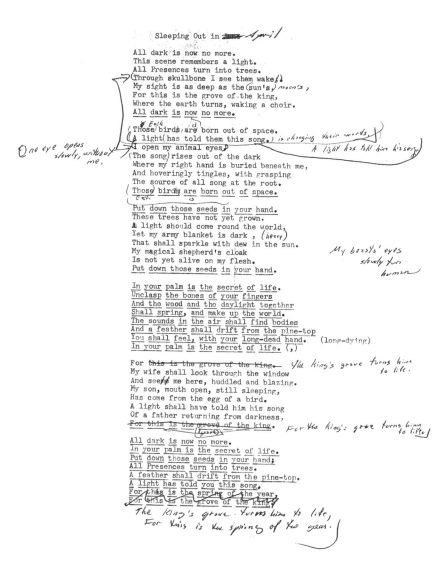

Figure 3: Third Draft, "Sleeping Out at Easter"

natural candidate for stage adaptation. Is it possible, one might wonder, to capture in performance the kind of immediacy that the poem can only suggest in print? If so, the interpreter of this poem indeed functions as a co-author, in more than the transactional sense suggested by Rosenblatt and others, extending the implied action of the poem into physical action in acoustic space.[15] The poem is *transformed* into visual and auditory action. The adaptation process of

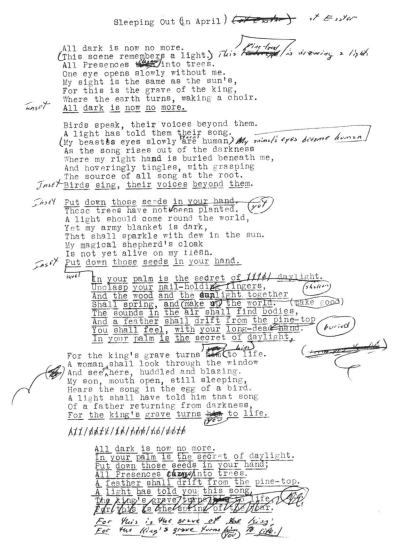

Figure 4: Fourth Draft, "Sleeping Out at Easter"

necessity must begin with a thorough understanding of the way in which experience is organized in the printed version of the poem, so that the scripting can be a responsible and true extension of the author's effort. The first stage of the coauthorship, then, begins with an analysis of the legacy provided by James Dickey to his readers.

Sleeping Out at Easter
by James Dickey

1   All dark is now no more.
This forest is drawing a light.
All Presences change into trees.
One eye opens slowly without me.
5   My sight is the same as the sun's,
For this is the grave of the king,
Where the earth turns, waking a choir.
    All dark is now no more.

Birds speak, their voices beyond them.
10   A light has told them their song.
My animal eyes become human
As the Word rises out of the darkness
Where my right hand, buried beneath me,
Hoveringly tingles, with grasping
15   The source of all song at the root.
    Birds sing, their voices beyond them.

    Put down those seeds in your hand.
These trees have not yet been planted.
A light should come round the world,
20   Yet my army blanket is dark,
That shall sparkle with dew in the sun.
My magical shepherd's cloak
Is not yet alive on my flesh.
    Put down those seeds in your hand.

25   *In your palm is the secret of waking.*
Unclasp your purple-nailed fingers
And the wood and the sunlight together
Shall spring, and make good the world.
The sounds in the air shall find bodies,
30   *And a feather shall drift form the pine-top*
You shall feel, with your long-buried hand.
In your palm is the secret of waking.

For the king's grave turns him to light.
A woman shall look through the window
35   And see me here, huddled and blazing.
My child, mouth open, still sleeping,
Hears the song in the egg of a bird.
The sun shall have told him that song
Of a father returning from darkness.

Figure 5 (above and opposite page):
"Sleeping Out at Easter," as published

40   *For the king's grave turns you to light.*

All dark is now no more.
In your palm is the secret of waking.
Put down those seeds in your hand;
All Presences change into trees.
45   *A feather shall drift from the pine-top.*
The sun shall have told you this song,
For this is the grave of the king;
For the king's grave turns you to light.

ANALYZING THE STRUCTURE OF EXPERIENCE IN "SLEEPING OUT AT EASTER"

John Hall Wheelock comments on the most recognizable experimental device of style in "Sleeping Out at Easter":

> [Dickey's] use of refrain . . . is especially individual, and he occasionally closes a poem with a sort of coda, or resumé, composed of the poem's key lines, a formal device that, in his hands, is amazingly effective. "Sleeping Out at Easter," the very beautiful opening poem in Mr. Dickey's collection, will illustrate one phrase of his method. The poem, which describes the coming of dawn, begins with a series of one-line statements, "All dark is now no more. / This forest is drawing a light. / All Presences change into trees," and so on. These, and certain other lines occurring later in the poem . . . are then repeated, sometimes in modified form, at the poem's close, thus constituting the coda.[16]

Dickey himself refers to the use of refrain in his first poem. "In . . . 'Sleeping Out at Easter,' I used . . . a kind of refrain technique that, so far as I know, I invented for the occasion."[17]

Harry and Agathe Thornton, however, in *Time and Style,* identify this kind of refrain technique as an example of Greek appositional style, a classical syntactical structure. Speaking of the works of Lucretius, the Thorntons summarize the major characteristics of the appositional style in literature:

> We have here the typical appositional movement of thought. . . . When his [the poet's] initial thought is satisfactorily differentiated and presented, the poet moves on to the next step in his argument which connects directly with the initial thought. Accordingly on the formal side we have a circular movement of thought which returns to its start, and a reference back past any amplifications, picking up the main thread of the thought-sequence.[18]

In the appositional mode, then, the poet makes a statement or observation and then proceeds to restate it—with slight modifications—until the initial statement or observation is finally shown in all its facets; only then does the poet move on to another major statement or observation, closely tied in meaning to the first, and elaborate on it. When all the differentiations are completed, the poet is likely to collect all the major thoughts into one unit of expression, as if tying all the threads of thought elaborations together into a meaningful whole. This mode of expression differs radically from the periodic syntactic mode, which is more common to English-speaking readers. "In the appositional mode, the inflections in the main look backwards, pointing to something already mentioned which they pick up again; in the periodic mode, they point forward to what is to come."[19]

The appositional style of "Sleeping Out at Easter" is the key to the organization and intensity of experience in the poem. Since language in apposition tends to build one moment on top of the next, it is clear why the Thorntons isolate intensity of emotional feeling as a central aspect of appositional style.[20] One restatement intensifies its predecessor, building lyrically on a single moment in time. Perhaps the very fact that Dickey has employed a kind of appositional style in "Sleeping Out at Easter" explains why Charles Monaghan is led to observe, "Dickey's . . . poems don't fly, they burn."[21]

"Sleeping Out at Easter" opens with a sense of time change. The first three lines, in apposition to each other, deductively center on the moment of awakening; as the persona suddenly comes into conscious terms with his environment, the vague "Presences" of half-sleep clarify into trees. The next line, "One eye opens slowly without me," may again refer to the strange sensation when half-sleep develops into conscious awareness: there is a sense that part of one is awake and the other part still asleep. The fact of the matter is, though, that the "one eye" had to have been opened from the first line of the poem, since the persona has been observing environmental changes since that time. "One eye opens slowly without me," then, is a restatement of an implied action in the first line. Analysis reveals, therefore, that the concept of at least two consciousnesses is introduced in line four, thus preparing us for the shift from first to second person in line seventeen.

All four opening lines are interested in the reciprocal relationship between subject and object rather than in the dominance of one over the other. As such, "Sleeping Out at Easter" is a good example of a strong phenomenological relationship between a perceiving self and nature. Since the implicit energies between self and natural objects seem to radiate back and forth, time becomes circular, not linear. Experience doubles back on itself. All four lines are devoted to describing the same moment of perception: when a half-awake persona comes into conscious contact with the newness of morning.

The next line, "My sight is the same as the sun's," could also be thought of as an appositional restatement of the fact that the persona is awaking to the world at the precise moment that the sun is lighting—or waking—the world. In this sense, both activities—that of the persona and that of the sun—merge into a moment of time. The "now" of the first line is therefore still the "now" of the fifth line. (In performance, *sun* can act as a double entendre with *son,* thereby establishing the religious experience of the poem far earlier than the printed version.)

The sixth and seventh lines of the first stanza, in contrast to the lines preceding them, are dependent clauses which elaborate significantly on the nature of the speaker's locale. In so doing, these lines are classically in apposition to what has gone before; they also introduce new aspects to the experience of the poem because they involve for the first time an oblique reference to Christ and are therefore instrumental in directing the poem toward its mythic dimension.

The apposition of the first stanza is completed neatly by the last line, which echoes the first, *"All dark is now no more."* All eight lines of the first stanza have been dedicated to an exploration of the natural relationship between the waking persona and the dawn he perceives. There is, however, a parallel relationship operating in this poem: the relation between the persona and Christ. The latter is expressed in mythic terms, because the man wakes up thinking that he is Christ. As Dickey describes the poem, "It's just about a man sleeping in back of his house and becoming another person on Easter through the twin influences of the Easter ritual and of nature itself. His rebirth is symbolized by nothing more or less than waking up in a strange place which is near a familiar place."[22]

Essentially, then, "Sleeping Out at Easter" is about one intensified moment in the life of the man speaking the poem: the moment of his mythical transformation into the person of Christ on Easter morning. Chronology is involved very seldom; events do not seem to succeed each other in the poem. One event happens, and it takes the entire poem to describe its character and ramifications fully. Appositional structure and cyclic time help to create the intensity of the experience, because lines seem to pile on top of one another as they restate the mystical experience which is taking place.

When Dickey gathers the key lines into discrete stanzas, he completes the appositional style of the whole poem, rather than of each stanza. In other words, the entire poem seems to operate on its own level of apposition because it restates the major word groups of the individual stanzas into two italicized stanzas, one in the middle and one at the end. The first italicized stanza is mostly about the relationship between the persona and Christ; the persona seems to have "become" Christ. The second italicized stanza unites the mythic experience with the conditions of nature (which are, appositionally, the same conditions as in the first line of the first stanza) and therefore unifies both relationships into one structured whole. Dickey explains, "The last or refrain lines of the stanza unite to make, themselves, a last stanza which sums up the attitude and action of the poem."[23]

Once the interpreter has come this far in the analysis process, the poem has become genuinely personal. Connotations, extensions, and interpretations are supplied by the reader, who *transacts* with the printed version of "Sleeping Out at Easter" to create the "poem," in Rosenblatt's sense. The next step, at least for the group interpretation director, is scripting.

INITIAL STAGES IN THE SCRIPTING PROCESS

Like the poet who translates an idea or raw experience into words, the interpreter translates the poet's worded version of the poem into *presentational form,* i.e., language and action in performance.[24] Both artists are conditioned by their implicit understandings of the eventual form the poetic experience will take—*words on a page* (the normal goal of the poet) or *action on a stage* (the normal goal of the adapter/director). The stages in performance scriptmaking parallel the manuscript stages of a printed poem, as the interpreter seeks to find a presentational voice and body for the poem.

At the outset of the scripting effort, five performance problems seemed to present themselves for solution by the performance script: (1) the immediacy of the experience in the poem; (2) the complex sound values of the poem, from implied environmental sounds to a "choir" of voices (a heavenly host, perhaps?); (3) the apparent duality of consciousness in the poem, as suggested by the change from first to second person; (4) the overlaying of Christian symbolism on everyday experience; and (5) the management of the appositional style, particularly the refrain, in performance.

The first performance script, written in 1969, tackled all five problems but was not uniformly successful in their solution. One of the most important contributions of the first performance script was in the area of problem 2, the sound values of the poem. The adapter arranged the poem to be sung or spoken by four voices (two male and two female)—Soprano, Alto, Tenor, Bass—and even worked in some *lautbilding*[25] on environmental sounds and keywords in the text. The script, as written, depended heavily on the improvisational skills of the performers, because tones and melodies were not recorded on paper at all. The opening stanza is representative of the first script version (fig. 6): In addition to the sounds out of which the first line emerged, Performance Script #1 incorporated several other sounds—such as swirling wind sounds to be produced under the second stanza and combinations of whispers, sung tonalities, and the spoken voice in stanza three—to create the environmental immediacy of the poem.

A fortunate inspiration during the writing of the first script helped to solve problems four and five with one stroke: As the line "In your palm is the secret of waking" echoed in the inner ear of the adapter, the rhythm of the line began to suggest, faintly, a familiar hymn tune. The familiarity persisted, but the actual tune annoyingly eluded the interpreter for days. Suddenly, it became clear. "In your palm is the secret of waking" is in the rhythm of "Christ the Lord Is Risen Today" and could be sung to that tune for an obvious symbolic extension of the line. Perhaps the connection may not have been made if James Dickey had not long ago changed the title to "Sleeping Out at *Easter*" (my italics). Once that tune was incorporated into the script, it helped make the refrain an actual melodic part of the poem; some lines such as "In your palm is the secret of waking" and "For the king's grave turns you to light" were sung

SLEEPING OUT AT EASTER by James Dickey
An Arrangement for Voices by Janet Larsen McHughes

V1:   Soprano
V2:   Alto
V3:   Tenor
V4:   Bass
ALL: Very faint, then louder: bird sounds. Overlay bird sounds with a low
       monotone hum, which gains in intensity (*V1 continue bird sounds*). Hum
       continues while "AH" begins (*V3 and 4*), first as mere exhalation, then
       voiced *sotto voce*. Lautbilding on "AH" sound, so that the first line of the
       opem grows from it.

V2, 3, AND 4:	Chant.	All dark is now no more.
	Build in pitch and vol-ume.	This forest is drawing a light.
		All Presences change into trees.
V1:	Cut bird sounds on *trees*	
V4:	Monotone, low chant:	One eye opens slowly without me
V1, 2, 3:	Lautbild on *slowly*	
ALL:	Lightly—Unison sing-ing, with emphasis on soprano and anapestic rhythm.	My sight is the same as the sun's,
		For this is the grave of the king,
	(Repeat in four-part har-mony two times, build-ing in volume.)	Where the earth turns, waking a choir.
		. . . waking a choir
		. . . waking a choir.
V4:	Full, deep voice:	*All dark is now no more.*

Figure 6: Performance Script #1 (1969): An Arrangement for Voices

to the tune, while other lines of the refrain were spoken above the humming
of "Christ the Lord Is Risen Today."

Performance Script #1 sounded good when recorded, but it failed to provide a visual-spatial dimension for the poem. To whom was this religious experience happening? Where is he in space? If there are two consciousnesses, who
are they and what is their physical or psychical relationship to each other? It
would take another script to answer those questions.

PERFORMANCE SCRIPT #2 (1978)

Nine years elapsed between the writing of the first script and the second.
In the meantime, the adapter had become fascinated with the process of script
orchestration[26] and returned to the "Sleeping Out at Easter" script to see
whether the poem would be enhanced in performance by some orchestration.
The second performance script retains all the sound qualities of the first ver-

sion, including the tune of "Christ the Lord Is Risen Today," but elaborates on them. Whereas the lines in the first script tend to be spoken in the exact order that Dickey wrote them (with one exception: the repetition of "waking a choir"), Dickey's lines are repeated freely in the second script. A madrigal arrangement was improvised for lines such as "My sight is the same as the sun's / For this is the grave of the king / Where the earth turns, waking a choir" and "The sun shall have told him that song / Of a father returning from darkness." The effect was a spectacular explosion of sound.

To help find more spatial analogues for the poem, the adapter added another performer, Voice 5—the voice of the persona. This performer does not sing at all but pantomimes the action in front of the singing choir of four voices, thereby creating two consciousnesses: the person himself and the chorus in the background. Voice 5 speaks all the lines in first person, which seem to emerge as moments of critical understanding during his religious experience, while the choir's second-person lines, such as "Put down those seeds in your hand," take on the dimension of an Other—perhaps an inner voice of the persona's or even angels speaking of God, depending on what the audience reads into their presence.

Another sound device incorporated into the second performance script is in direct counterpoint to the melodic tonalities of most of the poem. A prosodic study of the poem reveals that stanza two contains hard-hitting stresses, mostly in an anapestic rhythm, that stand in a kind of bas-relief to the legato rhythm of most of the rest of the poem. A drum beat was brought in, and Voice 5, who speaks all of stanza two, was directed to overstress the rhythm, matching word accents with the short-short-long beats of the drum. (See fig. 7). The effect is mysterious and other-worldly, just right for the kind of unexplained effects the persona seems to be perceiving at the moment.

The third most important addition in Script #2 worried the adapter from the start. An unwritten agreement in many adaptation processes is that the interpreter may repeat, delete, perhaps even reorganize, elements of the written poem (although no reorganization was needed for "Sleeping Out at Easter"), but may not add words not found in the original. It was with great uneasiness, then, that the adapter succumbed to the temptation to add the word *Alleluia*— from the chorus of "Christ the Lord Is Risen Today"—at various points near the end of the poem. But the singing of *Alleluia* in the hymn tune seemed so *right* for the poem, extending the Easter symbolism to the fullest degree the

```
        BIRDS        SPEAK     their VOI ces    be  YOND them
  -    -   X    -   -   X    -   -   X    -   -   X    -   -   X   -   -   X

        a   LIGHT     has TOLD them their SONG
  -    -   X    -   -   X    -   -   X    -   -   X
```

Figure 7: Percussion Accompaniment to Stanza Two, Performance Script #2

poem would permit. By adding *Alleluia,* the adapter paralleled the poet's progress through the manuscript stages: both "co-authors" gradually infused more and more religious symbolism into the poem by making small editorial changes.

A performance of Script #2 confirmed what the adapter saw and heard in her inner ear: the poem is a powerful and beautiful statement of the meaning of Easter. When the five performers presented the adapted poem from a church altar on Easter Sunday morning, the performance was an inspiring addition to the service.

PERFORMANCE SCRIPT #3 (1979)

Although Script #2 was artistically satisfying, the adapter suspected that the poem could be served by more infusion of music into the script. When she met a composer, Cheryl Ness Genette, who was interested in composing original music for the script, she welcomed the collaborative opportunity. Genette, greatly sensitive to the poem itself and to the adaptation process already completed, scored the poem at critical points in the poetic experience, thereby fully orchestrating the poem. The final performance script, reprinted in figure 8, stands in the same relation to the first performance script as Dickey's printed version does to his first manuscript.[27]

FULL PRODUCTION OF THE TRANSFORMED "SLEEPING OUT AT EASTER"

When negotiations to bring James Dickey to the Southern Illinois University campus began, the adapter decided to present an entire evening of Dickey's works. The five-minute script of "Sleeping Out at Easter" was to be the opening selection. The cast was expanded to a choir of eighteen voices located behind a scrim, with a single performer, dressed casually for camping out, as the persona. No set or props of any kind were used except the scrim; all action was pantomimed in an empty space, with pools of light creating the patterns on the stage floor. The scrim was completely unlighted at the beginning of the poem. Each chorus member, dressed in black to heighten the effect of darkness, carried a tiny pinpoint flashlight. As the faint bird sounds began, the performers intermittently flashed the firefly dots of light in the darkness, as though they were some active Presence observing the sleeping persona: a slow fade-up of lights behind the scrim created the dawning of light, but at no time did the choir ever get fully out of the shadows. The use of the scrim, with its separate lighting capability, also allowed the choir to disappear as mysteriously as it had appeared, leaving the persona inextricably changed.

Presenting staged literature for its author is a rare and fascinating experience for any director of Interpreters Theatre. The anticipation of Dickey's arrival heightened many artistic questions in the interpreter's mind. Are the adaptations truly in the spirit of the original works? What are the relationships of the performance scripts to the poet's original ideas as well as to the printed versions of those ideas? Are the interpreter and the poet indeed partners in a

SLEEPING OUT AT EASTER by James Dickey

An Orchestration for Voices by Janet Larsen McHughes
With Original Music by Cheryl Ness Genette

Voices:
- v1:   Male (tenor)   (*Note:* Multiple voices may be used, provided
- v2:   Female (soprano)   a balance is maintained for four-part
- v3:   Male (baritone)   harmony.)
- v4:   Female (alto)
- v5:   Male (medium range, but resonant, speaking voice. The voice of the persona).

ALL: Very faint, then louder: bird sounds; hums of the earth waking. Lautbilding on "AH" sound, so that the first line of the poem grows from it.
v1:   Chant: *All dark is now no more.*
v2:   Whispering, quicker: *All dark is now no more.*
v3:   Speaking sustained: *All dark is now no more.*

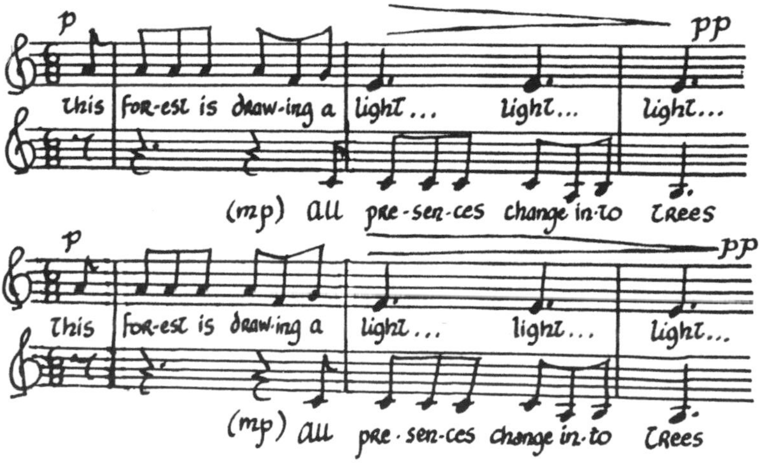

Figure 8: Performance Script #3: An Orchestration for Voices
(above and following pages)

V3, 5:   V5 pantomines action: monotone; low chant: *One eye opens slowly*
                                                       without me

V1, 2, 4:   Lautbild on *slowly*

V3:   Slowly, in fully resonant
      voice: *All dark is now no more.*

ALL: Drum rhythm, picking
      up the three-beat
      prosody of the stanza:

V5:   Over drum, speak the
      following lines: *Birds speak, their voices beyond them.*
                           A light has told them their song.

      Voice and drums
      build in intensity and   *My animal eyes become human*
      tempo: *As the Word rises out of the darkness*
                           Where my right hand, buried beneath me

      Rhythm "explodes"
      on *tingles* into a
      series of quick short
      beats: *Hoveringly tingles, with grasping*

      (Drum stops on *root*)   *The source of all song at the root.*

ALL:

ALL: Swirling wind sounds (under entire stanza):
V4:   Small voice, delicate
         legato: *Put down those seeds in your hand.*
V1:   Voiced whisper: *These trees have not yet been planted.*

V5:   Voiced whisper: *Yet my army blanket is dark,*

V5:   Speaking: *My magical shepherd's cloak*
                    Is not yet alive on my flesh.

V3:   Whisper: *. . . alive on my flesh.*

V3:
(May be transposed
one octave lower):

ALL:

                    "Alleluia" (continue humming tune)
V3:   Speaking: *Unclasp your purple-nailed fingers*
V2:   Speaking: *And the wood and the sunlight together*
                    Shall spring, and make good the world.
V1:   Speaking: *The sounds in the air shall find bodies.*
                    And a feather shall drift form the pine-top
                    You shall feel, with your long-buried hand.
                    (Humming swells)

ALL:

V2:   High-pitched chant: *For the king's grave turns him to light.*
       (continue chant)

V4:   Gently:

> A woman shall look through the window
> And see me here, huddled and blazing,
> My child, mouth open, still sleeping,
> Hears the song in the egg of a bird.

ALL: Four-part spoken
        madrigal
        improvisation:

> The sun shall have told him that song.
>   The sun shall have told him that song.
>   The sun shall . . . (etc.)
> Of a father returning from darkness,

V3:   Deep swell, almost
        chant:

> For the king's grave turns you to light.

V3:   Sustained chant:

> All dark is now no more.

V4:

V1:

V2:

V4:   Speaking:

> A feather shall drift from the pine-top.
> The sun shall have told you this song.

V5:   (Spoken in rhythm of
        "Christ the Lord Is
        Risen Today")

> For this is the grave of the king:

ALL:

full creative process, touching base at the printed page, almost as if a baton were handed from the poet to the interpreter?

As Deborah and James Dickey arrived in town and prepared to come to the theatre that night, the director was understandably excited and anxious. A needling worry was that something had been done in the adaptation of "Sleeping Out at Easter" unlike any of the other ten scripts. Nervously, the director approached the poet before the show.

MCHUGHES: Mr. Dickey, what you will see tonight is a creative *transformation* of your works. You see, we interpreters like to feel that we are creators of performance texts, almost as though we are partners with the poet.
DICKEY: Sounds good to me.
MCHUGHES: But—uh—I have one confession to make before you see what I've done with your poems. In one of the poems, "Sleeping Out at Easter," I did something we almost never do—I added a word.
DICKEY: *(Smiling)* What word?
MCHUGHES: Alleluia.
DICKEY: Alleluia, eh? *(Pause)* Hey, that's just right for that poem. Just right. Probably should have been there in the first place.

AN AFTERWORD BY JAMES DICKEY

There is a perhaps unfortunate belief among individual authors that their work exists on the printed page and only there, but this is obviously not true, for the work exists in the minds of people who come to it, and also it exists in the light which may be shed on it, or which may be made to shed, itself, in new ways, by the ingenuities and creative instincts of others who bring out these lights hitherto unknown to the author. In relation to the staged adaptation of my poem "Sleeping Out at Easter," I was much struck by the dimension of the choir and music, for the poem itself is a kind of song, or even a chant, and these qualities were emphasized by these devices and additions. I found my own understanding and experiencing of the poem was much enhanced by the adaptation and by the imaginative use of chorus and music.

I think there is a very real sense in which the director and author of such productions are the cocreators of a literary experience, and I for one am acutely aware of the enhancement of the work, of the bringing-out of various possibilities, the realizing of potentialities, that these imaginative renderings make available. Since words are the medium of poems, and since words have sounds, I believe that the oral interpretation of literary works, and especially of poetry, are of the utmost value. There is no substitute for the sense of a person's voice being part of a poem, whether it is my voice or someone else's. I am most grateful for the other voices than my own. Though they might be those of shadows or angels, I am gladdest that they are human, human voices.

NOTES

1. See Wallace A. Bacon, *The Art of Interpretation,* 3d ed. (New York: Holt, Rinehart, and Winston, 1979), 37–38. These ideas, in an abbreviated form, were introduced in the first edition of *The Art of Interpretation* (1966). In his most recent article Bacon refines the notion of the performed poem's separate existence by comparing it to the child of both parents, the poem and performer. "The performer is not a copier, taking in an impression and shooting it out again, but a creative participant in the creation of that 'child' which the poem's body seeks to make manifest. The child will resemble both parents, but it is a being in its own right." See Wallace A. Bacon, "An Aesthetics of Performance," *Literature in Performance* 1, no. 1 (1980): 2.

2. See, especially, Norman Holland, *Poems in Persons* (New York: Norton, 1973), 5; *Readers Reading* (New Haven: Yale University Press, 1975): "Transactive Criticism: Re-Creation through Identity," *Criticism* 18, no. 4 (1976). See also Louise M. Rosenblatt "Towards a Transactional Theory of Reading," *Journal of Reading Behavior* 1 (1969): 31–41; *The Reader, the Text, the Poem: The Transactional Theory of the Literary Work* (Carbondale: Southern Illinois University Press, 1978).

3. Rosenblatt, *Reader, the Text, the Poem,* 14.

4. *Interpreters Theatre* is used here as an umbrella term embracing both *Readers Theatre* and *Chamber Theatre.*

5. Beverly Whitaker Long, Lee Hudson, and Phillis Rienstra Jeffrey, *Group Performance of Literature* (Englewood Cliffs, N.J.: Prentice-Hall, 1977).

6. Marion L. Kleinau and Janet Larsen McHughes, *Theatres for Literature: A Practical Aesthetics of Group Interpretation* (Sherman Oaks, Calif.: Alfred Publishing Company, 1960), 39. This article will use the terms *work, text,* and *script* as they are defined in *Theatres for Literature.*

7. Collections this complete are somewhat unusual for a living poet. Arrangements for the acquisition of the Dickey materials by Washington University were made by poet Mona Van Duyn.

8. James Dickey, *Self-Interviews,* ed. Barbara and James Reiss (New York: Doubleday, 1970), 44.

9. Dickey, *Self-Interviews,* 85–86.

10. This manuscript, and the three following it, are reprinted by permission of James Dickey and the James Dickey Collection, Special Collections, Washington University Libraries, St. Louis, Mo.

11. Whereas this conclusion may be reasonably accurate for "Sleeping Out at Easter," evidence from the manuscript collection reveals that James Dickey often begins his poems with a "word list," a randomly typed collection of words or phrases that covers an entire page or more. Many of the words later become key images or actions in the finished poem. Although word lists are extant for many Dickey poems, there is no word list for "Sleeping Out at Easter," and it is therefore probably safe to assume that Dickey did not make a word list for this poem.

12. "Sleeping Out at Easter" was actually first published in the *Virginia Quarterly Review* 36 (April 1960): 218–19, just months before it appeared in book form as part of the Scribner's *Poets of Today* series.

13. Reprinted by permission of James Dickey and Wesleyan University Press, Middleton, Conn.

14. John Hall Wheelock, "Some Thoughts on Poetry," *Poets of Today VII* (New York: Scribner's Sons, 1960), 22–23.

15. By "acoustic space" is meant "the whole environment of the theatre auditorium, as well as . . . the imaginative space of the minds of the audience." For more discussion of acoustic space, see Kleinau and McHughes, *Theatres for Literature,* 6–8.

16. Wheelock, "Some Thoughts on Poetry," 24.

17. James Dickey, "The Poet Turns on Himself," in *Babel to Byzantium: Poets and Poetry Now* (New York: Farrar, Straus, and Giroux, 1968), 285.

18. Harry and Agathe Thornton, *Time and Style: A Psycholinguistic Essay in Classical Literature* (London: Methuen, 1963), 61–62.

19. Thornton and Thornton, *Time and Style,* 72.

20. Thornton and Thornton, *Time and Style,* 114.

21. Charles Monaghan, *Commonweal* (15 April 1966): 121.

22. Dickey, *Self-Interviews,* 86.

23. Dickey, "Poet Turns on Himself," 285.

24. For a discussion of presentational form, see Kleinau and McHughes, *Theatres for Literature,* 5–10; and chapter 7: "Presentational Action for Interpreters Theatre."

25. *Lautbilding,* translated as "structuring sound," is an orchestration technique for Interpreters Theatre whereby performers echo or expand sounds in a kind of improvisational play on words and their sound patterns.

26. For an explanation, with examples of several major orchestration techniques, see Kleinau and McHughes, *Theatres for Literature,* 54–66.

27. Musical scores are reprinted with permission of Cheryl Ness Genette. Scores for "Christ the Lord Is Risen Today" are from the Latin version of the hymn.

James Dickey's War Poetry:
A "Saved, Shaken Life"

RONALD BAUGHMAN

James Dickey repeatedly returns in his poetry to the experiences of World War II, trying, one imagines, to create the poem that will at long last clarify the war's meaning to him. His encounters with war have so deeply influenced both his view of life and his art that he continually pursues his self-definition in terms of his combat experiences:

> In World War II I was in some awfully harrowing action in the Pacific, and in some places I didn't think it would be possible to survive at all. The result is that now, far removed from those scenes, places, and events, I view existence pretty much from the standpoint of a survivor—sort of like a perpetual convalescent. Someone wrote an article on me once which was called, "James Dickey, the Grateful Survivor," and I can very well affirm that this is my attitude. It's really the only personal philosophical implication of the war that I can think of.[1]

Yet Dickey's survival causes him to experience more than just gratitude; it also drives him to reassess both his life as it presently is and his past as it was during those formative wartime years. As psychohistorian Robert Jay Lifton has convincingly documented, the combat veteran often approaches life with a psychological makeup not generally found in those who have not known the ordeal of war. Lifton's analysis of the war survivor's mind significantly illuminates Dickey's attempts to come to terms with the deep impression war has made on his "saved, shaken life."[2]

Lifton asserts that most combat veterans feel a "death imprint" referred to broadly as "survivor's guilt."[3] One who survives a war may believe that his life is saved at the cost of another's. Yet, even as he suffers the terrible loss of close comrades, the war veteran feels joy at his own survival; such contradictory emotions produce guilt, an enormous "turning inward of anger." This anger, Lifton believes, usually plunges the survivor into two successive forms of guilt,

---

Originally published in the *South Carolina Review* 15 (Spring 1983): 38–48. Reprinted by permission.

the "static" and the "animating." Static guilt is characterized by psychic numbing, which causes the veteran to have difficulty in making emotional investments in others. He retreats into a kind of emotional paralysis, a "self-laceration," and distrusts the ordinary, apparently trivial currents of civilian life that seem to ignore the destruction he has been through. He thus entertains a "profound suspicion of the counterfeit." In order to move to an animating guilt, that form of guilt which offers a measure of "self-knowledge" or self-illumination," the survivor goes through three stages in a "symbolic form of death and rebirth": first, he experiences "confrontation," a "sudden or sustained questioning . . . brought about by some form of death encounter"; next, he undergoes a "reordering" of his perceptions about the dead, a "breaking down of some of the character armor, the long-standing defenses and maneuvers around numbed guilt"; and finally he accomplishes a "renewal," a feeling that he can now be "the author of [his] own life story." Lifton's three stages in the movement from static to animating guilt—confrontation, reordering, and renewal—help define Dickey's progression from an initial state of uncertainty to an eventual measure of order in understanding his combat experiences.

Eight early poems illustrate the poet's varied approaches to confrontation, the perpetual questioning caused by his death encounters. "The Jewel"[4] announces his concern with the consequentiality of his life and actions both during and after the war. The protagonist is a man doubled strangely in time, caught in the vise binding his past and his present. On the surface of his present life, events seem orderly and contained; his secure smile is reflected by his coffee cup as he camps with his suburban family and recalls his satisfying detachment while he performed the technical maneuvers required within his bomber, his jewel. Beneath this emotional calm, however, arise the disorienting questions that occur in the poem's last stanza, questions that indicate his relentless anxieties about his present life and his past war responsibilities:

> Truly, do I live? Or shall I die, at last,
> Of waiting? Why should the fear grow loud
> With the years, of being the first to give in
> To the matched, priceless glow of the engines,
> *Alone, in late night?*

The protagonist senses that he may have been seduced by the beautiful machinery of war; he thus fears a psychic retribution for his acts, retribution defined by his anxieties about whether he is fully alive or instead a slowly dying casualty of war.

These profound apprehensions about his own possible guilt in inflicting war deaths drive the protagonist to seek solace or absolution from those who have been his most obvious victims, his Japanese enemies. In "The Enclosure," the speaker declares:

> It may have been the notion of a circle
> Of light . . .
> That led me later, at peace,
> To shuck off my clothes
> . . . and fall
> On the enemy's women
> With intact and incredible love.

His action is not intended as a violation of the women but instead as a gesture of love; the protagonist offers solace to the women, hoping that they will return a measure of solace to him, the psychologically imprisoned victor. Yet the love remains "incredible," finally ineffectual as a source of release. Similarly, in "A View of Fujiyama after the War" the speaker seeks insight into the knowledge and experience of his former enemy: "Can he know that to live at the heart / Of his saved, shaken life, is to stand / Overcome by the enemy's peace?" In such a pursuit, the protagonist suggests his own sense of guilt about the relationship of victor to the defeated, and, in so doing, he seems to be appealing for pardon at the enemy's shrines. Yet because neither absolution nor solace can be elicited from the defeated Japanese, the narrator is consequently forced to turn to his American comrades in his search for the meaning of his own survival.

The war survivor, Lifton asserts, believes that he is alive because someone else has died in his place. The survivor consequently tempers his joyful relief at his own escape from death by an agonizing concern for the dead. It is from those who have been sacrificed seemingly for him that the poet hopes to gain a meaningful forgiveness. While recreating in his poems the details of their deaths, he also draws a concrete portrait of his own amorphous guilt. Significantly, prisoners of war function as subjects for his homage to friends killed; in turn, the poet becomes another kind of prisoner to his friends' efforts and memories. In "The Performance" Donald Armstrong's acrobatics moments before he is beheaded dramatize the poet's admiration for his martyred friend. The cast of characters in this dreadful drama, however, expands to include not only Armstrong but also both the Japanese executioner, who must fulfill his role as beheader even though he breaks down in a "blaze of tears," and the narrator, who imagines with pained affection how Armstrong must have died. In "Between Two Prisoners," the same figures reappear, with the addition of another of Dickey's friends, Jim Lallery. In both poems, neither the American nor Japanese soldiers can escape their fates; death imprisons everybody, including the speaker. What transpires "between" the Americans and the Japanese, and ultimately among all the combatants, is the realization that death inevitably claims every soldier, either immediately or eventually. Armstrong's and Lallery's and the Japanese executioner's performances are all too brief; the writer's recreations of their ordeals, however, burn forever in his mind. These poems about prisoners and imprisonment mark the poet's true descent into his own piercing anxieties about death, and, rather than discovering a means of gaining forgiveness from dead friends, the writer finds that he has perhaps only intensified his awareness of the lacerating guilt that haunts him.

But as in desperate desire to find an escape from his imprisonment, the protagonist in "Horses and Prisoners" suddenly determines that he can triumph over death: "When death moves close / In the night, I think I can kill it." His belief that he can "kill" death as if it were an enemy soldier results from his strong identification with Japanese prisoners whom he observes firsthand. The prisoners sustain themselves by tearing apart and eating the raw meat of horses; for the narrator these men become not only an emblem of the soldiers' fierce struggles for life but also a symbol for all men who are "seeking a reason to live." The belief that one can kill death and therefore further preserve his own life is, as Lifton points out, "the other side of the survivor's death imprint—the sense of having defeated death and been rendered invulnerable to it. . . . This feeling of invulnerability . . . [is] fragile, and [masks] a more powerful sense of heightened vulnerability underneath" (106). The specter of men reduced to savagely gutting horses in order to stay alive does aid the protagonist in finding a "reason to live"; yet, of course, he cannot kill death any more than he can avoid his responsibility to those who have died as prisoners. Moreover, he knows that while he survives and continues into another life beyond war, death will be close; all the while he lives, his "grave-grass is risen without him."

The poet's strongest reasons to live are born out of the deaths of others, of strangers as well of friends, a realization that he voices in "The Island"[5] and "The Driver." These two poems illustrate the speaker's deep sense of obligation to the dead; he attempts not only to offer his personal homage to them but also to gain understanding about his own life from those who know what death is. In "The Island" the protagonist believes that "the dead . . . nourish me" and that "I, by them, must live." Here the speaker expresses most directly the important equation in the psychology of the survivor—that he is alive because someone else has died in his place. As the protagonist, marooned on an island, buries the war dead, he becomes himself an island, a prisoner, one alive among the dead. His self-imposed homage to these comrades occurs because of his personal attachment to the dead: "Each wooden body, I took / In my arms, and singingly shook / With its being, which stood for my own."

Such an identification with the dead causes the protagonist in "The Driver" to attempt a recreation of death, to enact his own symbolic death, by diving to a sea-buried half-track and adopting the "burning stare" of the drowned former driver. He himself comes close to drowning by staying too long underwater as he assimilates death while retaining consciousness. The closest the narrator can come to comprehending the world of the dead is through his reenactment of the driver's final realization: " 'I become pure spirit,' I tried / To say . . . ? But I was becoming no more / Than haunted." H. L. Weatherby states, in "The Way of Exchange in James Dickey's Poetry," that "to be haunted is to take upon oneself the condition of the dead, to be possessed by the dead, and that is what the swimmer does."[6] "Haunted" refers additionally to the narrator's tortured grief for the dead who pursue him into his troubled "new peace." The dead in "The Island" appear as a general abstraction to the protagonist. But in "The Driver," the speaker's attempt to become one with an actual drowned man seems to offer a source of real forgiveness or at least a vehicle for a less petrifying, more meaningful guilt. Instead, however, the narrator's close proximity to but eventual failure in joining with the deceased man increases his anxieties about the dead and his obligations to them.

The poet's "confrontation" with death involves a movement from a recognition, in "The Jewel," of his guilt to an examination, in the seven later poems, of possible sources of absolution or potential means of coping: asking for solace from enemies' women and shrines in "The Enclosure" and "A View of Fujiyama after the War"; seeking forgiveness or at least understanding by recreating the prisoners-captors' experience in "The Performance" and "Between Two Prisoners"; seeking a release through the extravagant notion that he can kill death in "Horses and Prisoners"; and ultimately trying to become one with the dead in "The Island" and "The Driver." The protagonist fails finally in these poems to achieve a complete oneness with the dead, but in "Drinking from a Helmet" he approaches success and thus initiates the process towards "reordering," in which he will begin to accept his guilt and to use it meaningfully.

The "reordering" process essentially involves a breaking down of the emotional numbing that may occur during "confrontation," and in this respect, the "reordering" moves the survivor towards, as Lifton states, "his simultaneous relationship to anticipated death and continuing life" (390). "Drinking from a Helmet" not only allows the protagonist to embody the last thoughts of one who is dead but also provides the speaker with a vision of earthly life beyond death. Once he has formulated such a vision of death and life beyond, the poet is able to probe directly his ambivalent feeling about himself and his war involvement in "The Firebombing." "The Firebombing" is in many respects the most important poem in Dickey's war canon because it both summarizes the themes presented in the earlier war poems and suggests a new focus for the poet's speculations. In this work, the writer attempts to answer directly the questions about his own self-forgiveness or self-punishment. That he is unable to make an ultimate judgment is understandable and is perhaps less important than the attempt itself. The "reordering" process concludes with "Haunting the Maneuvers," a poem that pictures the protagonist himself as the one who is dead. His death is a symbolic one, thus reflecting Lifton's contention that the survivor experiences various forms of symbolic death; yet undergoing this sort of personal death-experience prepares the protagonist for a rebirth, for his "renewal" into life set forth in "Victory."

In "Drinking from a Helmet," the central figure undergoes a psychological transformation as he transcends the boundaries between life and death through a visionary "exchange" of identities with a dead soldier. This transformation provides as well a means of communicating with the dead, the poet's long sought-after connection with death in order to clarify his own life, his own survival. When he drinks water from a dead man's borrowed helmet, the seventeen-year-old protagonist is struck with a flurry of surrealistic images signifying that a mystical occurrence has touched him; he inherits the legacy of the dead: "The dead cannot rise up, / But their last thought hovers somewhere / For whoever finds it." Richard Howard, in his essay "On James Dickey," points out that the word *helmet* derives from two archaic verbs referring to protection and concealment.[7] Joseph T. Shipley indicates, in his *Dictionary of Word Origins,* that the etymology also includes "the final hiding-place, *hell.*"[8] And certainly the young narrator's fears during combat indicate that he is in a hell for which he needs the helmet's special properties of protection and concealment. But now the helmet is also used as a vessel of communion and baptism, for when the protagonist drinks the water, he shares the "pain" and obtains the "wisdom" of the dead. He goes through the transition from youth to manhood, from a stark fear of death to a fledging understanding of the dead, from a lacerating agony to an animating acceptance of his own survival.

The dead man's final thought gives the speaker a vision of peace beyond the context of war. He inherits a serene scene of two brothers bicycling through California redwoods. Such thoughts, coming as they do in the moment before the soldier's death, offer the protagonist a lyrical, tranquil heaven which contrasts to his hell on the battlefields. The speaker is the one who suffers both the living hell of battle and the peaceful calm of death. This exchange and transformation is at once liberating and damning: the protagonist learns what the dead think and feel when he assumes their perspective as his own; at the same time, the momentary last thoughts of the dead man do not offer peace for the living speaker, especially once he returns to the actuality of combat. The protagonist decides that after the war he will find the dead man's brother "And tell him I was the man," echoing Dickey's quotation of Whitman in *Sorties:* " 'I was the man, I suffer'd, I was there.' "[9] This desire indicates a feature of "reordering" referred to by Lifton: "For the person undergoing this process is struggling to bear witness to the upheaval (death encounter) he has experienced, and to do so with autonomy and authenticity. Bearing witness implies being present to share pain and wisdom, and to take on the responsibility to 'tell the story' afterward" (392). After "Drinking from a Helmet," after moving from "confrontation" to "reordering," the writer is able to dramatize his own conflicts about his war involvement rather than having to depend upon others as agents for his self-exploration.

The movement within Dickey's war poems has been from an initial, relatively distant recollection of the experiences of others toward a deeper concentration on the role of the Self. In the early poems the writer clearly distinguishes between the dead and himself, between prisoners and himself, between executioners and himself. In "The Firebombing" these lines of separation dissolve as the reordering process reaches its zenith; the psychological

struggle Dickey undergoes throughout the war poetry achieves a major culmination in this poem. More than any other work, "The Firebombing" seems to
free the poet, allowing him to dramatize his pride, his fears, his amazement at
his own war involvement. The crucial feature of this work, however, is that the
narrator clearly identifies with both the victim and the executioner, and it is in
the consolidation of roles that the author is able, after writing the poem, to
move from a symbolic death to a spiritual rebirth, to his own self-illumination
about the war and its effects on him.

The strength of "The Firebombing" resides in the ruthless honesty Dickey
demands of himself in examining his reactions to bombing missions remembered twenty years later. The central figure attempts to reconcile two divergent
roles operating at once within himself. He is a cool "technical-minded
stranger" who glories in his own flying and bombing skills, a man in a position
to admire elaborately bursting bombs. On the other hand, years later he is an
American suburbanite who hides his private astonishment about war deaths
behind the bland mask of ordinariness, a man amazed at his former charge
over the lives and deaths of others.

Initially characterized as a "homeowner," the narrator is apparently in
league with other suburbanites, American and Japanese: "All families lie together." An immediate dichotomy destroys the unity of the homeowners, however, for some are "burned alive" while "The others try to feel / For them."
These first four lines present in microcosm the poem's and the speaker's conflict: as a bomber pilot, the narrator has delivered destruction to the Japanese
suburbanites; as a present-day American suburbanite, he shares the sense of
home's inviolability formerly enjoyed by his victims. Yet he can only *try* to feel
sympathy for them and remorse for his own actions. To probe the nature and
extent of his own responsibilities is a psychologically dangerous activity, and
thus he accumulates extra body fat as a physical insulation, a telling parallel to
his need for emotional protection from self-reproach. Yet, as he attempts to
"Starve and take off" fat, he clearly determines to lay bare the truth of his own
situation, shedding both pounds and protection.

The only direct punishment for his bombing missions as a war pilot has
occurred when a mosquito, drunk on altitude, bites him beneath his oxygen
mask while he flies over his target. The triviality of his punishment disturbs
him, for what he has done—destroyed homes and lives—should obviously meet
with appropriate consequences. Instead, he now enjoys the affluence of his
suburban existence; yet, in quiet moments he knows that, because of his actions, "my hat should crawl on my head" and the "fat on my body should
pale." The modal condition, *should,* suggests that the hat does *not* crawl nor
the fat pale. The speaker is unable completely to accept his actions as wrong
and consequently is unable to feel or to formulate an appropriate punishment
or guilt.

As a pilot the protagonist remains hidden safely in the blue-light of the
cockpit, as he was in "The Jewel," removed and protected from the bombs

dropping on people. The airplane he flies is described in human terms, as an extension of the narrator, and, conversely, the pilot adopts technical, unemotional, what Lifton calls "numbed," attitudes as he assumes the characteristics of a machine. He neither deeply feels nor morally judges his bombing performance. As a pilot, the narrator requires the personal distance involved in his powerful "charge" to kill others:

> It is this detachment,
> The honored, aesthetic evil,
> The greatest sense of power in one's life,
> That must be shed in bars, or by whatever
> Means, by starvation
> Visions in well-stocked pantries. . . .

Because he is forced to imagine what he cannot see actually, the poet internalizes the entire event of the bombing mission. He becomes not only the executioner of other people but also the victim of his own recreation of the destruction. And, because he becomes one with the victims as well as with the destroyer, it is impossible for him to pronounce judgment on his actions; he can neither completely absolve nor completely sentence himself. Rather, the poet must continue starkly and nakedly to confront the ambiguities of his situation. If he could choose either absolution or sentence, his emotional quandary would be solved. Instead, Dickey adopts a much more authentic but terrifying honesty; he is condemned to an unresolved ambivalence that will not let him achieve any peace.

Significantly, only after he has attempted connection with the dead in his earlier poems and after he has clearly seen that he is both the victim of and the executioner in war deaths does the poet dramatize himself as the one who is dead. In "Haunting the Maneuvers" the narrator's death is a symbolic one, the result of a mock-killing during a training-camp war game.[10] Instead of bombing others, the speaker is "bombed" by a sack of flour and becomes the "first man killed" during the war exercise. The whiteness covering him gives the protagonist an appropriately haunted or ghostly appearance. The poem's tone is, for a while, comic and ironic; since his is a sham death, being killed is "easy" and without blood. The tone changes, however, to a more solemn one when the protagonist ascends in "self-rising" sleep into his dream of death. As he moves in the night air above his comrades, he hears the mass laughter given to the "chaplain's one / Dirty joke," the cleric's false, romantic slogans about battle and death. The speaker perceives the truth behind such shams when he sees "nothing/ But what is coming." The glory that he had once thought possible in battle now turns into damnation in the "Hell" of combat. Lifton's perceptions of a symbolic death and rebirth are clearly suggested by this poem, for it is after this "death," prepared for by the exercises of his self-scrutiny in "The Firebombing," that the writer begins to move beyond death into what Lifton calls a "principle of improvement" (124–25). This "improvement" occurs in the final step moving the survivor from a static guilt to a more complete form of self-knowledge—"renewal." "Victory" may be seen as a manifestation of the poet's emotional "renewal" to life, accomplished by a symbolic rebirth after the war's end.

Dickey's process of "renewal" is dramatized in "Victory,"[11] a poem that presents a series of images of the Self's rebirth. Lifton states that "renewal" is "a process that, once established, can combine enduring forms with perpetual re-creation" (405); the survivor feels the assurance that his life will continue while simultaneously experiencing its varied moments as if for the first time. This reawakening to and assurance of life are, however, tempered by the death and suffering the survivor has endured. "Victory" is ostensibly a celebration of the Allied victory over the Japanese, but it is much more dramatically a personal rejoicing about the protagonist's successful escape from death and his opportunity for a renewed life. With his survival assured, he celebrates with whiskey two birthdays: the date of his actual birth and the occasion of his symbolic rebirth. As he drinks the whiskey, the narrator begins a transformation into his new life, his "life / After death." He feels his navel burn "like an entry-wound" as he drinks heavily and moves within himself toward the memory of home. Through this Dionysian baptism, the speaker hallucinates a snake's head coming out of the bottle and biting him, forcing a "brotherhood" between himself and this "angel/ Of peace." The brotherhood that the speaker and the snake share is comparable to the blood brotherhood dramatized between combatants and enemies, the sharing of life amidst and sometimes beyond death.

In his drunkenness, the protagonist indicates that he drinks not only to the war's end but also "to what I would do, when the time came, / With my body." What the narrator does with his body is to gain a new skin, the skin of a snake, in a tattoo parlor in Yokahama: "Naked I lay on their zinc / Table, murmuring 'I can't help it.'" The clause "'I can't help it'" is repeated three times at key moments of his struggle for rebirth, a repetition suggesting either that his transformation is beyond his control and volition or that he has consciously surrendered himself to the process. The tattooed snake coils over the speaker's body, beginning at his throat and cutting through the V sunburned on his chest; it encircles him as the "peaceful enemy" depicts scales on his side. As the snake design nears completion, the snake-skin begins to assume and consume the life of the protagonist: "I retched but choked / It back, for he had crossed my breast, and I knew that many- / colored snakeskin was living with my heart   our hearts / Beat as one."

Though the narrator's badge for his survival is ironically that of death— the snake is a figure that Dickey frequently uses as an emblem of the underworld—the protagonist is nonetheless resurrected into a new "life / After death." The new life that he gains depends upon his intense awareness of the ambiguities he will encounter, of both the jubilation and the guilt of his survival. He is the Lazarus-like figure who returns to life to face and to examine overwhelming complexities; he is the poet-seer who must face these complexities profoundly, not easily. He will never say simply that he is innocent or guilty, that war is good or hellish; he has witnessed and realized too much to reduce his knowledge to such small equations. He is reborn into life not with a psyche washed clean but rather with a mind immersed in the greater, more troubling comprehensions with which he must constantly confront the issues of his survival. By incorporating the actual and symbolic qualities of the snake into his own skin, the speaker experiences his "Second Birth"; this image, borrowed from the title of Dickey's 1964 essay, emphasizes the nature and the magnitude of the poet's artistic origin.

The writer's new life bears the results of war's paradoxes: the public glory and the private doubts of heroism, the excitement and the horror of bombing, the camaraderies of battles won and the isolation from friends lost, the joyful relief in and the agonizing guilt of survival. The poet acknowledges the unsettling questions about his life and the war he has survived, and in this respect, the war becomes a vehicle for his encounters with the terrifying truths about life and death that drive him toward profound answers. The insights into the war survivor that Robert Jay Lifton provides dramatize the depth of Dickey's exploration of the Self. It would be, however, misleading to assess Lifton's characterizations of the war survivor as flaws of a tragic figure or of an emotional cripple; rather, in regard to James Dickey, Lifton's research illustrates another kind of courage resulting from war encounters: the painful process of the poet's bringing himself to life again, experiencing a second birth into a profound, dark wisdom about his "saved, shaken life."

NOTES

1. James Dickey, *Self-Interviews,* recorded and edited by Barbara and James Reiss (Garden City, N.Y.: Doubleday, 1970), 135.

2. James Dickey, "A View of Fujiyama after the War," *Drowning with Others* (Middletown, Conn.: Wesleyan University Press, 1962), 51–52.

3. Robert Jay Lifton, *Home from the War: Vietnam Veterans: Neither Victims nor Executioners* (New York: Simon and Schuster, 1973), 126–32. This summary of Lifton's analysis comes from *Home from the War.* Pages 126–32 cover the characteristics of survivor's guilt, while pages 388–408 define the three stages in the movement from static to animating guilt.

4. James Dickey, "The Jewel," *Poems 1957–1967* (Middletown, Conn.: Wesleyan University Press, 1967), 28–29. All subsequent quotations come from the poetry, except those otherwise noted, will be from this volume.

5. James Dickey, "The Island," *Drowning with Others,* 53–54.

6. H. L. Weatherby, "The Way of Exchange in James Dickey's Poetry," *Sewanee Review* 74 (Summer 1966): 669–80.

7. Richard Howard, "On James Dickey," *Partisan Review* 33 (Summer 1966): 414–28, 479–86.

8. Joseph T. Shipley, *Dictionary of Word Origins* (Totowa, N.J.: Littlefield, Adams, 1967), 179.

9. James Dickey, *Sorties* (Garden City, N.Y.: Doubleday, 1970), 159.

10. James Dickey, "Haunting the Maneuvers," *Harper's*, January 1970, 95.

11. James Dickey, "Victory," *The Eye-Beaters, Blood, Victory, Madness, Buckhead and Mercy* (Garden City, N.Y.: Doubleday, 1970), 38–41.

Ezra Pound and James Dickey:
A Correspondence and a Kinship

LEE BARTLETT AND HUGH WITEMEYER

James Dickey visited Ezra Pound at St. Elizabeths in August of 1955. Their correspondence began near the end of that month and lasted until November of 1958. The fact that Dickey later described it as "an enormous correspondence" suggests more about its importance to him than about its actual volume.[1] When he met Pound, Dickey had published only eight poems in well-known magazines.[2] As one of *les jeunes*, he adopted a filial stance toward the venerable figure whom he addressed as "Cher Maître" and "Uncle." From Pound he seemed to receive a sense of parental support and approval: "The kind of contact I had with Ezra Pound was simply the contact of an older dad who talked to you like . . . like you would be talked to by your own crackpot father. . . . Ezra Pound is like your own crazy, intelligent father."[3] To Pound, in turn, Dickey may have seemed a potential son and disciple, who could be instructed to carry on the great battle for a civilized cultural and economic order. The initial tone of the correspondence is personal and literary, but during the second year a proselytizing note enters unmistakably into Pound's letters. Dickey responds to this persuasion with increasing reticence and eventual silence. Fond though he was of his "crazy, intelligent father," Dickey was never thoroughly converted either to Pound's economics or to his poetics. Yet Dickey has spoken eloquently in recent years of the qualities in Pound's poetry which have inspired his own creative work.

In August of 1955, James Dickey was on his way home to Atlanta after spending a year in Europe as the recipient of a Sewanee Review Poetry Fellowship. Before that, he had spent two years as an English instructor at Rice University, and he was about to take up a similar position at the University of Florida in Gainesville. He stopped in Washington, and visited Ezra and Dorothy Pound in the company of William Pratt, a college friend who later became a prominent historian and critic of the Imagist movement.[4] In his first letter to Pound, written from Atlanta near the end of the month, Dickey establishes two grounds of mutual interest: the craft of poetry and the experience of repatriation to America. Pound answered within a week. The major topics of the

Originally published in *Paideuma* 11 (1982): 290–312. Reprinted by permission.

correspondence during 1955 are the whereabouts of Pratt, the works of René Crevel and Basil Bunting, Morrison's Chinese dictionary, and a sweater that Mrs. Maxine Dickey was knitting for Pound.[5]

† † † † † † †

29 August 1955
Atlanta

Dear Mr. Pound,

A few weeks ago Bill Pratt and I came out to see you; I have been meaning to write to you ever since, though I have nothing particular to say beyond mentioning that I enjoyed meeting you and your wife very much, and that I should like very much to hear from you.

Now that "l'année de la poésie" is over and we have reentered the buried life via the gates of the University of Florida, American life has us by the throat again, as before we discovered Europe, stuffing a tiny salary into one hand and nailing the other to the blackboard. Europe seems very far away and inaccessible, and poetry has come again to have the attributes of a personal weapon rather than those of artisanship. All this has no real cause to interest you, but I hope it does, for I remember the time spent talking with you and Mrs. Pound as somehow indicative of a new orientation toward America for me, coming down as we had done through the vast, lucid (but withal bewildering, despite everything) tangle of highways and super-highways out of New York.

My best regards to Mrs. Pound. Meanwhile, I plunge through the brickwork and cactus-blossoms of the University of Florida, in search of the Head of the English Department. Ave Caesar, morituri te salutant!

Write, if you wish.

Yours,
James Dickey

† † †

[6 September 1955]

Kindly curse HELL of out Pratt for falling into
one of the lousiest habits brought in during reign of Sowbelly the damned.

i.e. puttin adress on envelope and NOT on his letter.

Under VERY eggceptional circs / one may omit an address
BUT
to do it in accord with present era of defilement is
NOT proper.

How the HELL am I expected to answer his quite bright effusion?
Or tell Giovanni to send him a copy of. . . .

DO people file ENvelopes????

    Tell him its not that Ruskin didn't SAY it / it is that the
Meyers, Marbles, Sulzbuggers, Belmonts promptly wipe
it out of the public mind, AND endow scholarships
      by the Washinton Posts and other sewages of
their times.
          as soon as ANYone says it /
  Antoninus Pius wiped out of the ms /
Byzantium had a bad prss
         has   press, vide Canto 96

              † † †

                         30 September, 1955
                         Gainesville, Fla.

Cher Maître,
    Bill Pratt's address (after so long a time) is Box 41, Station B, Nashville,
Tennessee. I hope to be forgiven for the delay. There are reasons, but I don't
believe in reasons, really, and feel that I should have written straight through
the middle of them, and shall, from this on.
    We hear it is cold in Washington, though nobody in Florida would ever
believe it; or gets cold in Winter. My wife and I are collaborating on a kind of
project (she works, and I goad) to knit you a sweater, or I guess it will be a
kind of sweater, though at the present stage it knows more what it is trying to
be than we do. Would you like the Gaudier sketch worked in, if we can (we
can't guarantee artistry, but can fumble at similarity) work it in? It will be a
heavy sweater, anyway, so that if it really does get cold there, it can go ahead
and do so.
    My regards to René Crevel, if he should happen to wander in, dressed as
a ghost. I am reading Mon Corps et Moi.
    I have written a long, over-violent and pretty good poem, which I shall
send you after a few more weeks, if you like.
    My best to Mrs. Pound.

                         Yours,
                         James Dickey

1720 N.W. 7th Place
Gainesville, Fla.

              † † †

                         [October 3 1955]

3 Oct / THAT
        is wot was called under the "deplorato" un' ~~Mixzi~~

iniziativaaaa.

        meeting with my highest commendation

the MING YUN (vide a destra) having started the
weakening at the edges of the OLE REEliable /
the probbulum had begun to present itself.

命
運

May I suggest that Madame make it WITHOUT sleeves /
That will both simplify her labours   fit the need of
the beneficiary /
             the waning garment is double wooolllll

grampaw had arruv at the borders of cent kilO / has now
got a BIT nearer human form /
              do yu want MEASUREMENTS?

at any rate fer XrizaChe don't make it short. nowt more
annoying   that a GAP betaeen pantZZ' top and bo'm
of the warmth purrjuicer.

OMIT fancy adornments / trouble enuf to git the garmink
   constructed

"Pieds dans le plat" / best Crevel.
             O.K. send the poEM /

yu had earlier strokes / and Corsini artl / ?

"New Times" orstraliar has trans/ of P. Domenique on "L Homme
                              de Yalta"

   AND the Giovannini on Ez / wot "America" goofed
after faithful promises to G.

[Page two, in Pound's holograph]

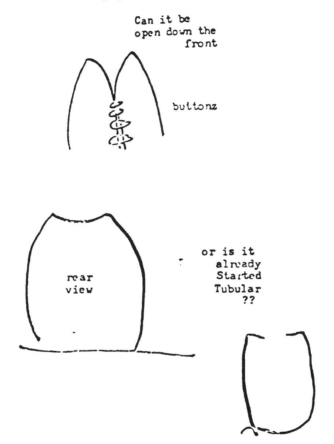

Can it be
open down the
front

buttonz

or is it
already
Started
Tubular
??

rear
view

[appended in Dorothy Pound's holograph]

Woolley most
acceptable
idea! I was
mending the
old one two
days ago—

Saluti
    D. P.

† † †

25 October, 1955
Gainesville, Fla.

Dear Uncle,

Thanks for the continued attention, which I fear I am repaying but illy and tardily. I thought of asking for measurements for the sweater, and all that, but I think the garment might have a better chance on its own, with only my wife's intuitions working and her attention nodding. We will put on the Gaudier head, which we have been at some pains to work out, on sheets of grocery paper, with rulers, pins, and a good many revisions. We have the thing started in gray, leaving you open down the front, as you say. If you want another color, speak up, and we'll try for a barber-pole effect with the (as yet) unknown color.

The poem is not ready yet, but I will send it when I find out myself, what it wants to do.

Where dost get a hold of B. Bunting's poems? I saw a review one time of a Selected or Collected Poems published by something called the Cleaners' Press, but I can't locate either the press or the book. He seems to me to be mighty good, in what I have read, and I'd gladly steal any volume or portion of one I could, or even buy it.

I have not heard from Bill Pratt for a good long time. If you are in epistolary or psychic range of him, tell him I resent his negligence.

Love to your wife. Winter Plans for Clothing and Shelter proceeding at all speed and dispatch, sir, I am

Yr O'bt Sv't
James Dickey

† † †

[Postcard, addressed: Jas Dickey / 1720 N.W. Seventh Place / Gainesville / FLA]

[October 30, 1955]

the Bunter sent to save time, yu
owe Dave one buck ($) payable via me
in postage stamps or come vuoi
I go'r big Morison in woptaly (5 guineas.
SIX vols/ or is it 7. where t'll dju
fink I learned ANY abaht ids/ ??
Only man EXcept W. M. H. who has read all the
4, arranged by roots / since the proofreader.
vols

By February of the next year, Dickey was in trouble with the University of Florida authorities because of a lecture/reading he had given to the American

Pen Women's Society.[6] But he was pleased enough with his recent work to call to Pound's attention a poem and a review-article.[7] He also praised Pound's *Section: Rock-Drill: 85–95 de los cantares,* which was published by New Directions in March. At the end of the spring term, Dickey quit teaching and went to work in New York for the advertising agency which handled the Coca-Cola account. By August, when the sweater was finally finished (though without the Gaudier design),[8] Pound began to hint that Dickey's troubles at Gainesville were due to an economic and cultural conspiracy against clear-thinking men of letters, and that Dickey ought to become active in Pound's campaign to reform the "ethic and civic" of contemporary society. Dickey apparently resisted these hints, and the correspondence became, as Pound put it, "de SULTory."

20 February, 1956
Gainesville, Fla.

Dear Uncle,

I render herewith the annual report of Florida sweater-growers, to say the one we (my wife, especially, but myself also, to some extent: you will recognize the holes) have been most concerned with. The winter is nearly gone now, and we are still "making progress"; that is, we aren't through with it yet. But it will be a warm one when finished, and you can use it forever. And it <u>is</u> almost finished.

There is not much else to say from here, except that a whole generation of Florida students is being brought up on the *ABC of Reading,* much to the astonishment of the Cerberi of the English Department. Also, I lectured, I mean "lectured," to the American Pen Women's Society so furiously (and, I guess, controversially) that their National President wrote to the president of <u>this</u> place and demanded that I be kicked out. I haven't been, yet, but the U. of Florida may martyr me still. I rather hope so, though it may just be possible that I am doing one or two people some good here.

There is a poem of mine to appear in the *Partisan Review* you may want to look at. It is the only one that comes anywhere near doing what I want to do. Others have appeared, but on reading them over I can't for the life of me think they're what I want. But there are some new ones still baking that seem to have some of it. Also, there is a long omnibus review of poets in the Spring *Sewanee* that gets in some good licks against a man by the name of Jarrell, whose work has been to some extent influential, in a bad and sentimental way, here for the last few years. He should read Bunting, and either change or kill himself.

All my love to Mrs. Pound. We think of you often, up to our waists in sand, and burned by the winter (for it is a hot one here.) And we <u>will</u> finish the sweater, if I have to wear out a wife a day working on it.

By the way, is there any news of Pratt? He won't write to me, though I heard some way or other that he now has a child, a girl, specifically.

Yours,
James Dickey

1720 N.W. 7th Place
Gainesville, Florida

† † †

15 August, 1956
Atlanta, Ga.

Dear Uncle,

We mailed the sweater we made, and you should have it in a few days, if you don't already. It is good and strong, and should keep the <u>Cantos</u> warm this winter, and thereafter. I reckon it is heresy of some kind to send a <u>sweater</u> in this kind of season, but when you unstow it this fall I hope it will go round you warmly, and with the other kind of warmth, too.

I left the University of Florida <u>in medias res</u>, "all accusations refuted but that of being the bohemian type." I am in Atlanta working, and teaching and I (at least in the sense of my getting paid for it) are through. It is probably a good thing for both of us.

Can you get me in touch with Bunting?

My love to Mrs. Pound.

I have read the last ten <u>Cantos</u> and they are mighty good. But you sure don't need me to tell you that.

Have not heard from Pratt in five months.

Work going well. Book promised (tentatively) in Spring.

Yours,
Jim Dickey

† † †

[August 18, 1956]

Thanks for information that the sweater has been swatted.

As for touching the Bunting
                    his address is

    242 New Burn Rd. Throckley, Northumberland (wich iz in England)

the best way is with a bag of oatmeal.   (*)

Further details on why those who can't, teach
might be added to gramp's anthropoligical data, or as hist / moeurs
contemp/

no need for laconism on part of the Dickey

as yr / correspondence   is   de SULTory, I take it yu letch not for
numerous pen pals.

(*)

all depending on how serious you are AND   on what you work
FOR, in terms of currency.

[appended in Dorothy Pound's holograph:]

DP. adds:—
Enclo: re BB
came to surface by
chance
yesterday.

† † †

[August 30, 1956]

J. D. the sanity of the woptalian regime was shown in its
Anschauung that a writer (artist) at least at certain level
was more use doing his own job than doing anything else.

At present I shd/   receive information / and reply only
to questions not already answered in print , as from 1908
onward.

The irre-ponsibility ethic and civic of most of my godamned
"licherary" contemporaries, is food for thought on part of yr /
generation.
            The   possibility of being irritated at grampaw's
  prolonged incarceration   alzo eggzists.

Lamentable lack of polemic skill and acumen on part of
my well-wishers. Pearce properly enraged by the infamies of
  the Galimerdacious Panoramic Brown, but am not sure he will
  make bullseye in attack .
                      not if he bases it on mere taste
    instead of Brown's repetition of N.Steal puppyganda lies.

If yu are sighing for action, and god knows we need a super ku klu
  klux.

      You might note the simult.

The other "piece of mail," as they call it that arruv with yrs/
I enc.

[page two]
        2/
Whether yu wd/ git into any serious trouble by TELLING

Mr Parton , that the man who STARTED on Jeff/Van Buren and
                                                        Adams

some years ago , has been in jug ten years for doing so
while the Spewiltzers have been engaged in debasing the
coinage of criticism and of american writing in general.

(or whether yu b'er omit at least the 2nd. observation.

Whether yu think the heritage is safe in the hands of the spwlitw

spewlitzers, guitar players, gibson goilz and other
analagous fauna ,

                etc, at least as subject for correspondence

it that's wots lacking in Atlanta.

            yrs in strict anonymity.

    Pound's suggestion that Dickey enlist in a super Ku Klux Klan was fol-
lowed by a hiatus of nine months in their correspondence. Pound broke the
silence in May of 1957 with a letter promoting *Edge,* a little magazine published
in Australia by Noel Stock and others who were sympathetic to Pound's work
and ideas. Dickey answered politely, sending both personal and literary news,
repeating his praises of *Section: Rock-Drill,* and requesting Pound's advice
about books on monetary reform.[9] Pound's reply, one of his uglier anti-Semitic
effusions, effectively ended the correspondence. Pound sent postcards from
Brunnenburg in June and November of 1958, asking for "nooz" of Southern
politics; but Dickey apparently chose not to answer them.

                                        31 Maggi [May, 1957]

        Edge has now printed Zielinski "La Sibylle," compleat in
                                        one issue.

        will do Neame's Cocteau "Leonne"
    Junzaburo poem of interest.

        if broke can send yu ming/ item of No 4.

Dare say he wd/ accept $10 for   three stubs/ at any rate club
                                                                        scription not
    eGGzorb/t

Little Rev. finally sold for $750   the set / tink of   phosterity

Punch reviving under Muggridge.   Large notice on banks ,
                                                                    10Ap/

Wotchu heard re/ General Educ/ Program kahal'd from
                                                        COlumbia ? has it
got to Ga/ as well as teX ?

any line on Niebuhr ?

† † †

5 June, 1957
Atlanta, Ga.

Dear Uncle,
    Good to hear from you. I will write the <u>Edge</u> people and see what they
have.
    I don't know whether I told you, but I am out of teaching. Had bad luck
there and a passel of "Pen Women" got me booted. I am now making a living
by half-successfully disguising myself as a "business man," coming down town
to work in an office from nine to five each day, and banging away at lunch
hour and evenings at poems and a few reviews. <u>Partisan Review</u> people say they
will bring out a book for me if I can finish a manuscript by Nov. 15th, and I
tell myself I am working toward that, though it goes very slowly.
    Have a good letter from Bunting, though he sounds discouraged and says
he cannot write because of the work he has to do. He says there is no more of
his work besides the Galveston volume you sent and a long poem a few years
ago in <u>Poetry</u>. It is hard to think that <u>he</u> thinks there will be no more. Can you
prevail on him to get going on some new stuff? I would like to, but since I
don't know him, can't, really.
    Rock-drill good. I think the image about the water-spider (or whatever)
and the flower of shadow on rock is the best single image in Cantos. Would
not want to stand off Kenner and the others on this, but will hold to opinion
anyway.
    Nothing "cultural" here. Have a house where I can put books. Should like
to read up on monetary reform. Can you recommend? I know nothing about
money except that it is hard to come by, but not so hard as when teaching gave
it.
    Heard from W. Pratt. He tells me you say good things about Lloyd Fran-

kenberg's poems. Have F's "Red Kite." The stuff is good, but strikes me as more or less usual. Has Pratt got the name right?

Good, again, to hear from you. Let me know what you need, and wife and I will try to supply.

My best to Mrs. Pound. Thank her (belatedly) for sending me the Angold. I had not known him. Some very good clumsyish poems.

Can't find anything of René Crevel.

Yours,
James Dickey

2930 Westminster Circle
Atlanta, Ga.

† † †

[June 6, 1957]

6 Giugn 57

J.D

if Pen Women mean P.E.N. club wimmen / yu have been ditched by one dirty jew gang to be taken up by another / be prudent and dont mention my name till the bastards have actually printed you /

but better try a clean outfit / sometimes they cop a work merely to putt it into a cellar,

P.E.N. started in London / talmudic principle of degradation (F.D.R. praxis), rot of Paris under Cremieux , presumably of the family of the s.o.b. famous in story of french corruption.

Bunting a lump/ immovable /

Dont know Frankenburg's poetry / it was an anthology not too bad /

Econ/ start with enc / Text Book/

IF you can find any clearer statement than in my ABC, and the six pamphlets printed by Russel /

Horton had some copies .)
let me know /

After that / Gesell and C.H.Douglas.

Plus of course Del Mar and Benton.

You have or haven't the Sq S series /

no one educated NOW who
hasn't at least that basis of educ.

somebuddy   told the" Season's Debutante" (T.S.E. acc/   last
account)   that Frobenius wasn't quite the thing / idem   re/
Crevel in different Gebiet ,

he did print my obit in final issue of
Critterarium

  Angold dead too soon / naturally didn't get to full exposition of
what he had in him. morto in guerra.

Recent letter from Italy, re visit from "Italy's 2nd best poet"
says:

Conferma that USIS and such organizations are definitely run
by communist jews, and when they can't give scholarships etc.etc
to jews they give them to communists—or any way   pinks with
not even guts to be communists.

I hear a nobl Georgian by name Simmons has writ a Impeachment
of the SOUPreme court / can yu git me a cawpy
Georgia Impeachment Resolution?

Iago motive/ Aragon praising suicide, Crevel sickened and did /
same with kike wailing to mezzo/kike de Bosis /

Mebbe yu better write to The Point , , 12 Bow St. Cambridge 38
Mass,   Not for sale but they will send to INDIVIDUALS

[page two]

   had some nice quotes from St Ambrose, last sept/
yu needn't say yu ain't a cawflik

Hotter organization/ Alerte
Advocates of our Lady bx 3554 South Bend
Ind.

kahal principle: irresponsible oligarchy / need not be opposed
on grounds of race / but objectors will probably be
branded antikike.

Stock reports Elsom, Lightening over Treasury Building /
  cypher letter in Booth 's trunk decoded from code in possession
of Judah .P.Benjamin.
as might be eggspekted

Lot of stuff in Australian N.Times / you cd/ get the vol/ of last
year, I suppose /

bringing Gesell and CHD up to date

You had Accademia Bulletin No 2 ?   if not will send you a copy

All I want is to have these vestiges of the free press maintained
toward restoration of the U .S.Consterooshun

benedictions an best to deh lady

alzo try to keep Pratt communicating with someone

Crevel / Les Pieds dans le Plat / yu'l have helluva time to find copy
I think Possum even omitted the obit from his selection of EZsays

Ask Point for their Ambrose issue , sometime last autumn.

Dante's method of thought/ not outmoded , but much needed / I
dont mean necessarily re/ political conclusions but the Anschauung /
Swabey , possibly Theobald and G.G. in future EDGE

not dodging thought .i.e. violating the post Conde-Nast system.

[appended in Pound's holograph:]
J.R Elsom
Lightning over
   Treasury
   Building

   ─────

Meador
   1941
   ─────

write to Elsom
who was @
~~39~~ 329 E 111th ST
   Los Angeles **3**

† † †

[Postcard with Pound's photograph, addressed: Jas Dickey / 2930
Westminster Circle N.W. / Atlanta / Ga. / U.S.A.]

[June 23, 1958]

Hotel Italia, Rapallo

got any NOOZ from Loozianaa?
   a state in yr/ vicinage

yrz

z

23 June

best to yr consort , its wearin

fine.

† † †

[Italian picture postcard, addressed: Jas Dickey   esq / 2930 Westminster Circle / N.W. / Atlanta Ga. / U.S.A.]

7 Nov[ember 19]58

Grey sweater resisting alpine blasts and Agassian geog/ formations.

send some nooz of the real south , and how it feels to have so many dem/ cong/men

yrz E.P.

† † † † † † †

Although his correspondence with Pound ended on a strained note, James Dickey's interest in Pound's work remains vigorous and undiminished. To be sure, he has never modelled his own poetic style upon that of Pound. Not even at the outset of his career did he directly imitate the diction and rhythms of his "cher maître." Nor did he submit any of his poems to Pound's criticism, though he spoke at one point of doing so. This early avoidance may have resulted from anxiety on Dickey's part about the possible effects upon his nascent poetic identity of Pound's influence. If so, the anxiety has not persisted in the mature Dickey, who freely acknowledges that he has found a steady source of inspiration for more than twenty-five years in Pound's vision and articulation of human experience. In *The Water-Bug's Mittens: Ezra Pound: What We Can Use*, delivered as the fifth annual Pound Lecture in the Humanities at the University of Idaho on 26 April 1979, Dickey identifies and celebrates the features of Pound's work that have meant most to him.

The title of the lecture comes from the passage in *Section: Rock-Drill* that Dickey praised in his letter to Pound of 5 June 1957: "Rock-drill good. I think the image about the water-spider (or whatever) and the flower of shadow on rock is the best single image in Cantos." The image occurs twice in the cantos Dickey was reading at the time, and once in the later *Drafts and Fragments of Cantos CX–CXVII* (1970):

As the water-bug casts a flower on stone
             nel botro,

One interaction. Tĕ   interaction. A shadow?

(87/574)

The water-bug's mittens
                   petal the rock beneath,
The natrix glides sapphire into the rock-pool.

(91/616)

The water-bug's mittens show on the bright rock below him.

(Addendum for C/800)

These lines represent, according to Dickey, "the kind of untrammeled and primitive observation and careful, simple wording that the best of Pound's own poetry exemplifies and encourages . . . *Mittens!* The *water-bug's* mittens! How curious, and how exactly, exactingly, observably and unforeseeably right! For that is what the water bug's invisible tracks—his feet, his fingers—look like, transformed by the sun and water and rock into shadow. It is an amazing picture, an amazing image, and I for one would not want to do without it."[10]

This image was created, Dickey says, by "the Ezra Pound that I can most truly, effectively and permanently use"—an Ezra Pound who insists "on the mind-object relationship and the word's plain-speaking of it." Pound's poetry opens up to Dickey "the possibility of catching an observable or imaginable part of the world in fresh, clean language that would be simple without being thin and ordinary: that would have the forthrightness of assertion, and be given in language having a strongly marked rhythmical pulse, somewhere near the Anglo-Saxon, and consequently, the sound of a voice saying something both simple and extraordinary, the tone of a thing *meant,* which is also the tone—the *tone*—of a delivered truth." Dickey illustrates these qualities by quoting the fly-tying passage from Canto 51. Such passages, he says, help him to write poetry with "a corresponding imaginative forthrightness, strong rhythm—rhythm using rather more double-stresses, spondees, than is usual—and an unhesitant sound of authority, a tone of truthfulness and 'no-nonsense': a tone of 'this is it, and don't argue.' I like that kind of assertiveness, especially when it is personal and imaginative as well as assertive, and Pound's example has been of immense help to me in formulating passages in which these qualities were dominant."[11]

It is impossible to say just what "passages" of his own work Dickey has in mind here, but the qualities of clear perception, fresh diction, strong rhythm, and authoritative tone which he praises in Pound's work are intermittently present in "The Father's Body," the poem of Dickey's which offended the American Pen Women's Society in Gainesville. As the poem opens, a boy is about to step into a pinewood shower stall, where his father is already bathing.

The boy is standing, dry and blue,
Outside the smoke-hole of water,
The ink-cut and thumb-ball whorls of planks
About him like the depth in a cloud
Of wire, dancing powerfully.[12]

Although the passage is not miming an identifiable model, the images and rhythms of the second and third lines may well owe something to Dickey's reading of Pound. After the boy enters the shower and closes his eyes under the pouring water, he envisions a numinous, paradisal grove,

a wood

Where nothing pours. Grass comes gently
Down into being, in a ring.
He steps forward, deeper,
In the descended brow-light of a shell
Spreading the nerves of sound into itself.

The paradisal groves of *The Cantos* may have helped Dickey to evoke this atmosphere of translucent radiance and intensive silence, with its unexpected but precise and effective image of the "brow-light of a shell."

Amidst this sacred wood, the protagonist of Dickey's dream-vision is initiated into manhood by his father. In a ritual reminiscent of the biblical account of the creation of Eve, the father shapes a girl out of the boy's ribs and tongue. The boy's subsequent coupling with this girl is no doubt what upset the Pen Women, and led to Dickey's resignation from the University of Florida faculty:

He parts the girl's terrible legs; he shouts
Out silence; his waist points
And holds and points, empowered
Unbearably: withheld: withheld—

A loom is flooded with threads,
Showing him stretched on the nails
Of the inward stars of noon, released.

He has died, and his father flickers out
In the lengthening grass where he and the girl
Have been crowded down and crowned.

One does not feel Pound's presence behind these lines. The metaphors may have shocked Gainesville in the mid-1950s, but they seem confused and evasive when compared with the straightforward language of Pound's fertility-ritual cantos, 39 and 47, published in the mid-1930s. Dickey's own dissatisfaction with "The Father's Body" has since led him to exclude it from collected editions of his poetry.

Both "The Father's Body" and his reaction to meeting Pound suggest that

Dickey was preoccupied around 1955–56 with the question of fathers and sons. It is as though he was seeking the support of a father from whom he could yet remain independent, a father by whom he, like the boy in the poem, could be at once "crowded down and crowned." At first Pound seemed to be such a father, accomplished yet accepting. But when Pound began to demand the younger man's support for his own cases, Dickey refused to identify himself with them. "I don't have the integrity of Pound," he later concluded, "at least not that kind. I think integrity and fanaticism are probably two sides of the same coin. I don't have that at all. My orientation is completely different from his. He fails as only a large figure can fail, you know?"[13] His encounter with the "large figure" of Pound was nevertheless both nurturing and liberating for Dickey. In his 1979 lecture he contends that Pound's influence upon younger writers has been "not only beneficial but releasing and exhilarating."[14] In his own case, it would seem, that influence has also been deep and enduring.

NOTES

1. "James Dickey: Interview," *Unmuzzled Ox* 3, no. 2 (1975): 77. The surviving correspondence between Ezra Pound and James Dickey consists of fifteen items, nine from Pound to Dickey (including three postcards) and six from Dickey to Pound. All of the correspondence is typewritten, with an occasional holograph note by Ezra or Dorothy Pound. The Pound letters are housed in the James Dickey Collection at Washington University, St. Louis, Missouri; the Dickey letters, in the Ezra Pound Archive, Beinecke Rare Book and Manuscript Library, Yale University. The directors of those collections provided Xerox copies of the originals, and it is from these copies that we have worked. All of Dickey's letters are dated. Pound often neglected to date his, but we have been able to establish the proper chronology through both postmarks and internal evidence in the correspondence itself. We have left Pound's spelling, punctuation, and typography intact. The letters are published by permission of James Dickey, the Ezra Pound Literary Property Trust, the Washington University Library, and the Beinecke Library. We are grateful to Mr. Dickey, Timothy D. Murray, Mary Maturo, Mary de Rachewitz, Noel Stock, Hamlin Hill, John Walsh, and Donald Pearce for their assistance in the preparation of this article.

2. See Franklin Ashley, *James Dickey: A Checklist* (Detroit: Gale Research Company, 1972), 49.

3. "James Dickey," "Interview" 77–78.

4. Dickey later recalled visiting Pound "a few times" ("James Dickey: Interview," 77), but the correspondence does not mention more than one visit. Of Pratt, Dickey writes: "Bill is a professor of English at Miami University of Ohio. He was a colleague of mine at Vanderbilt, and is a poet, translator, literary critic and historian. At the time we visited Pound at St. Elizabeths Bill was in the Navy, on duty somewhere in or around Washington" (letter from James Dickey to Lee Bartlett, 25 January 1982).

5. See René Crevel, *Mon corps et moi,* 2d ed. (Paris: Editions du Sagittaire, 1926); and *Les pieds dans le plat* (Paris: Editions du Sagittaire, 1933). In his letter to Dickey of 6 June 1957, Pound mentions his obituary article, "René Crevel," *Criterion* 18, no. 71 (January 1939): 225–35. See also Basil Bunting, *Poems 1950* (Galveston, Tex.: Gleaner's

Press, 1950); and Robert Morrison, *A Dictionary of the Chinese Language, in Three Parts,* 6 vols. (Macao: East India Company, 1815–23).

6. Dickey writes: "There was a confusion on Ezra's part about the organization I spoke to down there. [See Pound's letter of 6 June 1957] Ezra thought it was the PEN bunch, when it was actually a much less formidable—and I daresay, less interesting—group called the Pen Women of America, which is hardly more than a large garden club. As I remember, I read some poetry to them, none of it mine, and then at their insistence read part of a poem called 'The Father's Body,' which I had in my pocket and was working on. This had some sexual references that the (Pen) Women didn't like, and they made complaint. I refused to apologize, left the University, and went to work in New York for McCann-Erickson, on the Coca-Cola account. The poem was later published in *Poetry,* though I never collected it" (letter from James Dickey to Lee Bartlett, 25 January 1982). On "The Father's Body," see n. 12.

7. See "The Swimmer," *Partisan Review* 24 (Spring 1957: 244–46; and "Some of All of It," *Sewanee Review* 64 (April–June 1956): 324–48. The last ten pages of the *Sewanee* essay contain a review in dialogue form of Randall Jarrell's *Selected Poems.* The book of poems mentioned by Dickey in his letter of 15 August 1956 and again in his letter of 5 June 1957 was finally published as "Into the Stone and Other Poems" in *Poets of Today VII,* intro. John Hall Wheelock (New York: Charles Scribner's Sons, 1960). The enclosure mentioned by Dorothy Pound in Ezra's letter of 18 August 1956 is a short article by Basil Bunting, "Note on Persian Reading—1." *Four Pages,* 2, no. 1 (October 1950).

8. Letter from James Dickey to Lee Bartlett, 25 January 1982. The authors are indebted to Noel Stock for his help in identifying the "Brown" and "Pearce" mentioned in Pound's letter of 30 August 1956. John Lackey Brown wrote *Panorama de la littérature contemporaine aux États-Unis* (Paris: Gallimard, 1952), in which he spoke of Pound's "dadas economiques et sociaux (le 'social credit,' par example)" and described Pound's activities in Italy as follows: "Coupé maintenant des courants de son temps, il devient aigre et de plus en plus excentrique. Il se fait alors le propagandiste de Mussolini, écrit des pamphlets politiques et sociaux (dont il vaut mieux ne rien dire) et, pendant la guerre, parle à la radio fasciste" (280, 277). Pound wanted Donald Pearce, a scholar of Yeats and modern literature who was then associated with the University of Michigan, to publish a rebuttal of Brown's account, which Pound described as "a DIRTY job by a measly ex-prof, in frog . . . sloppy journalistic survey of yankdom in letters (AND fetters) . . . american puppy-gander, STILL parroting, on official salary, Spew Deal lies" (letter from Pound to Donald Pearce, 26 July 1954). Pearce wrote a critique of Brown's *Panorama* but it was never published (letter from Pearce to Hugh Witenmeyer, 30 March 1982).

9. The items mentioned in Pound's letter of 31 May 1957 are: Thaddeus Zielinski, "The Sibyl: Three Essays on Ancient Religion and Christianity," trans. Henry Swabey, *Edge,* no. 2 (November 1956): 1–47; Jean Cocteau, "Leoun," trans. Alan Neame, *Edge,* no. 6 (June 1957): 1–18; and Nishiwaki Junzaburo, "January in Kyoto," *Edge,* no. 5 (May 1957): 1–2. The authors are grateful to Noel Stock for this information. In connection with Dickey's letter of 5 June 1957, see Lloyd Frankenberg, *The Red Kite* (New York and Toronto: Farrar and Rinehart, 1939); and *Pleasure Dome: On Reading Modern Poetry* (Boston: Houghton Mifflin, 1949). See also John Penrose Angold, *Collected Poems* (London: Peter Russell, 1952). Angold (1909–43), English poet and essayist, wrote for Orage's the *New English Weekly,* Pound translated some of Angold's

economic writings into Italian during World War II; see C. David Heymann, *Ezra Pound: The Last Rower* (New York: Viking Press, 1976), 140; and Charles Olson, *Charles Olson and Ezra Pound: An Encounter at St. Elizabeths,* ed. Catherine Seelye (New York: Grossman Publishers, 1975), 110, 140.

10. James Dickey, *The Water-Bug's Mittens: Ezra Pound: What We Can Use* (Moscow: University of Idaho Press, 1979), 4.

11. *Ibid.,* 9–10.

12. James Dickey, "The Father's Body," *Poetry* 89 (December 1956): 145–49.

13. "James Dickey: Interview," 78.

14. *Water-Bug's Mittens,* 4.

The Momentum of Word-Magic in James Dickey's *Eye-Beaters, Blood, Victory, Madness, Buckhead and Mercy*

ROBERT KIRSCHTEN

In the late 1960s, when he collected his first five books of poetry into one volume, James Dickey had reached such a considerable level of literary success that Louis Untermeyer claimed that *Poems 1957–1967* "is the poetry book of the year, and I have little doubt that it will prove to be the outstanding collection of one man's poems to appear in this decade." While Peter Davison and James Tulip ranked Dickey and Robert Lowell as the two major poets in the country, John Simon was even more enthusiastic when he declared, "I place Dickey squarely above Lowell." However, in 1968, with the appearance of Dickey's very next book, *The Eye-Beaters, Blood, Victory, Madness, Buckhead and Mercy,* critics seemed annoyed, even dismayed, at the new direction of his highly experimental collection of verse. Herbert Leibowitz noted that the "balance of pure abandon and meticulous observation breaks apart in Dickey's latest volume," and, further, that a "stagy, unpleasant hysteria enters the poems." Benjamin DeMott charged that the "poet runs on unrestrainedly," giving "no shapely object to delight in, little refinement of feeling or subtlety of judgment, no intellectual distinction, no hint of wisdom." Even as staunch an early supporter as Richard Howard lamented that "The look of these poems on the page is disconcerting: forms are sundered, wrenched apart rather than wrought together." Howard concluded with a statement of considerable strength, "The cost to [Dickey's] poetry is tremendous, for it has cost him poems themselves—there are not poems here . . . only—only!—poetry."

Despite the severity of these appraisals, *Eye-Beaters* contains at least seven of Dickey's major poems, and constitutes one of the central transitional texts in Dickey's poetic canon.[1] During this period, his experiments in two basic areas, form and diction, opened a number of technical, poetic doors that opened the way to his remarkable and controversial book-length poem *The Zodiac* in 1976 to major achievements in the 1980s in *Puella* and *The Eagle's Mile,* two of his best volumes of verse. In *The Eye-Beaters,* Dickey still kept his

Originally published in *Contemporary Literature* 36 (Spring 1995): 130–63. Reprinted by permission of the University of Wisconsin Press.

eye at times on a classical sense of narrative—the story-based poem on which he built such a wide following of readers; however, he also began to highlight word-groups that radically altered his techniques of telling and gained him especially dramatic entrance to the world of darkness and terror that strongly unsettled Leibowitz, DeMott, and Howard. These word groups reveal fundamental methods in Dickey's word-magic and the subsequent momentum of his poetic thought, which, to my mind, has been misrepresented by many of his negative critics. These critics look for intellectual or discursive thinking in a poet who is not understandable only to the rational mind, and, as a result, they find Dickey's poems lacking in elements that are completely irrelevant to his poetic program.[2] Dickey's best poems in this book are not hysterical, unrestrained, unshaped, unsubtle, or wrenched apart, but are intricately constructed forms generated by a mode of thinking that is rooted in anthropological and mythopoeic criticism—namely, contagious magic.

Presupposing an ancient, universal law of contact between animate and inanimate objects, even those which are geographically distant such as the moon and stars, contagious magic seems, at first, primitive, simple, or scientifically mistaken. However, when developed through the complex combinations within his extraordinary diction, Dickey's version of this practical causal principle allows him to reinvent a world in which magic not only seems plausible, but natural and even necessary. For, out of his animated series of "natural" connections, Dickey constructs a diverse range of rituals, ranging from sacrificial rites to linguistic acts of creation, which, reflexively, depend on his magical ontology for their effectiveness. When properly constructed, these rites reveal special, therapeutic powers designed to bring some measure of human control to the catastrophic, real worlds of "blood" and "madness." The plausibility of Dickey's word-magic takes its authority from its appeal to deeper reaches of the human mind that are closed to more discursive modes of lyric action. Not "deep image poetry" exactly, his poetry operates through archetypal images within a deeply appealing and personal mode that also engages and alters the social self, especially the self traumatized by war. While his verbal and formal magic has distinguished precedents in the work of Hart Crane, Dylan Thomas, Theodore Roethke, and even Samuel Taylor Coleridge, critics often fail to judge Dickey by those principles which have been used to canonize these writers. To establish critical criteria—especially those in a mythopoeic mode—more accurately attuned to Dickey's true poetic vision in *The Eye-Beaters,* we need to focus on a number of issues that preoccupied the poet at this point in his career: his construction of poetic form in relation to word-magic, the subsequent shift of formal momentum in his poetry from action to image, and the shaping elements in at least one of the historic genres in which he was writing.

I

To initiate his keynote speech to the South Atlantic Modern Language Association in November of 1982, Dickey borrowed a distinction from the

Notebooks of poet Winfield Townley Scott.[3] Centering on two kinds of poetry, or, rather, two kinds of poetic diction, this distinction is simple enough yet reveals much about Dickey's own poetic practice. The first type of poetry is, according to Scott, literalistic and marked by its capacity for moving, external reference. It is "a commentary on human life so concentrated as to give off considerable pressure." Two of its central practioners are Wordsworth and Hardy, and it "is represented by [Edwin Arlington] Robinson's [line]: 'And he was all alone there when he died.' " The second and opposite type, less literal and more evocative in character, "is a magic gesture of language" (*Night Hurdling*, 125), among whose proponents are Poe and Rimbaud; this second type is illustrated by lines from Hart Crane's poem "Voyages":

> O minstrel galleons of Carib fire,
> Bequeath us to no earthly shore until
> Is answered in the vortex of our grave
> The seal's wide spindrift gaze toward paradise.
>
> (*Poems*, 36)

For Dickey, the key word in these lines is *spindrift*, whose peculiar qualities place Crane among what Dickey calls, following Scott, the "Magic-Language exemplars" of poetry. Instead of a literal or essential component of the seal's manner of seeing, *spindrift* belongs less to the "reality world" of animal vision than the "word world" of verbal association (126), or what Crane calls, in his well-known phrase, the "logic of metaphor" (221). Dickey explains that " 'Sprindrift' is sea-foam, wave-foam, usually wind-blown along beaches, and, though the seal's eyes may be wide, and his gaze toward Paradise, 'spindrift' is really not, cannot be part of his vision: the word is word only, associational and in its way beautiful, but word" (126).[4]

   Instead of inventing poems characterized by statements that have an empirical or external referential direction, the poets of word-magic work from inside a reverberating, self-generating world of linguistic interplay. According to Dickey, these writers are less interested in realistic narratives or personal anecdotes which convey maxims about the world of human action and ideas than in the evocative powers and suggestions of words themselves. This word-play may be further understood by considering its opposite—namely, that kind of diction that belongs to poets whom Dickey calls "the literalists." Unlike the "magic-language practitioners," "literal-minded poets" believe "in words as agents which illuminate events and situations that are part of an already given continuum" (*Night Hurdling*, 131). For example: "The Robinson line . . . is simply factual. There are only plain words in it: a statement. Plain words in ordinary order; nothing unusual, much less exotic. The line puts the reader into contemplation of something that happened to someone, and the condition of the happening; it is the clear pane of glass that does not call attention to itself, but gives clearly and cleanly on a circumstance" (126). On the other hand, word-magicians do not give primacy to plot or to the discursive revelations of character, but to a dream-mode or some kind of surrealistic space in which the powers of reason have little importance. Although Dickey's remarks were made with *Puella* (1982) in mind, the book with his fullest use of word-magic and to which this article is a preliminary study, these observations reveal much about his own magical approach throughout his poetry. This approach is evident as far back in Dickey's work as the opening poem, the magical chant "Sleeping Out at Easter," in his first collection of poems, *Into the Stone* (1960). Of word-magicians, Dickey said in 1982: "For the Magicians, language itself must be paramount: language and the connotative aura it gives off. . . . The words are seen as illuminations mainly of one another; their light of meaning plays back and forth between them, and, though it must by nature refer be-yond, outside itself, shimmers back off the external world in a way whereby the world—or objective reality, or just Reality—serves as a kind of secondary necessity, a non-verbal backdrop to highlight the dance of words and their bemused interplay" (*Night Hurdling,* 126–27).

However magical Dickey's interests became at this point, he never fully divorced himself from his commitment to literal-mindedness or his belief in the necessity of basic storytelling. For, in the same essay, he criticizes purely magical poetry for its considerable limitations. In magical poetry divorced from public concerns, Dickey says, "the *world* is lacking" and where "the buzz of language and the hit-or-miss-metaphor-generation is everything; the poem it-self is nothing; or only a collection of fragments" (*Night Hurdling,* 138). Al-though he admits to being "profoundly interested" in "the absolute freedom" that the magical making of metaphors" offers the poet, Dickey also wants lyrics "bound into one poetic situation, one scene, one event after the other" (139). A further problem with the magical method, especially in the surrealistic school, is that it invents without discovering, as Wallace Stevens noted. It does not reveal the contents of the unconscious but, instead, mere phantasms. Also it has no *"drama,"* for it *"cannot build."* Of poems in this style, Dickey observes that they have no narrative, no logic, no idea-development, no transformation, no "publically available" themes (137).

If one wonders in which camp Dickey places his own poetic language, he provides what appears to be a decisive response earlier in his essay. Although he greatly admires the best of them, he claims, "I am not of the party of the magic-language practitioners" (*Night Hurdling,* 129). At first glance, this self-classification seems true. Because so much of Dickey's early poetry depends on anecdotal narrative and extrinsic reference to topics and events from his own life (world war, family, animals, even a Southern Baptist preacher), he seems justified in placing himself among those poets whom he calls "literal-minded" (129)—e.g., Robert Frost, Edgar Lee Masters, and Randall Jarrell. From a sty-listic or linguistic point of view, however, Dickey's poetry also suggests an ex-tremely strong magical orientation. In the mid- and late 1960s, in particular, Dickey began to experiment with word-groups bunched together by means of techniques such as the "block format" and the "split line."[5] At this time, words themselves and their "connotative aura" (*Night Hurdling,* 127) became singularly featured on the pages of his lyrics. In "May Day Sermon," "Falling," "The Shark's Parlor," "The Fiend," and to some extent in "The Firebombing," he built "wall[s] of words" (*Night Hurdling,* 116) out of distinctive visual and semantic combinations that were not only striking to behold but, more important, approximated, as Dickey says, "the real way of the mind as it associates verbally . . . in bursts of words, in jumps" (*Self-Interviews,* 184).

One major effect of the method (or "real way") of these mental word-"bursts" and "jumps" is the construction of an emotionally immediate, if not obsessive, universe in which the magical contiguity of natural forms of life and death is conveyed by Dickey's imagistic contiguities. He calls the semantic aspect of this magical contact "apparently unjustifiable juxtapositions" and "shifts of meaning or consciousness" (*Self-Interviews,* 185). These juxtapositions may be rationally "unjustifiable," but, from a poetic and emotional point of view, they enable the objects inside his visually bracketed word groups to exchange (or share) properties in an especially dramatic and vivid manner. These stylistically fused traits build scenes so rich in texture that they constitute the animating ground of the poem's action and thus possibility for Dickey's characters. "May Day Sermon" provides an especially vivid example of how the poet's word-magic "jumps" across the page with a stunning momentum that energizes the woman preacher who delivers the lines. This momentum also animates the objects of nature in Dickey's universe and reveals how he thinks magically through them:

> Sisters, understand about men and
>   sheaths:
> About nakedness: understand how butterflies, amazed, pass out
> Of their natal silks   how the tight snake takes a great breath   bursts
> Through himself and leaves himself behind   how a man casts finally
> Off everything that shields him from another   beholds his loins
> Shine with his children forever   burn with the very juice
> Of resurrection . . .

> (*Poems,* 7)

In this section Dickey's word-magic builds the poem's (and nature's) momentum by means of his striking grammatical strategies of predication, strategies that, as we will see, are also central to his magical method in "Pine." In the arrangement of word blocks in "May Day Sermon," nouns such as *butterflies, tight snake, man,* and *his children* share the ejaculatory, universal motion of sheaths and nakedness, which "pass out," breathe, burst, "shield," behold, "[s]hine," and "burn . . . with resurrection." This sharing is effected by an elaborate series of delayed predicates in parallel constructions in which the poet omits punctuation and connectives in favor of breath spaces. By keeping mechanical interrupters and conjunctions to a minimum, Dickey creates an oratorical and ontological momentum marked by "fluidity and flux" (*Voiced*

Connections, 155) which is his own specification of William James's famous stream of consciousness.[6] Dickey's poetic flow—more like a tidal wave in this poem—makes objects exchange attributes by making the mind "jump" between nouns and predicates such that a verb (and its textual traits) in one clause may be plausibly predicated of two or more preceding subjects. In the lines cited previously, the subject of *burn* is *loins* but may as well be *children,* for both *loins* and *children*—albeit in different modes—"burn" "with the very juice / Of resurrection." Dickey does not only use this technique for single terms. Because he begins his word blocks with dynamic verbs, gerunds, and present participles, he drives these blocks forward in a stream of sexual, natural, and grammatical motion while simultaneously allowing the eye to linger upon visually separated word groups so that entire groups of words appear to serve as nouns for several series of subsequent verbals. Several lines later in "May Day Sermon," it is a trout which flows and slides upstream, but Dickey's spatial arrangement of his word groups makes it appear that the trout's "cold Mountain of his birth" does the same, for the trout "heads upstream, breathing mist like water, for the cold / Mountain of his birth   flowing sliding in and through the ego- / maniacal sleep of gamecocks" (*Poems,* 7). The metaphysical mechanism behind these shared predicates is a mode of connection that Sir James Frazer calls "contagious magic" in *The Golden Bough*—namely, "that things which have once been in contact with each other are always in contact" (13). In Dickey's poetic universe, these grammatical and ontological connections produce a magical animism, in which, to use Joseph Campbell's phrasing, "there is no such thing as absolute death, only a passing of individuals back and forth, as it were, through a veil or screen of visibility, until—for one reason or another—they dissolve into an undifferentiated ground that is not of death, but of potential life, out of which new individuals appear."[7]

Not only objects and groups of objects are animated by mental word-magic in Dickey's world. Dickey's word-magic also drives the emotionally animating end of "May Day Sermon," which is nothing less than the resurrection in springtime of nature, sexual instinct, and the vocalized anima (or soul) of the victimized daughter, all under the aegis of the oratorical triad of energized women: preacher, audience, and subject of the sermon (the daughter). The daughter of the abusive, backwoods, Bible-reading father is able to return from the dead each year precisely because, in Dickey's lyric universe, "there is," in Campbell's words, "no such thing as absolute death." Dickey's is a world in which life and death cyclically and magically dissolve into and out of each other and in which the animating power of the woman preacher's eternal logos—like "men" and "nakedness"—also "bursts," "Shine[s], and "burn[s] with the very juice / Of resurrection." The daughter does not die for her sexual freedom but dies as a fertility goddess who transcends death each spring like the earth itself by riding the eternal continuum of decay, regeneration, and rebirth, empowered in Dickey's worldview by the words of women and the poet's magical modes of "resurrection." The very possibility for the daughter's archetypal transcendence is thus rooted in a magically empowered and conceived setting which eternally energizes her.

If the ritualized methods and the ground of action in Dickey's lyrics take on a special primitive power in the mid-1960s, the effects of his word magic and its reverberating linguistic momentum become even more pronounced in the late 1960s and the early 1970s. His magical diction is primarily effected through catalogues of tactile, concrete metaphors, hypenated word-combinations, and explosive, staggered groups of action-packed gerundives. When working in a distinctively surrealistic or hallucinatory dream-mode, Dickey distances himself even further from his earlier formal strategies, realistic anecdotes and the relatively sober revelations of romantic perception, in favor of an exuberant emphasis on magical imagery. For instance, in "The Eye-Beaters," the narrator does not go inside the minds of blind children for internal revelation when he visits a home for the children in Indiana but, instead, externalizes his imagined vision of what they see as he addresses himself.

> Smudge-eyed, wide-eyed, gouged, horned, caved-
> in, they are silent: it is for you to guess what they hold back inside
> The brown and hazel   inside the failed green   the vacant
> blue-
> eyed floating of the soul.[8]

At first, there appears to be little here of what could be traditionally called a complicated plot which changes the fortunes of its characters. Neither the children nor the narrator can change. Try as he may, the speaker cannot alter the condition of the blind children, who beat their eyes in frustration. In a sense, then, the animating end of this poem is the realistic failure of the poet's magical, elaborate, techniques of animation. This failure, however, is only half the equation. After acknowledging the therapeutic limits of his poetry, the speaker frantically continues to build his fictional wall of mythic images for his own sake and for that of the real "vision" of the children. He argues rationally that in spite of their blindness, these children are still important, and that "what they see must be crucial / To the human race." Despite his claim to reason, Dickey's magic produces nothing more than a semi-hysterical nightmare of his own darkness and rage as the poet tries to see what is "under their pummeled lids" (54).

His word-magic is thus closer to word-madness than magic. Yet this madness has its own, peculiar visioning power. In "May Day Sermon," while partially maddened by her belief system, by abuse to the farmer's daughter, and by Dickey's inflamed rhetoric, the woman preacher nonetheless effects an optimistic, mythopoeic reincarnation of the victimized girl. In *The Eye-Beaters,* Dickey's word-madness seeks a magic that at first appears ineffective. This magic is built out of nothing but the "sheer / Despair of invention" in the real world where the narrator's poetic powers cannot heal. However, what comes most alive in this world—even more than plot and character—is the poet's mental cave of magical images—i.e., the cave of "perversity" and "madness"—constituted by Dickey's wall of words. It is as if he has taken us inside Plato's cave of illusions or inside one of the Paleolithic caves at Montesquieu-Avantes in the Pyrenees and left us in the dark. In such a world "Half-broken light flickers" briefly and shows us partial images of "ibex   guagga . . . cave bear aurochs   [and] mammoth" (51). However, this is a mental world which is even darker and more claustrophobic, where the poet's "reason" has "gone / Like eyes," and only his primal images offer him solace from despair. We thus come closer to experiencing the dark world of these children than we ever would have without Dickey's disturbing and dazzling poem, at the heart of which is yet another of his extraordinary, primitivistic exchanges. This exchange transforms speaker and reader by linking sighted readers to blind children, even though the mode of shared "vision" is only—or, to use Richard Howard's exclamation that we saw earlier, "only!"—poetic.

As we trace the evolution of Dickey's use of magical language, what is important to note in "The Eye-Beaters"—as well as "Mercy," "Victory," and "Pine" in the same volume—is that Dickey's walls of words are so powerful that their contagious, magical energy appears to displace plot, character, and revelation as emotionally central parts of his poetic action. These traditional shaping elements are, of course, still prominent in his work of this period. However, we may well be able to claim—using Dickey's own description of poetic word-magicians—that, in these boldly experimental poems, he has gone farther than ever toward giving primacy to "language and the connotative aura it gives off." This new primacy of parts enables him to invent a new poetic "reality [that] . . . serves as . . . backdrop to highlight the dance of words and its bemused interplay" (*Night Hurdling,* 127). To put it another way, Dickey's radically magical walls of reality establish settings which not so much displace thought and character as they take on the functions of character, revelation, and the solution (or opposition) to the protagonist's driving needs. In "May Day Sermon," magical word groups not only create the physical setting but also the animating ground of change and motivation for the woman preacher. Yet they also constitute a formal revolution, what would in contemporary criticism be called a "deconstruction," in which Dickey's word magic achieves a parity of power with the classic, Aristotelian elements of thought and action, and even becomes the central pattern of thought and action. By focusing on "the action of words upon each other, for whatever meaning or sensation they may throw off, evoke" (131), Dickey uses these networks of "meaning or sensation" not to remain mired in sensation but to invent what is for him a new kind of poetic form. Insofar as his new diction produces a "connotative aura" that radically alters his speaker's fundamental mode of perception while also shaping and guiding the reader's point of view, Dickey's mythical language becomes both his poetic action *and* his basic method of representation. This collapse—or fusion—of analytic distinctions is true for all poetry insofar as poetry's shaping causes are synthesized within its verbal materials. But, for

Dickey, his distinctive change in emphasis yields especially vivid insights into a new way of thinking through words which themselves revolutionize his poetry.

II

If, in this middle period of his career, Dickey begins to think in a radically mythomagical mode while quite consciously moving away from anecdote and narrative, we see yet another reason why his poetry upsets the Aristotelian causal hierarchy which privileges plot the way Dickey did in his early work. The very nature of thought manifested in Dickey's word-magic demands this formal shift. For, as Ernst Cassirer notes, "mythical consciousness . . . knows nothing of certain distinctions. . . . [I]t lacks any fixed dividing line between mere 'representation' and 'real' perception, between wish and fulfillment, between image and thing."[9] Further, by using a mode of thought which burkes classical logical axioms and assumes instead magical principles—such as "the part not only *stands for* the whole but positively *is* the whole" (61)   Dickey confounded many critics in the late 1960s and early 1970s by inventing an "aura" that baffled them when they applied discursive or meditative criteria. For, when Dickey's linguistic aura became a dominant force, it produced a dreamworld like that of the undifferentiated reality of primitive consciousness; thus many readers dismissed the poems in *The Eye-Beaters* as formless or poorly constructed. On the contrary, these poems are intricately constructed, and, further, they are designed to convey the atmosphere of nightmares or dream consciousness, the very nature of which is cloudy or phantasmic.

One magical mode, the conversion of properties or attributes of objects into bodies, appears in the scenic imagery of "Mercy," a nightmare poem about the narrator's lover, Fay, a nurse at a hospital in "slum Atlanta," whom he picks up at the nurses' dormitory called "Mercy Manor." By mixing hypostatized, imagistic traits of love, mortality, blood, and banal pop culture in a dazzling scene of surrealistic transformation, Dickey converts Fay into a contemporary Persephone, macabre yet heroic. While "perfume and disinfectant battle / In her armpits" (*Eye-Beaters*, 15), she straddles the worlds of life and death, goddess-like, when, in the poem's conclusion, the speaker imagines himself "Collapsed on the street," having a kind of heart (or love) attack: "I nearly am dead / In love." Herself a stark contrast in the colors of healing and of death, Fay leans over him as he calls for her kiss to silence the cry of mortality from his lips and to bear him safely from the world of darkness into the "mercy" of St. Joseph's hospital:

> She would bend
> Over me like this   sink down
> With me in her white dress
> Changing to black   we sink
> Down flickering
> Like television   like Arthur Godfrey's face

        Coming on   huge   happy
            About us   happy
        About everything   O bring up
    My lips   hold them down don't let them cry
  With the cry   close   closer   eyeball to eyeball
            In my arms, O queen of death
            Alive, and with me at the end.

                                                        (16)

If Fay, like Persephone, possesses a goddess-like power of healing and renewal, she does so because the poet rescues her from a convincing technical,
pop cultural hell that enervates yet simultaneously animates her. As he does in
"The Eye-Beaters," Dickey builds another dynamic wall of words—this time,
down the middle of the page—that makes the night world of hospitals come
alive in a sensuously dark dream-scene. This scene is not static. As the drama
develops, the setting not only gains emotional power by means of the affective
accumulation of Dickey's detail; it propels the action forward by providing an
overwhelming opponent of "night" and "mortality" against which the speaker
battles for "care" and "love." In the night world of this hospital, "love," if not
life, has never felt more vulnerable. One cause of this vulnerability is the massive sense of indifference that the setting—indeed, the world—evinces toward
the speaker. This anomie is reflected in Dickey's magical, imagistic hypostatiza-
tion of Arthur Godfrey's smiling, television face, whose mind-numbing,
"happy" countenance benignly smiles over the night world of pain and death
with the comic indifference of a plastic Halloween mask. Cassirer says that in
magical thought, "The 'image' does not represent the 'thing'; it *is* the thing; it
does not merely stand for the object, but has the same actuality, so that it
replaces the thing's immediate presence" (*Mythical Thought,* 37). We do not
confuse Arthur Godfrey with his image. Rather, Dickey so animates the banality of the image that its preposterous happiness becomes an oppressive, real,
actual body. In this animated, surrealistic space, the poet turns a complex of
cultural and technological relations into "a pre-existing material substance" in
which, in Cassirer's words, "all mere properties or attributes . . . become bodies" (55). By magically making banality a substance, Dickey provides one element in the poisoned substratum of a contemporary, urban scene against
which the energized passion of a goddess-woman offers temporary redemption
from the speaker's hysterical "wail" and the dark, cold world of mortality and
indifference.

    In this stage of Dickey's poetic career—which may be labeled a magical
period in which he makes a radical move from action to image—voice, points
of view (reader's and speaker's), and plot seem less like specific, separable literary devices than undifferentiated aspects of the dreamy aura of his word selection. These strategically constructed word groups reveal the movement of his
mind from linguistic block to block in modes of non-discursive, nonanalytical

thought that Ernst Cassirer discusses in his chapter on "Word Magic" in *Language and Myth:*

> Mythic ideation and primitive verbal conception [involve] a process of almost violent separation and individuation. Only when this intense individuation has been consummated, when the immediate intuition has been focused and . . . reduced to a single point, does the mythic or linguistic form emerge, and the word or the momentary god is created. . . . [T]he process of apprehension aims not at an expansion, extension, universalizing of the content, but rather at its highest intensification. . . . The conscious experience is not merely wedded to the word, but is consumed by it. Whatever has been fixed by a name, henceforth is not only real, but is Reality.[10]

In the momentum of Dickey's thought in the best poems from *The Eye-Beaters,* objects and events are individuated through narratives that antagonize and separate agents. Things and acts are also individuated through strategic spatial separations (different from the split line but an off-shoot of it) and through emphases of his arrangement of words on the page. His word blocks isolate images in focussed impressions that, when grouped in his distinctive series of sequences, give the sense that a name and its referent are magically connected; indeed, that reality is built out of momentary bursts of tangible, tactile names. These names not only share the properties of what they signify but also feel as if they are some essential part (or the whole) of their referents while simultaneously amplifying the emotional impact of those parts. At times, Dickey's focussed images give us an animal's surrealistic, enlarged perspective of heads and eyes in word groups that themselves enlarge the objects represented. For example, in "Madness," a family hound is bitten by a rabid female fox, and the experience of sound and pain is conveyed and enlarged in a poetic form marked by the isolation of intensified moments from the story:

she bit down

Hard on a great yell
To the house being eaten alive
By April's leaves. Bawled; they came and found.
The children cried

Helping tote to the full moon
Of the kitchen   "I carried the head"   O full of eyes
Heads kept coming across, and friends and family
Hurt   hurt
The spirit of the household, on the kitchen
Table being thick-sewed . . .

(*Eye-Beaters,* 48)

To no small degree, the basic representational device in this poem progressively becomes the form of the poem. That is, the strategic isolation of the names of fragments of events results in a magic pointillism that fixes as its primary patterned reality the surrealistic aspects of the core event that pattern depicts. Summarized under the title of "Madness," the basic narrative is simple: a family dog is bitten, becomes rabid, is hunted down, then beheaded. However, the stylized, magical story is considerably more complex, primarily because of the way it is told: the conversion of a family hound into an energized, manic god of the hunt and kill, who, through a narrative of hallucinatory frenzy marked by the contagious, explosive escalation of sexuality and violence, dies a divine death as a non-retaliatory scapegoat; the humans in the poem project their own mimetic desire for violence upon this sacrificial monster who is expelled from the circle of domestic safety then closes the poem's process of over-flowing violence with his own execution. Dickey's verbal methods of separation, individuation, and amplification are essential to the monster-making process because they amplify the dog's bizarre and dangerous traits into monstrous proportions so that his sacrificial death, dramatically mandated, purges the stable world that he himself has infected and threatened. One instance of this amplification process occurs after the dog is bitten. It is carried into the family kitchen, and the phrase "O full of eyes" floods the moment with what Dickey construes to be the animal's vision yet also isolates that moment with an image in which eyes seem disembodied and bizarre, as would befit a being which is in the process of transgressing normal social boundaries. That the poem is so effectively disturbing and dark reveals that Dickey's vibrant word magic makes fully tangible the traits of surrealistic monstrosity which the poem requires for its sacred drama.[11]

Although there is none of the archetypal pairing of the intensely dramatic mythopoeic opposites of sex and violence in the three-page lyric "Pine," this poem reveals several other aspects of Dickey's remarkable—and difficult—mode of magical meditation.[12] Cast in a sequence of "successive apprehensions" (or "four ways / Of being") with a fifth, concluding, single-word section ("Glory"), "Pine" examines a pine tree by means of four senses: hearing, smell, taste, and touch. At first glance, the poem's process of thought appears to be built out of compounds—or, to use Dickey's own term, "a dark / Flood"—of traits which the speaker is "Opening one by one." Each section features, though not exclusively, one sense which Dickey examines by means of a series of percepts, analogies, intuitions, and visceral experiences of the body. This flood of synaesthetic experience combines to form a whole of some kind, when, at the end, Dickey claims:

> A final form
> And color at last comes out
> Of you alone putting it all
> Together like nothing

> Here like almighty
> V
> Glory.

                                                    (*Eye-Beaters*, 46)

To some extent, Dickey's mode of perception resembles the kind of accumulation that, according to Denis Donoghue, constitutes "the self" in Walt Whitman's lengthy catalogues:

> he begins by saying, Let x equal the self. Then x equals A plus B plus C plus D plus E . . . where each letter stands for a new experience contained and possessed, and the self is the sum of its possessions. This is the law of Whitman's lists. If you say that the self—x—is the sum of its possessions . . . then the more you add to the righthand side of the equation, the more you enrich the left, and you do this without bothering about the "nature" of the x. You assume, as most Romantic poets did, that the self is not at any moment fixed, complete, or predetermined, and then you are free to develop or enlarge it at any time by adding to its experience.[13]

The Romantic aspect of Dickey's poetic identity certainly coincides with the latter part of Donoghue's observation about flow and indeterminacy. However, Dickey's mental method of accumulation—and, consequently, his conception of his poetic self—does not depend on a mere unity which is the "sum of its possessions." Dickey does not build his perceptual objects out of discrete properties only, but, instead, conceives a different kind of whole constituted by an empathic mode of consubstantiality. One may best see the method in his word-magic in the Melanesian concept of "mana," which is a general, undifferentiated power that appears in different forms and different objects in a sacred, rather than a profane, world. In such a realm, not every animate thing possesses mana, only certain objects that evoke a sense of wonder and delight. Sacred wonder and delight in the world of physical sensation and magical things (especially animals and natural objects in motion) are constants in Dickey's lyric universe, the various elements of which are bound together by a principle of shared power that Ernst Cassirer calls the "law of concrescence or coincidence" (*Mythical Thought,* 64): "Mythical thinking . . . knows such a unity neither of combination nor of separation. Even when it seems to divide an action into a number of stages, it considers the action in an entirely substantial form. It explains any attribute of the action by a specific material quality which passes from one thing in which it is inherent to other things. Even what in empirical and scientific thought appears to be a mere dependent attribute or momentary property here obtains a character of complete substantiality and hence of transferability" (53).

Even though the major parts of "Pine" are divided by individual sense, Dickey builds the poem's progression out of a fluid "merging of properties"

(*Mythical Thought,* 77) which is effected by collections of hypenated compounds and jammed fragments of thoughts and feelings. These compounds—especially Dickey's phrase *sift-softening*—and his fragmented, syntactic shorthand recall the opening lines from the fourth stanza of Gerard Manley Hopkins's "The Wreck of the Deutschland":

> I am soft sift
> In an hourglass—at the wall
> Fast, but mined with a motion, a drift,
> And it crowds and it combs to the fall.[14]

Hopkins's "soft sift / In an hourglass" serves to remind him that his body decays with time and that he can achieve redemption only by "Christ's gift" of eternal salvation, "proffer[ed]" in the Gospel. In "Pine" Dickey's "sift-softening" does not stand for the "motion" and "drift" of a heightened sense of personal mortality. Rather, "sift-softening" is one stage in his poetic process of rendering both sensible and transferable the motion of the wind through pine needles. If yet another mark of magical thinking is that substance and force are not sharply distinguished, then Dickey's fusion of force and thing demonstrates even more fully his mythopoeic mode of transforming relations between objects into tactile, living presences which he offers to perception. For instance, here is Dickey's flow of compounded properties which he unifies—or, in his own word, "assign[s]"—as he makes the force of the sound of pine sensuous and, therefore, substantial:

> Low-cloudly it whistles, changing heads
> On you. How hard to hold and shape head-round.
> So any hard hold
> Now loses; form breathes near. Close to forest-form
> By ear . . .
> Overhead assign the bright and dark
> Heels distance-running from all   overdrawing the only sound
> Of this sound   sound of a life-mass
> Drawn in long lines in the air   unbroken   brother-saving
> Sound merely soft
> And loudly soft just in time   then nothing and then
> Soft   soft and a little caring-for   sift-softening
> And soared-to.

(Eye-Beaters, 44)

Because the form of the sound of pine is difficult to grasp—as Dickey says, "any hard hold / Now loses"—he hypostatizes the pine's "sound of a life-mass" by inventing a sequence of modes of motion, each of which is assigned a distinctive trait such as sifting, soaring, and whistling. By giving even the softest sound a tangibility, Dickey makes his own poetic process of perception, and thus his poetic form, substantial. What was "hard to hold" now has elements which can be held, and can be held in a discernible sequence or form. Further, by making sound a mode of motion shared among the fragments of his "apprehension," Dickey also makes these substantial traits transferable from one part of the apprehension to another, and thus to the whole percept. The form of the stanza is the flow of the traits of felt motion commingling and building toward a whole. The process of substantiation and consubstantiation begins to culminate in the phrase "O ankle-wings lightening and fleeing," which represents the magical fusion of the substantiated properties of the "sound" of pine; these properties include speed, lightness, evanescence, alternation, and texture. A few lines later, in its conclusion, the stanza reveals one whole, unified aspect of pine in terms of hearing. Pine's basic properties merge in the figure of "footless flight," which the reader understands can both be heard yet is difficult to hear—like the sound of pine—for it is "coming and fleeing / From ear-you and pine, and all pine" (44).

Another way to examine the poem's formal momentum is to think of Dickey's cataloging and combining of properties as a mythopoeic mode of predication—that is, as a preliminary process of naming, and thus dividing, an undifferentiated subject into specific predicates from which he builds a differentiated reality. As an analogue of this preliminary, linguistic stage of cognition, Dickey's poem makes pine feel like "mana," in that it emerges through his word groups with what feels like its own mysterious energy and power. Like the Sioux conception of Wakanda (i.e., Great Spirit or world creator or mystery or grandeur or sacred—the term is nearly untranslatable in English), the spirit-force of pine grows magically through animated substances, and, in Dickey's case, toward an ultimate, imaginatively conceived unity which differentiates it from its ground of perception. In his primitive predication of properties and in his conception of an animated whole, Dickey's poetic method is radically perspectival. As Cassirer notes: "for mythical thinking, the attribute is not one defining the aspect of the thing; rather, it expresses and contains within it the whole of the thing, seen from a different *angle*" (*Mythical Thought,* 65). Not only is each perceptual sense in each major part of "Pine" "a different angle"; each tangible attribute of each sense is also "a different angle." Further, as we saw, each "angle" reveals and incorporates the whole by means of Dickey's complex movement of concrete imagery. These new angles are themselves new views, new names of aspects of pine rendered plausible, determinate, and separable from the pre-conscious welter of sensation out of which pine reveals itself to consciousness.

In his verbal act of distinguishing perspectives, Dickey calls pine into being through the magical power of naming. With regard to this constitutive, predicative dimension, Dickey's perspectival form is a linguistic act of Creation. Like the narrative thrust in many primitive creation myths, the direction of Dickey's mythic speech moves a differentiating human preconsciousness away from the chaotic condition of heaven and earth before things had names and thus could be verbally distinguished. What is magical and sacred about this naming is that, in Dickey's poem, names do not merely signify but convey the potential powers of the things named and thus symbolically created. In "Pine," Dickey's series of imagistic potencies—e.g., "Your skull like clover   lung-swimming in rosin" (*Eye-Beaters,* 45)—literally become the poetic essence of the identity of pine as the speaker's whole being, not just the rational component of the human mind, engages the world of nature and its emerging objects through his nascent language. No better description of the epistemological implications of Dickey's unity-effecting word-magic can be found than in an analogy between the primitive process of object formation and its relation to language, taken from the biblical narrative of Creation. Cassirer recalls that after the Word of God separated darkness from light to produce heaven and earth, the distinctively human element then entered the linguistic process of genesis:

> The names of earthly creatures are no longer given by the Creator, but have to wait their assignment by man. . . . In this act of appella-tion, man takes possession of the world both physically and intel-lectually—subjects it to his knowledge and his rule. . . . This unity, however, cannot be discovered except as it reveals itself in outward form by virtue of the concrete structures of language and myth, in which it is embodied, and from which it is afterward regained by the process of logical reflection. (*Language and Myth,* 82–83)

Dickey's one-word conclusion to "Pine" thus signals his sacred finale to the linguistic process of inventing a "momentary god." In this kind of "holy" and "mythico-religious" atmosphere, the unity-effecting name and the god's nature (or power) are thus felt, however evanescently, to be one: "Glory."

III

Another formal achievement derived from the momentum of word-magic and magical thinking in *The Eye-Beaters* is the most dramatic aspect of Dickey's neoromanticism—namely, his reinvention of the ode of terror. To be sure, Dickey has explored the world of nightmares and dream consciousness from the very beginning of his work in poems such as "The Vegetable King" (1960) and "The Firebombing" (1964). However, in "Mercy" and "Madness," his word-magic in this volume signals his fullest and most frightening contribution to a genre of poetry which was extremely popular in the late eighteenth and early nineteenth centuries. Represented on Coleridge's dark side by "The Rime of the Ancient Mariner" and "Dejection: An Ode," this genre took its criteria for excellence from Longinus' classic treatise "On the Sublime," especially that aspect of the sublime that focuses on 'the most striking and vehement circum-stances of passion" (16). Because, in Edmund Burke's opinion, the sublime produces "the strongest emotion which the mind is capable of feeling," and because terror was felt to be an emotional corollary of the feeling of religious dread occasioned by nothing less in importance than "the supreme evil," the ode of terror was held by many to be the highest form of lyric. Although there is no explicit theodogical component in "Victory," this historic genre—"so wildly awful, so gloomily terrific," as the eighteenth-century critic Nathan Drake enthusiastically put it—combined a number of traits that bear directly on Dickey:

> To excel in this species of Ode demands a felicity and strength of genius that has seldom been attained; all the higher beauties of poetry, vastness of conception, brilliancy of colouring, grandeur of sentiment, the terrible and the appalling, must combine, and with mysterious energy alarm and elevate the imagination. A lightning of phrase should pervade the more empassioned parts, and an awful and even dreadful obscurity, from prophetic, or superhuman agency, diffuse its influence over the whole.[15]

"Terrible" and "appalling" with a "mysterious energy" that appears to issue from a "superhuman agency," "Victory" is Dickey's striking nightmare poem about one of the most "supreme evil[s]" of human experience: world war. The poem recounts the story of a GI in the Pacific Theatre who anticipates the surrender of the Japanese on V-J Day (2 September 1945), two years before the actual fact. "[T]wo birthdays // back, in the jungle, before [he] sailed high on the rainbow / Waters of victory," the soldier drinks whiskey sent by his mother as a present, then explains to her—apparently, in a letter—how he later found himself drunk in a tattoo parlor in Yokahama, with "four / Men . . . bent over me," who tattoo his entire torso with a brightly colored snake that follows the contours of his body:

```
                                              it was at my throat
          Beginning with its tail . . .
                                        moving under
              My armpit like a sailor's, scale
          By scale. . . .
                                  I retched but choked
          It back, for he had crossed my breast. . . .
              Oh yes and now he lay low

          On my belly, and gathered together the rainbow
        Ships of Buckner Bay. I slumbered deep and he crossed the small
                    Of my back    increased
        His patchwork hold on my hip        passed through the V between
                    My legs, and came
Around once more        all but the head   then I was turning        the
snake
              Coiled round my right thigh and crossed
          Me with light hands . . .
                                            (Eye-Beaters, 40–41)
```

The soldier's experience with this all-devouring, demonic snake warrants immediate comparison with two turbulent moments from Coleridge's odes of terror. Dickey's snake-filled, nightmare world in "Victory"—especially, "the dark side / Of the mind" (*Eye-Beaters,* 40)—recalls Coleridge's "viper thoughts, that coil around my mind, / Reality's dark dream!" from "Dejection: An Ode."[16] When Coleridge turns from these viperous thoughts to "listen to the wind," he hears, with greater terror, the "groans . . . of trampled men, with smarting wounds— / At once they groan with pain, and shudder with the cold!" Likewise, Dickey's world of war is filled with the pain of men, that of his living "buddies," "ready," as he is, "to sail . . . toward life / After death," along with the memories of "others long buried / At sea" (38). Even more important, the retching and choking of Dickey's soldier at a time of war suggest the sixth stanza from "Ode to the Departing Year" which records Coleridge's rage and shock at human slaughter carried out in the name of Liberty during the French Revolution and at the Massacre of Ismail in 1770. After experiencing a nightmare vision "on no earthly shore" of the Departing Year, whose past events and "robe [are] inscribed with gore" (*English Romantic Poetry,* 388), this Romantic poet awakes to find that his predatory dream continues to flood traumatically through his soul to the same degree that World War II traumatically pervades Dickey's poetry and fiction (even a half-century later in Dickey's best and most recent novel, *To the White Sea*). One has only to place sections side by side from "Victory" and "Ode to the Departing Year" to note the emotional frenzy and pain shared by the two writers.[17] Here are Coleridge's words, still striking after two hundred years:

> Yet still I gasp'd and reel'd with dread.
> And ever, when the dream of night
> Renews the phantom to my sight,
> Cold sweat-drops gather on my limbs;
>   My ears throb hot; my eye-balls start;
> My brain with horrid tumult swims;
>   Wild is the tempest of my heart;
> And my thick and struggling breath
> Imitates the toil of death!
> No stranger agony confounds
>   The Soldier on the war-field spread,
> When all foredone with toil and wounds,
> Death-like he dozes among the heaps of dead!
>   (*English Romantic Poetry,* 389)

While terror signals the presence of an emotionally animating form in both poems and indicates the genre to which each belongs, the method of closure in each differs considerably, and this difference sheds further light on the momentum of Dickey's word-magic. To be sure, both poems close with a suffocating terror that demands release. Each poet has worked his way through considerable psychological pain; however, to remain in a state of such dread is emotional, moral, and political paralysis. In short, the pervasive terror in the body of each ode demands the poet's return to action in his conclusion, lest the momentum in each piece remain mired in pathetic tragedy.[18] This two-step process—stasis and renewal—occurs in Coleridge's ending, when he warns England that it has been protected from the political terrors of the Departing Year primarily because of the military value of its geographic isolation. Threatened even as he closes, Coleridge hears "the Birds of warning sing" then personally resolves to be "unpartaking of the evil thing" and to remain alert, "Cleans'd from the vaporous passions that bedim / God's Image" (*English Romantic Poetry,* 390).

Dickey, also acutely aware of catastropic evil in human nature, needs to be "Cleans'd" from his exposure to the atrocities of war, which, like Coleridge, he personifies in animal form.[19] Although both poets subscribe to a harmonious pantheism that incorporates historic calamity as fully realistic material for the poetic imagination, Dickey postulates nothing like a Divine Providence—as does Coleridge when he "recentre[s] his "immortal mind"—as a subsumptive or unifying principle to which he can appeal for relief. Instead, on a personal level, Dickey dramatizes an inferred, magical animism in which life and death are not exclusive opposites but shared moments in a cycle of perpetual motion. In a world in which life and death constantly emerge into and out of each other, Dickey's snake—unlike Coleridge's birds, "the famish'd brood of prey"—has a double nature. First, the boa constrictor–like coiling and physical mutilation of the snake constitute a "confrontation" or "death encounter" for the speaker, a poetic event that has an emotional analogy with his vast experience of death from war and simultaneously stands for his desire for the symbolic death of his mutilated war self. With what appears at first to be an "appalling" movement, the snake then enters its subject from behind, and an opposite movement begins—namely, the renewal of the soldier which is initiated in the poem's final line. Strangely enough, the motion of the snake alters—indeed, redeems—both serpent and host, for the snake acquires, in Drake's terms, a "mysterious energy" that transforms the soldier, Christlike, into "the new prince of peace":

> I felt myself opened
> Just enough, where the serpent staggered on his last
> Colors   needles gasping for air   jack-hammering
> My right haunch burned by the hundreds
> Of holes, as the snake shone on me complete   escaping
> Forever   surviving   crushing   going home
> To the bowels of the living,
> His master, and the new prince of peace.

> (*Eye-Beaters,* 41)

As is the case with Dickey's animals in many of his poems, such as "Approaching Prayer," "Eagles," "Reincarnation I and II," and "The Sheep

Child," the snake now functions redemptively by assuming the role of what is a shamanic commonplace in anthropological literature—namely, a power animal. In keeping with the classic, mythological character of a power animal, Dickey's snake acquires a "mysterious power" that is both malignant and benign. On the one hand, as a cross-cultural symbol of the range of human evil (including war), the snake is a traditional object of terror. Joseph Campbell says: "In its threatening character, as a traveling aesophagus, the serpent is . . . an image of the consuming power of the . . . will [in nature], foreboding death to all that lives." On the other hand, Campbell notes: "The ability of the serpent to shed its skin and thus to renew itself, as the moon is renewed by sloughing its shadow, has recommended it, throughout the world, as an obvious image of the mystery of the [same] will in nature, which is ever self-renewing in its generation of living beings."[20] This ancient mythological connection between snake and moon thus enables the serpent to play its double role by providing it with the "self-renewing" power that is passed on to the soldier. In "Victory," as in "May Day Sermon" and "The Eye-Beaters," Dickey establishes yet another magical setting in which his poetic agent is energized as he tries to overcome overwhelming odds. On the road of this momentous psychic journey, Dickey's soldier struggles forward to rid himself of war by acquiring traits of natural objects which are really rhetorical, self-animating aspects of his own mind.[21] That nature should seem beneficent and helpful, rather than another debilitating oppressor, adds considerably to the momentum of the healing process.

Consequently, in Dickey's ritual scene the moon is not static but carries with it a renewing, ancient, magical light. For example, "two birthdays / Ago" in "Victory," when the soldier got drunk—drunkenness being another variation of the hallucinatory state of shamanic transition—he did so at night when "the moon burned with the light it had when it split // From the earth" (Eye-Beaters, 39). Dickey's soldier, like this moon, has been "split" by war from the human and emotional ground that he desperately requires. However, this moon retains the "light," or energizing possibility, to split then become something different and uniquely powerful, a possibility and process that bear direct analogy to the soldier's ritual journey of healing and self-empowerment. While expressing a dynamic relation between life and death, metaphors throughout the poem further bind the motions of snake and moon, suggesting once more that, in Dickey's world, there operates something analogous to Frazer's principle of a power-exchanging, contagious magic. When the soldier says, "I reached for the bottle. It was dying and the moon / Writhed closer to be free," the dying energy of whiskey's liberating hallucination gives rise to the snakelike motion of the moon, which sheds its animating light on the soldier's "smile of foreknowledge" that he will survive the war. Similarly, just before the visionary snake emerges from the bottle, the speaker indicates another, closer, lunar connection between snake and moon that images the archetypal movement of life out of death: "Had the Form in the moon come from the dead soldier / Of your bottle, Mother?" (39). Finally, even during the tattooing process, the passive host gives himself over to the animating, magical motion of the snake. Earlier he described the snake by saying "the angel / Of peace is limbless" (39–40). Yet, as the snake covers his body, the soldier identifies with the shape and motion of this "dreadful . . . superhuman agency" (Drake's terms) and so takes on its sustaining and renewing moon energy, as he notes, "limbless I fell and moved like moonlight / On the needles" (40).

Even though Dickey's poem suggests that the "Form in the moon" (which I read to be an incipient image of the "snakehead") comes from a masculine source (albeit from his mother: "the dead soldier / Of your bottle" [*Eye-Beaters,* 39]), and though the form's shape suggests a phallocentric image, the serpent is, by no means, a universal sign of masculine power. As an instrument of self-revelation and transformation, the serpent is conceived in many cultures as a feminine totem that symbolizes modes of coming to consciousness that bear directly on central religious components in Dickey's poem. For example, Campbell notes that in "India's Kundalini Yoga . . . the energy of life—all life—is symbolized as . . . a female serpent." In this sect,

> The aim of the yoga is to wake this Serpent Maiden, coiled in upon herself, and bring her up to the spine to full consciousness, both of herself and of the spiritual nature of all things. She is awakened by the sound of the energy of the light of consciousness (the sound of the syllable "om"), which is brought to her first on the rhythm of the breath, but fully heard only when she has uncoiled and ascended to the center of the heart. (*World Mythology,* vol. 2, pt. 3, 291)

As it does in this Indian ritual initiated through feminine power, the snake in "Victory" covers the soldier's body with a motion that constitutes a hypnotic, somatic meditation, a meditation that, like Dickey's poem, involves the total transformation and awareness of its participant. Examples of the movement of Dickey's snake warrant repeating here to confirm this striking analogy: "the snake . . . was at my throat / Beginning with its tail . . . moving under my armpit . . . He coiled around me . . . I turned with him side / To side . . . he grew . . . I lay and it lay / Now over my heart . . . and I knew that many- / colored snakeskin was living with my heart   our hearts / Beat as one" (40–41).

In Campbell's citation, the symbolic purpose of the Indian snake is to unify all of man's emotional and psychic centers, whether at the lowest point in the genitals or at the higher reaches of the human heart. This somatic concordance then leads each center along the "One Way Trail" to full consciousness at "the crown of the head" (*World Mythology,* vol. 2, pt. 3, 291). To carry the whole man—sensory and cognitive, conscious and unconscious—through a comprehensive healing process, Dickey's serpent enters the soldier's bowels with the ritual motion of the mythic ouraboros, the serpent eating its own tail in the eternally circular process of separation and return to an energizing source. When Dickey's serpent passes the navel (that part of the body which Campbell interprets as a mythological symbol of "the will to power, aggression") and enters the soldier, we may read this event as the poem's climactic moment, a culmination of the fully conscious, circular transformation by the aggressive, wartorn, and exhausted phallus into an instrument of peace and renewal. Thinking through the physical imagery of the male body, Dickey transcends the merely physical by concluding in the mystical tradition of T. S. Eliot in "East Coker." While we may see a pun equal to Kenneth Burke's word-play in his essay on the bodily tropes, we also see a standard, religious oxymoron in Eliot's words that locates Dickey's poetic attitude in a well-documented series of theological traditions—namely, that "In my end is my beginning."[22]

If one thinks that this kind of closural magic (or, indeed, the formal, snakelike movement of Dickey's poem down the page) is trivial or may be reduced to static, sensory experience, one needs only to examine similar forms of "religious" meditation in other cultures, ranging from that of the Hopi Indians to certain Oriental religions.[23] Consistent with the worldviews in many of these beliefs, Dickey's magical method in "Victory" is not a form of escapism but rather a non-dualistic way of clearing the ego of earthly pain in order to stand outside dominating sensation and emotion, and thus to free oneself from their tyranny. In many ways, the animating emotional form of "Victory" is analogous to the utterance of the mythic syllable "AUM," which carriers its practitioner through levels of consciousness, beyond myriad mental opposites, to the infernal and celestial vision deep within one's own soul. Dickey's magical, religious method of closure is thus both ancient and cross-cultural; it is directed to an external narrative of traumatic historical events yet also inner-directed to the most sensitive reaction to these events by the human body. That this method should involve a sexual component becomes even more intelligible when related to certain basic religious principles, shared by Buddhist and Hindu sects. As Campbell notes of the Sahajiya cult in the Pala Dynasty from Bengal, between A.D. 7 and 1200.

> It was held that the only true experience of the pure rapture of the void was the rapture of sexual union, wherein "each is both." This was the natural path . . . to the innate nature (*sahaja*) of oneself, and therewith of the universe: the path along which nature itself leads the way.
>
> So we read . . . "This sahaja is to be intuited from within." "It is free from all sound, colors, and qualities; can be neither spoken of nor known." "Where the mind dies out and the vital breath is gone, there is the Great Delight supreme: it neither stands steady nor fluctuates; nor is it expressible in words." "In that state the individual mind joins sahaja as water water." "There is no duality in sahaja. It is perfect, like the sky."
>
> . . . One knows then: "I am the universe: I am the Buddha: I

am perfect purity: I am non-cognition: I the annihilator of the cycle of existence."[24]

"Victory" originally appeared in the *Atlantic Monthly* in 1968. Twenty-five years later, in fall 1993, Dickey dramatized yet again his paramount interest in mystical momentum by using word-magic to conclude *To the White Sea.* Here, his hero-predator, the American tail gunner Muldrow, shot down over wartorn Japan, is killed by Japanese soldiers. As their bullets go through him, he does not die exactly, but rather enters a desireless, objectless, bodiless world, like the Sahajiyaian realm of supreme rapture, in which "the mind dies and the vital breath is gone," which "neither stands steady nor fluctuates," and in which there is "no duality," for "the individual mind joins [nature] as water water." This absolute, circular flow—the union of life and death, waking and dreaming, pain and the absence of sensation—then hypnotically transports him to a kind of waking trance beyond even these harmonious opposites. In the novel's final lines, Muldrow's predatory quest ends when he closes his eyes and the individuality of his speaking voice dissolves into a darkened silence, which Campbells calls the "fourth element" of AUM, "the sphere of bliss," described in the *Mandukya Upanisad* as "neither inward- nor outward-turned consciousness, nor the two together . . . neither knowing nor unknowing . . . the coming to peaceful rest of all differentiated, relative existence: utterly quiet: peaceful-blissful."[25] In the purity of his motionless motion this soldier, like the soldier in "Victory," is propelled by the momentum of Dickey's extraordinary word-magic into the ecstatic silence that is his and its own final form:

When I tell you this, just say that it came from a voice in the wind:
a voice without a voice, which doesn't make a sound. You can pick it up
any time it snows, where you are, or even just when the wind is
from the north, from anywhere north of east or west. I was in the place
I tried to get to. I had made it in exactly the shape I wanted to be in,
though maybe just a little beat up. But the main thing was that
I had got to the landscape and the weather, and you can remember me
standing there with the bullets going through, and me not feeling a thing.
There it was. A red wall blazed. For a second there was a terrific heat,
like somebody had opened a furnace door, the most terrible heat,
something that could have burned up the world, and I was sure I was gone.
But the cold and the snow came back. The wind mixed the flakes,
and I knew I had it. I was in it, and part of it. I matched it all.
And I will be everywhere in it from now on. You will be able
to hear me, just like you're hearing me now. Everywhere in it,
for the first time and the last, as soon as I close my eyes.

(274–75)

NOTES

1. Poems that I should like to nominate as major in this collection are: "Under Buzzards" (pt. 2 of "Diabetes"), "Mercy," "Victory," "Pine," "Madness," "The Eye-Beaters," and "Turning Away."

2. For example, "the stagy, unpleasant hysteria" with which Leibowitz faults Dickey may, in fact, be an emotional sign that Dickey has formally achieved exactly the kind of poem he intended to produce with "hysterical" effects totally appropriate to its genre. See my discussion of "Madness," "Mercy," and "Victory." Also, Ernest Suarez deals perceptively with the considerable critical misperception of Dickey (*James Dickey and the Politics of Canon: Assessing the Savage Ideal* [Columbia: University of Missouri Press, 1993], esp. chap. 4). See also Romy Heylen's valuable distinction between "reflection poetry" and "a participation poem or performance poem that quite simply must be experienced," with Dickey falling under the latter heading.

3. "The G.I. Can of Beets, the Fox in the Wave, and the Hammers over Open Ground" was presented in November 1982 at the South Atlantic Modern Language Association in Atlanta, Ga. This essay is collected in *Night Hurdling: Poems, Essays, Conversations, Commencements, and Afterwords* (Columbia, S.C., and Bloomfield Hills, Mich.: Bruccoli Clark, 1983), 124–40; hereafter cited parenthetically in the text.

4. Whether or not we agree that "Spindrift" cannot be part of the seal's vision— one recalls Crane's own vigorous defense of his language in a famous letter to Harriet Monroe (*The Complete Poems and Selected Letters and Prose of Hart Crane,* ed. Brom Weber [Garden City, N.Y.: Anchor, 1966], 234–40; hereafter cited parenthetically in the text)—Dickey's comments on Crane's word selection lead to further considerations about magical wordplay in poetry, which is relevant for the beginning of our inquiry.

5. James Dickey, *The Central Motion: Poems, 1968–1979* (Middletown, Conn.: Wesleyan University Press, 1983), v; *Self-Interviews* (New York: Dell, 1970), 184–85; hereafter both texts cited parenthetically in the text.

6. For Dickey's view of William James, see Ronald Baughman, ed., *The Voiced Connections of James Dickey: Interviews and Conversations* (Columbia: University of South Carolina Press, 1989), 155; hereafter cited parenthetically in the text.

7. Joseph Campbell, *Historical Atlas of World Mythology,* vol. 3: *The Way of the Seeded Earth,* pt. 1: *The Sacrifice* (New York: Harper, 1988), 9; hereafter cited parenthetically in the text.

8. James Dickey, *The Eye-Beaters, Blood, Victory, Madness, Buckead and Mercy* (Garden City, N.Y.: Doubleday, 1970), 50; hereafter cited parenthetically in the text.

9. Ernst Cassirer, *The Philosophy of Symbolic Forms,* vol. 2: *Mythical Thought,* trans. Ralph Manheim (New Haven: Yale University Press, 1955), 36.

10. Ernst Cassirer, *Language and Myth,* trans. Susanne K. Langer (New York: Dover, 1946), 56–58.

11. Dickey calls this mode of lyric "country surrealism" (*Sorties* [Baton Rouge: Louisiana State University Press, 1984],100).

12. My own reading of "Pine" differs from, yet is indebted to, Ernest Suarez's analysis (*James Dickey,* 134–36).

13. Denis Donoghue, "Walt Whitman," in *Leaves of Grass,* ed. Sculley Bradley and Harold W. Blodgett (New York: W. W. Norton, 1973), 964.

14. Gerard Manley Hopkins, "The Wreck of the Deutschland," *Poems and Prose of Gerard Manley Hopkins,* ed. W. H. Gardner (Baltimore: Penguin, 1953), 13.

15. Edmund Burke, cited in Ronald Crane, ed., *Critics and Criticism: Ancient and Modern* (Chicago: University of Chicago Press, 1952), 446, 447.

16. Samuel Taylor Coleridge, in *English Romantic Poetry and Prose,* ed. Russell Noyes (New York: Oxford University Press, 1956), 389; hereafter cited parenthetically in the text.

17. If we apply Drake's criteria as well as conventional standards of the ode to "Victory" and "Ode to the Departing Year," we find that both poems qualify as singular representatives in the genre of terror. First, both poems are long—Dickey's at 131 lines, Coleridge's at 161—which enables each to develop a considerable vastness of conception regarding war and the toll it takes on human emotion. Further, both possess an occasional reference of considerable, if not ceremonial, importance, Dickey's to V-J Day, Coleridge's to the year of 1796 and a preceding, tragic history; each occasional reference produces the feeling of an elevated status of public utterance, even though every poem is represented in a profoundly personal mode of address. Both poems entail elaborate stanzaic organization, exquisite detail and coloring, and a somewhat similar style of indentation, although Dickey's is more pronounced and much less regular than Coleridge's. While Dickey uses no rhyme and his tone is less heightened, both lyrics convey a considerable seriousness that slowly alters and transports the reader into a state of impassioned dread. Rhetorically, this dread aids the political position of each poet by giving each a vulnerable sincerity that makes them sympathetic and morally convincing.

18. Arguing for the value of "poetic" rather than merely "semantic" meaning, Kenneth Burke puts the issue in a poignant statement that could well represent Dickey's poetic stand against certain self-indulgent aspects of confessional poetry:

> I wonder how long it has been since a poet has asked himself. . . . Suppose I did not simply wish to load upon the broad shoulders of the public medium my own ungainly appetites and ambitions? Suppose that, gnarled as I am, I did not consider it enough simply to seek payment for my gnarledness, the establishment of communion through evils held in common? Suppose I would also erect a structure of encouragement, for all of us? How should I go about it, in the sequence of imagery, not merely to bring us most poignantly *into* hell, but also *out* again? . . . Must there not, for every flight, be also a return, before my work can be called complete as a moral act? (*Philosophy,* 138–39)

19. As critic Ronald Baughman points out in "James Dickey's War Poetry: A 'Saved, Shaken Life' " (South Carolina Review 10 [April 1983]: 38–48), it is not just the snake that terrorizes Dickey, but also a veteran's residual terror of surviving the war. It is a well-known biographical fact that Dickey spent the formative years of his young adulthood (1942–46) serving in the U.S. Army Air Force in the South Pacific. After Dickey flew nearly one hundred missions with the 418th Night Fighters, after he saw his American colleagues killed and mutilated by the enemy, and after he was an integral part of the killing mechanism of war, it is little wonder that so much of Dickey's poetry is driven by his internal need to deal emotionally with the shock of combat.

20. Joseph Campbell, *Historical Atlas of World Mythology,* vol. 2: *The Way of the Seeded Earth,* pt. 3: *Mythologies of the Primitive Planters: The Middle and Southern Americas* (New York: Harper, 1989), 378; hereafter cited parenthetically in the text.

21. This self-enabling rhetoric is extremely important, especially on a personal and emotional level. The reader has only to ask how many times he or she has had to fight back from psychological or physical attack, whether in a major social arena such as world war or in the wars conducted on the battlegrounds of one's profession, family, or love life, where the threat of failure is the constant enemy. For a similar rhetoric, though presented in a more explicit mode of direct address, see Whitman's poem "A Noiseless Patient Spider" (Walt Whitman, *Leaves of Grass,* ed. Sculley Bradley and Harold W. Blodgett [New York: Norton, 1973], 450). See also "Rhetoric and Primitive Magic" and

the "Realistic Function of Rhetoric" in Kenneth Burke, *A Rhetoric of Motives* (Berkeley: University of California Press, 1969), 40–46.

22. Kenneth Burke, "The Thinking of the Body" and "Somnia ad Urinandnum," *Language as Symbolic Action* (Berkeley: University of California Press, 1966), 308–58. See also William James's famous chapter on "Mysticism" in *The Varieties of Religious Experience* (London: Collier, 1961), 299–336.

23. See Joseph Campbell's description of the Hopi Indian Snake Dance, which occurs in late August in the lunar month called "the Big Feast Moon" (in *World Mythology,* vol. 2, pt. 3, 290).

24. Joseph Campbell, *Oriental Mythology: The Masks of God* (New York: Viking, 1962), 351.

25. Joseph Campbell, *Creative Mythology: The Masks of God* (New York: Viking, 1968), 666.

REFERENCES

Baughman, Ronald. "James Dickey's War Poetry: A 'Saved, Shaken Life.'" *South Carolina Review* 10 (April 1983): 38–48.

———, ed. *The Voiced Connections of James Dickey: Interviews and Conversations.* Columbia: University of South Carolina Press, 1989.

Burke, Kenneth. *Language as Symbolic Action.* Berkeley: University of California Press, 1966.

———. *The Philosophy of Literary Form: Studies in Symbolic Action.* New York: Vintage, 1957.

———. *A Rhetoric of Motives.* Berkeley: University of California Press, 1969.

Campbell, Joseph. *Creative Mythology: The Masks of God.* New York: Viking, 1968.

———. *Historical Atlas of World Mythology.* Vol. 2: *The Way of the Seeded Earth.* Pt. 1: *The Sacrifice.* New York: Harper, 1988.

———. *Historical Atlas of World Mythology.* Vol. 2: *The Way of the Seeded Earth.* Pt. 3: *Mythologies of the Primitive Planters: The Middle and Southern Americas.* New York: Harper, 1989.

———. *Oriental Mythology: The Masks of God.* New York: Viking, 1962.

Cassirer, Ernst. *Language and Myth.* Trans. Susanne K. Langer. New York: Dover, 1946.

———. *The Philosophy of Symbolic Forms.* Vol. 2: *Mythical Thought.* Trans. Ralph Manheim. New Haven, Conn.: Yale University Press, 1955.

Coleridge, Samuel Taylor. *English Romantic Poetry and Prose.* Ed. Russell Noyes. New York: Oxford University Press, 1956.

Crane, Hart. *The Complete Poems and Selected Letters and Prose of Hart Crane.* Ed. Brom Weber. Garden City, N.Y.: Anchor, 1966.

Crane, Ronald, ed. *Critics and Criticism: Ancient and Modern.* Chicago: University of Chicago Press, 1952.

Davison, Peter. "The Difficulties of Being Major: The Poetry of Robert Lowell and James Dickey." *Atlantic Monthly* 220 (October 1967): 223–30.

DeMott, Benjamin. "The 'More' Life School and James Dickey." *Saturday Review* 53 (28 March 1970): 38.

Dickey, James. *The Central Motion: Poems, 1968–1979.* Middletown, Conn.: Wesleyan University Press, 1983.

———. *The Eagle's Mile.* Hanover and London: Wesleyan University Press, 1990.

————. *The Eye-Beaters, Blood, Victory, Madness, Buckead and Mercy.* Garden City, N.Y.: Doubleday, 1970.

————. *Night Hurdling: Poems, Essays, Conversations, Commencements, and Afterwords.* Columbia, S.C., and Bloomfield Hills, Mich.: Bruccoli Clark, 1983.

————. *Poems 1957–1967.* Middletown, Conn.: Wesleyan University Press, 1967.

————. *Puella.* Garden City, N.Y.: Doubleday, 1982.

————. *Self-Interviews.* New York: Dell, 1970.

————. *Sorties.* Baton Rouge: Louisiana State University Press, 1984.

————. *To the White Sea.* New York: Houghton Mifflin, 1993.

Donoghue, Denis. "Walt Whitman." In *Leaves of Grass.* Ed. Sculley Bradley and Harold W. Blodgett, 962–72. New York: W. W. Norton, 1973.

Eliot, T. S. *The Complete Poems and Plays: 1909–1950.* New York: Harcourt Brace, 1952.

Frazer, Sir James George. *The Golden Bough.* New York: Macmillan, 1963.

Heylen, Romy. "James Dickey's the Zodiac: A Self-Translation?" *James Dickey Newsletter* 6, no. 2 (Spring 1990): 2–17.

Hopkins, Gerard Manley. *Poems and Prose of Gerard Manley Hopkins.* Ed. W. H. Gardner. Baltimore: Penguin, 1953.

Howard, Richard. "Resurrection for a Little While." *Nation* 210 (23 March 1970): 341–42.

James, William. *The Varieties of Religious Experience.* London: Collier, 1961.

Longinus. "On the Sublime." In *Criticism: The Foundations of Modern Literary Judgment.* Ed. Mark Schorer, Josephine Miles, and Gordon McKenzie, 10–24. New York: Harcourt Brace, 1948.

Leibowitz, Herbert. "The Moiling of Secret Forces: *The Eye-Beaters, Blood, Victory, Madness, Buckead and Mercy.*" In *The Imagination as Glory: The Poetry of James Dickey.* Ed. Bruce Weigl and T. R. Hummer. Urbana: University of Illinois, Press.

Simon, John. *Commonweal* 87, no. 9 (1 December 1967): 315.

Suarez, Ernest. *James Dickey and the Politics of Canon: Assessing the Savage Ideal.* Columbia: University of Missouri Press, 1993.

Tulip, James. "Robert Lowell and James Dickey." *Poetry Australia* 24 (October 1968): 39–47.

Untermeyer, Louis. "A Way of Seeing and Saying." *Saturday Review* 50 (6 May 1967): 55.

Whitman, Walt. *Leaves of Grass.* Ed. Sculley Bradley and Harold W. Blodgett. New York: Norton, 1973.

The Eye and the Nerve: A Psychological Reading of James Dickey's *Deliverance*

HAROLD SCHECHTER

Put on the river
Like a fleeting coat,
A garment of motion,
Tremendous, immortal.
Find a still root
To hold you in it.
Let flowing create
A new, inner being.
—James Dickey, "Inside the River"

Explore thyself. Herein are demanded the eye and the nerve.
—Henry David Thoreau, *Walden*

In a book about the relationship between literary value and popular appeal, the case of James Dickey is an interesting and particularly apt one, since he is a writer who has not only enjoyed both critical and commercial success but also seems to have pursued both art and media celebrity with equal gusto. A poet who rose to literary prominence within a few years of the publication of his first collection, *Into the Stone* (1957), a National Book Award winner in 1966 (for *Buckdancer's Choice*), and former poetry consultant to the Library of Congress, he seems, at the same time, to be totally captivated by Hollywood glitter. Not even Norman Mailer has played opposite Burt Reynolds in a movie (as Dickey did in the film version of his best-selling book, *Deliverance*) or squired Cher Bono Allman to a presidential ball.

When I first saw the full-color photograph of Dickey and Cher which *Newsweek* printed as part of its coverage of Carter's inauguration and which fairly resonated with allegorical significance—suggesting any number of morals about the seduction of the American artist by glamor and fame—I was reminded not so much of Mailer as of Mailer's hero, Hemingway, who, with a

Originally published in *Seasoned Authors for a New Season: The Search for Standards in Popular Writing*, ed. Louis Filler (Bowling Green, Ohio: Bowling Green University Popular Press, 1980), 4–19. Reprinted by permission.

fine Emersonian scorn for foolish consistency, wrote savagely about selling out (in "The Snows of Kilimanjaro") while feeling no aversion to picking up a few extra dollars by doing endorsements for Ballantine Beer ("You have to work hard to deserve to drink it. But I would rather have a bottle of Ballantine Ale than any other drink after fighting a really big fish").[1] The resemblances between Dickey and Hemingway, of course, run far deeper than their common taste for stardom; indeed these similarities go right to the heart of the issue with which this essay is concerned: namely, determining the artistic value of *Deliverance,* a book which has been a big commercial success and has also generated a fair amount of critical controversy over the question of its merits. (Though there is some divergence of opinion about Dickey's poetic achievement, the problem which the present volume addresses—that of the connection between "popularity and value in modern creative writing"—does not arise in relation to his poetry, simply because, like almost all the serious poetry written in this country, its appeal is limited to a small, "elite" audience. I intend, therefore, to devote this essay to *Deliverance,* taking his poems into account only insofar as they bear on the themes of the novel.) The qualities which critics and readers alike have found increasingly off-putting in Hemingway's work are the very ones which unsympathetic reviewers denounced in *Deliverance:* the obsessive machismo, the preoccupation with proving one's manhood (a preoccupation which may or may not conceal a strain of latent homosexuality) by pitting oneself against nature and other men in situations of great stress, danger, and violence. Writing in *Saturday Review,* Benjamin DeMott took Dickey's novel to task on precisely these counts, deploring its "shoot-'em-up mindlessness" and dismissing it as an "emptily rhetorical horse-opera played in canoes"—an opinion echoed by several other reviewers, one of whom, discussing Dickey's literary antecedents, claimed that the main influence on the novel was not the writing of Hemingway but "that of Edgar Rice Burroughs, who is much more fun."[2] In a sense, Dickey himself must be held at least partly accountable for judgments like these, not only because of his own pronouncements about the book—his insistence that it be regarded primarily as a simple "adventure yarn," "an exciting story"[3]—but also because of the he-man image he has always been at pains to project, the hunter-soldier-athlete-poet persona played up in his dust-jacket biography: "James Dickey is a former star college athlete, night fighter pilot with more than 100 missions in World War II and the Korean conflict, hunter and woodsman . . ." etc., etc. This kind of thing encourages us to respond less to the art than to the anamolie, as we might, paraphrasing Samuel Johnson, to the sight of a dog walking on its hind legs: What's really impressive is not the poetry but that a former fighter pilot and college jock should write poetry at all.[4]

In any event even Dickey's detractors tended to concede that the novel was entertaining, if trivial and wildly improbable. His admirers, on the other hand, regarded *Deliverance* as a brilliantly done thriller—a masterpiece of suspense, ranking, as L. E. Sissman wrote in his *New Yorker* review, "up among such classics of the form as 'The Thirty-Nine Steps,' 'The Wages of Fear,' and 'Rogue Male'."[5] Various critics and reviewers attested to the book's powerful, visceral impact. "It will curl your toes," declared Evan S. Connell on the front page of The *New York Times Book Review*.[6] It will "make your hands cold," said Donald W. Markos in the *Southern Review*.[7] "I felt every cut, groped up every cliff, swallowed water with every spill of the canoe, sweated with every draw of the deadly bowstring," Nelson Algren wrote in *Harper's*.[8] Even those people who praised the novel, however, saw little in it besides a compelling plot and some fine descriptive prose. L. E. Sissman, for example, though he called *Deliverance* "a suspense story that transcends its genre," read it basically as a commentary on the crazy, random violence which, more and more, is coming to characterize life in America, whereas other critics tended to interpret the book's concerns strictly in terms of the recurrent themes of Dickey's poetry: the call of the wild, the dangers of cutting oneself off from the primal energies of nature (from the "moiling of secret forces" beneath the surface of things which Dickey evokes in his poem "The Shark's Parlor"), and so forth. Moreover, many of the people who liked the book shared with those who didn't some serious reservations. One recurrent complaint had to do with the quality of the characterizations, which reviewers in general found to be two-dimensional. Lucy Rosenthal, for instance, though basically enthusiastic about the book, nevertheless thought that the characters were "almost interchangeable with one another," while Algren commented that "the characterization is thin-running to types.[9]

My own response to *Deliverance* was similar to the one described by Connell, Markos, and Sissman. I too found it extremely gripping—and not just while I was reading it. Dickey's novel has possessed my imagination for a long time now, and in a way which cannot be wholly or even primarily accounted for by its effectiveness as a "page-turner." In fact, over the course of several rereadings, the construction of its plot has come to seem just a little *too* slick to me, the work of a man out to write a very calculated best-seller who not only has all the formulas down pat but also the artistry to conceal the contrivance. And yet, despite my growing awareness of the book's more mechanical qualities, its power has remained essentially undiminished for me. That *Deliverance* does indeed have a strange compelling effect on readers can be seen in some of the extreme reactions it has produced. Leslie Fiedler put his finger on this feature of the novel when he remarked once that *Deliverance* is a book which has killed people. (Dickey himself was obliged to make a public announcement urging readers not to attempt to duplicate the canoe trip described in the novel, after several people had already died trying.) Needless to say, not many books have the power to move people so deeply. The question, then, is: What is the source of this power?

Paradoxically, it is one of the book's weaknesses which supplies us with a clue to the mystery of its strength. For to say that *Deliverance* is long on action and short on fully developed characters is really to say nothing more than that it possesses one of the typical traits of what Richard Chase describes as the classic American romance. The romance, writes Chase, "following distantly the medieval example, feels free to render reality in less volume and detail" than the novel does. "It tends to prefer action to character, and action will be freer in a romance than in a novel, encountering, as it were, less resistance from reality. . . . The romance can flourish without providing much intricacy of relation. The characters, probably rather two-dimensional types, will not be complexly related to each other or to society or to the past." Another characteristic of this form, as Chase defines it, also corresponds to one of the "flaws" of Dickey's book—its supposedly "impossible" plot. According to Chase, we may expect the plot of the romance "to be highly colored. Astonishing events may occur, and these are likely to have a symbolic or ideological, rather than a realistic, plausibility. Being less committed to the immediate rendition of reality than the novel, the romance will more freely veer toward mythic, allegorical and symbolic forms."[10]

Chase's definition provides us, I believe, with a yardstick for measuring Dickey's achievement in *Deliverance*. It is my contention that Dickey's bestseller is a work very much in the tradition of the "American prose romance"—a tradition whose development Chase traces from its beginnings in the "haunted, nocturnal" melodramas of Charles Brockden Brown, through the symbolic classics of Hawthorne and Melville, and up to the Gothic masterpieces of Faulkner. Like the work of these authors, *Deliverance* derives its special power, I believe, less from the excitement and suspense of its plot than from the richness of its mythic or archetypal imagery. Though the novel begins in a very realistic and precisely evoked social setting, it quickly turns into one of those "projective fictions" (to use a phrase Leslie Fiedler applies to Charles Brockden Brown's *Edgar Huntly*)[11] which seem "not so much written as dreamed." This type of fiction, writes Fiedler, deals "with the exaggerated and grotesque, not as they are verifiable in any external landscape or sociological observation of manners and men but as they correspond in quality to our deepest fears and guilts as projected in our dreams or lived through in 'extreme situations.' Realistic milieu and consistent character alike are dissolved in such projective fictions, giving way to the symbolic landscape and the symbolic action, which are the hallmarks of the mythopoeic novel."[12]

What Chase calls the "dark romance" and Fiedler the "mythopoeic novel," Carl Jung labels "visionary literature." The visionary novel, he observes, usually consists of "an exciting narrative that is apparently quite devoid of psychological exposition." It portrays events which "astonish" us, "evokes a superhuman world of contrasting light and darkness," reminds us of "nothing in everyday life, but rather of dreams, night-times fears, and the dark recesses of the mind that we sometimes sense with misgiving." "Mythological themes clothed in modern dress," he writes, "also frequently appear."[13] What distinguishes Chase's "dark romance," Fiedler's "mythopoeic novel," and Jung's "visionary literature," then, is a dreamlike—or more properly, nightmarish—

atmosphere, plus a wealth of primordial imagery: a mythic dimension which resonates with that deeply impressive force which Jung calls "numinosity." And these, I believe, are precisely the features which distinguish *Deliverance* and give the book its "curiously compulsive power."

The mythic substructure underlying *Deliverance* is easy enough to sketch, since the story corresponds in every respect to the archetypal pattern commonly known as the "night sea journey" (Leo Frobenius), the "monomyth" (Joseph Campbell), or the hero's quest. Responding to a "call for adventure"—a summons of some sort which rouses him from the comfortable, if stifling, routines of his life—the hero leaves the workaday world behind and crosses a threshold into a region of darkness and danger (the Descent into Hades, or Nekyia).[14] Within this alien realm he passes through a series of initiatory ordeals ("The Road of Trials"), achieves the boon of spiritual illumination ("The Treasure Hard to Attain"), and returns, transfigured, to the daylight (Rebirth). Ed Gentry, the hero, undergoes just such an archetypal adventure. But in addition to the mythic imagery in *Deliverance,* there is the psychological meaning of the myth. Dickey himself, in the interview in which he declares that his purpose in writing the novel was "to tell an exciting story as simply as I could," also remarks, "I think it's important, as you get older, to discover . . . different parts of yourself."[15] My psychological reading of *Deliverance,* therefore, relies primarily on the insights of Carl Jung, not only because he is the person who dealt most extensively with the psychological significance of myth but also because, in his own practice, he concentrated on the treatment of patients very much like Ed Gentry, a middle-aged businessman, successful in his career but increasingly dissatisfied with his life and conscious of encroaching old age, who must, if he is to survive the "mid-life crisis" he is passing through, undertake the perilous journey of self-exploration to "discover the different parts" of his own inner world.

In *Deliverance* the story proper is preceded by a pair of epigraphs, one describing the narrator's problem, the second suggesting a solution. The first, from Georges Bataille, says, "Il existe a base de la vie humaine un principe d'insuffisance"—"There exists at the base of human life an element of incompleteness." That Gentry is indeed feeling that his life lacks something essential is made very clear in the opening section of the book. This prologue, entitled "Before,"[16] introduces us to a character suffering from that malaise which, according to Jungian psychologists, commonly afflicts men and women during the second half of life—that depression which descends upon "middle-aged people who, having been successful in their chosen career, suddenly awake to a feeling of emptiness and lack of meaning in their lives."[17] "We had grooved as a studio" (16), he thinks, referring to the thriving advertising agency he runs with his partner, Thad Emerson. "We had made it as it was; we had made it" (23). But, as he walks back to his office from a lunch date with some friends, this "middle-aged responsible" man—"Vice-President Gentry" (18)—is suddenly hit by a deep sense of his own mortality: "Going under a heavy shade tree, I felt the beer come up, not into my throat but into my eyes. The day sparkled painfully, seeming to shake on some kind of axis, and through this a leaf fell, touched with unusual color at the edge. It was the first time I had realized that autumn was close. I began to climb the last hill," he says significantly (a little too significantly; Dickey is usually a good deal more deft in his handling of symbols). Inside his office, Gentry is again overcome by "the old mortal, helpless, time-terrified human feeling": "The feeling of the inconsequence of whatever I would do, of anything I would pick up or think about or turn to see was at that moment being set in the very bone marrow. How does one get through this? I asked myself" (19). "It seemed like everything just went right by men, nothing mattered at all" (29).

Gentry, it is clear, is going through what is commonly called, in these days of pop psychology, a "mid-life crisis." All the classic symptoms are there: the feeling of being trapped ("I was not really thinking about their being my prisoners," he says at one point, referring to his employees, "but of being my own") and the restlessness that accompanies it; the sense that, though he has won all the right prizes—the station wagon, the house in the suburbs, the color TV—his life adds up to nothing, that it is rich in material possessions but empty of meaning. He has a sexual infatuation with a model half his age and a marriage which, though decent and loving, no longer holds much excitement for him (in an early lovemaking scene with his wife, Martha, it is she who takes the active role, manipulates and issues commands, while Ed remains passive and detached, dreaming of the model and commenting on his wife's "practical approach to sex" (29). Everything about his life seems sterile and unfulfilling. Though he works as the art director of his ad agency, for instance, he does not consider himself to be at all creative: "[My wife] insisted on believing that I had talent as an artist, though I had none. I was a mechanic of the graphic arts, and when I could get the problem to appear mechanical to me, and not the result of inspiration, I could do something with it" (28).

This sense of emptiness, meaninglessness, psychic sterility, is, Jungians tell us, the result of the one-sided psychological development that social adaptation demands—the necessity for sharpening consciousness while repressing one's instinctive nature. Ed Gentry is a prime example of the civilized man whose superior rationality is "won at the expense of his vitality."[18] He has become dangerously dissociated from his instinctual self, from the primitive energies of the psyche which society forces us to deny. Images evoking the tension between nature and culture abound in the book: a view of the trees in Ed's back yard, "wild, free things . . . in a domestic setting" (33); a vision of "domestic animals suddenly turning and crushing one against the splintering side of a barn stall" (52); a quick glimpse of the primitive forces "moiling" beneath the tidy surface of a happy suburban household, as Ed's son Dean "playfully" stalks his father with a sheathed Bowie knife after father and mother have made love, and Ed suddenly grows conscious of the vulnerability of his naked genitals beneath his bathrobe.[19] All these things—along with repeated references to the "monkey fur" on Ed's body, the vestigial mark of his animal ancestry—are symbols of the narrator's plight, of his deeply felt distance from the instinctual roots of his being.

What is the answer to this problem? The solution is suggested by the second epigraph which Dickey prefixes to his story: "The pride of thine heart hath deceived them, thou that dwellest in the clefts of the rock, whose habitation is high; that saith in his heart, Who shall bring me down to the ground?" (*Obadiah*, v. 3). While some critics have read this as an allusion to the mountain men who figure in the story ("thou that dwellest in the clefts of the rock"), it makes more sense to me as a reference to Ed, the upper-middle-class city dweller, a member of the "gentry" (as his name suggests),[20] who must, in order to be cured of his complaint, be "brought down to the ground"—made aware of an important connection to the natural world. Read in this way, the epigraph applies not only to the external action of the story—the "back-to-nature" plot—but also to its psychological action. In psychological terms, the epigraph may be taken to refer to a consciousness which has become too highly developed and must be put back in touch with the "lowly" instinctual level of the psyche from which it has become detached.

How can such a reattachment be achieved? Reestablishing a connection between the various parts of the psyche is precisely the goal of analytical psychology, and is accomplished by means of what is known in Jungian terminology as *individuation*—a process of self-realization which acts "to abolish the separation between the conscious mind and the unconscious, the real source of life, and to bring about a reunion of the individual with the native soil of his inherited, instinctual make-up."[21] And this psychological process is precisely what *Deliverance* portrays. Dickey's novel is essentially a visionary work which depicts a night journey into no-man's-land—"the country beyond the ego"—and the confrontation with the alien powers of the deep unconscious. Moreover, and this is unusual for a work of American fiction, *Deliverance* represents a *successful* hunt for selfhood, a hero's quest which culminates in a genuine rebirth.

"In dreams or myths," writes the Jungian analyst Joseph Henderson, "individuation most frequently presents itself as the lively, urgent wish to undertake a journey"[22]—and in the opening section of *Deliverance* Dickey introduces us to four southern suburbanites planning a weekend canoe trip into the backwoods of Georgia. Ed himself expresses a "lively" desire to go—"I . . . felt ready for something like this" (8)—but the urgency is communicated more by his companion Lewis Medlock, who, playing the role of the mythological "herald," announces his determination to travel down the "wild rippling water" (36) before the river is dammed and the Cahulawasee is transformed into Lake Cahula, a "real estate heaven" of "choice lots . . . marinas and beer cans" (7). The other two members of the group, Bobby Trippe and Drew Balinger, have reservations about the journey, don't feel any particular need for it. "The whole thing does seem kind of crazy," Bobby says (10). But, like Ahab on the quarter-deck, Lewis goads them on.

There are, as a matter of fact, interesting similarities between *Deliverance* and *Moby-Dick*. In many ways, Drew is just like Starbuck. Staid and steadfast, domestic and devout—"The only decent one; the only sane one" (186)—he is incapacitated by his own normality: a man whose "mere unaided virtue or right-mindedness" affords him no protection against "spiritual terrors" and who is invariably destroyed by the voyage to Hades.[23] Bobby, on the other hand, resembles Stubb, the typical Melvillean bachelor, jolly and obtuse—the clown who can journey into the heart of darkness without understanding anything at all about the experience; whose smug satisfaction with the world is a sign of his spiritual shallowness:

> Bobby, particularly, seemed to enjoy the life he was in. He came, I believe, from some other part of the South, maybe Louisiana, and since he had been around—since I had known him, anyway—had seemed to do well. He was very social and would not have been displeased if someone had called him a born salesman. He liked people, he said, and most of them liked him—some genuinely and some merely because he was a bachelor and a good dinner or party guest. . . . He was a pleasant surface human being. (11)

Lewis, the leader of the expedition, is, as I have suggested, similar to Ahab. Driven, obsessed (12), fanatical (40), "insane" (230), he sees the canoe trip not simply as a weekend jaunt, but, as "A Way"—a quest for immortality:

> Lewis wanted to be immortal. He had everything that life could give, and he couldn't make it work. And he couldn't bear to give it up or see age take it away from him, either, because in the mean-time he might be able to find what it was he wanted, the thing that must be there, and that must be subject to the will. He was the kind of man who tries by any means—weight lifting, diet, exercise . . . to hold on to his body . . . to rise above time. (12)

Lewis, I believe, is suffering from a neurotically extreme fear of dying. This may seem strange, given his compulsive daredeviltry. But, after all, neurotic phobias often express themselves in paradoxical ways, so that a person suffering from a pathological fear of speed, for instance, may never set foot in a car or, alternatively, may become a professional racer. The two responses are just the flip sides of a single coin. Lewis's craving for immortality is simply a desperate desire not to die. At the same time, as Ed himself is well aware, Lewis's accident proneness reveals an equally desperate desire *to* die, as if he is eager to relieve himself of the burden of his terrible fear (12). After fracturing his thigh in the rapids, however, Lewis finally comes to "know something that I didn't know before" (194)—"that dying is better than immortality." No longer compelled to play superman, he becomes "a human being, and a good one" (235), at peace with himself at last. Thus, though he and Ahab both suffer crippling leg injuries—"It feels like it broke off," Lewis gasps (126)—the significance of the wound is very different for each man: for Lewis, it means the end of his quest, for Ahab the beginning.

Like Ishmael, who is carried away with the rest of the crew by the "irresistible arm" of Ahab's rhetoric, Ed listens to his friend and feels himself "getting caught up . . . in his capricious and tenacious enthusiasm" (9). For Gentry the canoe trip is also "A Way," though not to physical fitness. Whereas Lewis regards the Georgia wilderness as a testing ground for his body, Ed looks at a map of the area and sees something else: "It was certainly not much from the standpoint of design. The high ground, in tan and an even paler tone of brown, meandered in and out of various shades of green, and there was nothing to call you or stop you on one place or another. Yet the eye could not leave the whole; there was harmony of some kind" (13). Right from the start, the region of the unknown holds out the promise of spiritual wholeness, psychic serenity, self-realization, to Gentry. Just as the narrator of *Moby-Dick* must leave the "insular city of the Manhattoes" and travel into "the mystic ocean," "the dark side of the earth," to cure his spiritual sickness—the "damp, drizzly November" in his soul[24]—the narrator of *Deliverance* is impelled to journey into night country in order to dispel his *hypos*. Like the schoolteacher Ishmael, whose spiritual quest unites him with the neglected instinctual side of his psyche, embodied by the cannibal Queequeg, Gentry must make the inner voyage to confront those primitive qualities which, when assimilated, will revitalize his existence.

As he sets out for the valley, Ed expresses some skepticism about the trip. He defends "the way of civilization," of order and comfort and rationality, while Lewis extols nature and asserts that city life is "out of touch with everything" (42). "You don't believe in madness, eh?" asks Medlock.

> "I don't at all. I know better than to fool with it."
> "So what you do. . . ."
> "So what you do is go on by it. What you do is get done what you ought to be doing. And what you do rarely—and I *mean* rarely—is to flirt with it."
> "We'll see," Lewis said, glancing at me as though he had me. "We'll see. You've had all that office furniture in front of you, desks and bookcases and filing cabinets and the rest. You've been sitting in a chair that won't move. You've been steady. But when that river is under you, all that is going to change." (40)

Ed's reservations about the wilderness experience—"I'll still stay with the city," he insists (46)—reflect the conscious mind's natural resistance to entering the realm of the irrational. But, as all heroes must, Ed responds to the "call" of the unconscious and takes the plunge. That his journey is indeed a dream trip, a symbol of the descent into the darkness of the unconscious, becomes clear as soon as he enters the river: "A slow force took hold of us; the bank began to go backward. I felt the complicated urgency of the current, like a thing made of many threads being pulled, and with this came the feeling I always had at the moment of losing consciousness at night, going towards something unknown that I could not avoid, but from which I would return" (65–66).

As Gentry travels farther into the woods, he begins to make contact with the alien forces of his psyche—a situation symbolized by a dreamlike experience he has on the first night of the journey. Lying in the blackness of his tent, deep in the forest, he is startled when something slams against the roof. He snaps on a flashlight and runs "the weak glow up from the door."

> I kept seeing nothing but gray-green stitches until I got right above my head. The canvas was punctured there, and through it came one knuckle of a deformed fist, a long curving of claws that turned on themselves. Those are called talons, I said out loud.
>
> . . . .
>
> I pulled one hand out of the sleeping bag and saw it wander fraily up through the thin light until a finger touched the cold reptilian nail of one talon below the leg-scales. I had no idea of whether the owl felt me; I thought perhaps it would fly, but it didn't. Instead it shifted its weight again, and the claws on the foot I was touching loosened for a second. I slipped my forefinger between the claw and the tent, and half around the stony toe. (78)

This strange, hallucinatory scene represents, as Donald W. Markos points out, "the penetration of the wilderness into human consciousness"[25]—i.e., the breakdown of the barrier between the ego and the unconsciousness. The owl, a creature associated with night vision and wisdom, symbolizes Ed's increasing insight into the darkness of his psyche.

In a perceptive essay on *Deliverance* Donald J. Greiner discusses the book in terms of Ed's growing self-knowledge and maintains that Dickey's central concern is bestiality: "In *Deliverance* Dickey goes beyond the violent action and he-man acrobatics to suggest that each of us harbors in the deepest recesses of himself an unknown part which we are afraid to face because we might be forced to acknowledge our own bestiality." The narrator's spiritual development, Greiner argues, depends precisely on his ability to accept that "unknown part," to "call forth the monster within . . . to meet [his buried self] face to face." "The adventure in the big woods teaches [Ed] . . . that self-awareness means an acknowledgment of and harmonious relationship between the two sides of his nature, the bestial and the human."[26] Though Greiner's approach is not Jungian, his insights correspond very closely to archetypal theory. For according to that theory, self-realization invariably begins with the recognition of "the monster within"—that dark embodiment of bestial qualities which Jung calls the *shadow archetype*. "The meeting with oneself," he writes, "is at first the meeting with one's own shadow."[27] In *Deliverance* that meeting takes place early in the second day of the trip when, "in the intense shadow" of the woods (98), Ed and Bobby encounter a pair of grotesque mountaineers:

> They came forward, moving in a kind of half circle as though they were stepping around something. The shorter one was older, with big white eyes and a half-white stubble that grew in whorls on his cheeks. His face seemed to spin in many directions. He had on overalls, and his stomach looked like it was falling through them. The other was lean and tall, and peered at us as though out of a cave or some dim simple place far back in his yellow-tinged eyeballs. (95)

For Gentry this second man is indeed "the Other"—the Enemy, the Hostile Brother: that figure who represents the hidden side of Ed's personality, "its lower, primitive, instinctual, sensual half."[28] Ignorant, incomprehensibly brutal (98), animal-like (102), "repulsive-looking" (170), he is the personification of the city man's "inadmissable" impulses—of sheer, unbridled carnality and aggression. The utter bestiality of the mountaineers—"Pull your shirt-tail up, fat ass" (99)—is the antithesis of Ed's civilized behavior, of his sensitivity and rather passive sexuality.

Confronted with the horrors of his shadow's repellent urges, Ed resists his insight at first, strives to assert his rationality: "The lean man put the point of the knife under my chin and lifted it. 'You ever had your balls cut off, you fuckin' ape?' 'Not lately,' I said, clinging to the city" (98). It soon becomes clear, however, that, if Ed is to survive, it will be necessary for him not merely to face his shadow but to come to terms with it. In order to be reborn, in order to achieve deliverance, Ed must become a savage himself—i.e., incorporate the shadow archetype into his conscious personality.

The process of accepting his inherent animality, of acknowledging the primitive impulses which constitute the shadow, begins when the first mountaineer is slain and Ed approves Lewis's plan to bury the corpse in the woods. As the four men drag the body upstream, their civilized veneer is stripped away, and Gentry finds himself transformed into a beast: down on all fours in the "squelchy" muck, panting and digging wildly with his hands (117). Ed's metamorphosis is made explicit a few pages later when Drew is (apparently) shot in the head and the canoe overturns, spilling the narrator into the rapids: "I got on my back and poured with the river, sliding over the stones like a creature I had always contained but never released" (124). Attempting to right the canoe, he thinks of himself as "an out-of-shape animal" (127). Here, he is beginning to identify himself with his antagonist, who had leaped into the forest "like an animal" (102) when his partner was killed; an identification which signifies Ed's conscious realization of his shadow side, his recognition of a connection with the archetype. Indeed, as Ed crouches at the bottom of the gorge beside Lewis and Bobby, trying to figure out a way to save them all from the "murderous hillbilly" above (135), his "hidden" personality rises to consciousness and he experiences the Other within:

> "I think," I said, "that we'll never get out of this gorge alive."
> Did I say that? I thought. Yes, *a dream-man* said, you did. You did say it, and you believe it.
> "I think he means to pick the rest of us off tomorrow," I said out loud, *still stranger* than anything I had ever imagined.
> . . . .
> "What can we do?"
> "What can do three things," I said, and *some other person* began to tell me what they were. (129–30; my italics)

Liliane Frey-Rohn, describing the emergence of the shadow into consciousness, writes that "In such cases one often has the impression that the psyche is being controlled by a 'stranger' who appears as a 'voice.' "[29] Ed has started to know his shadow, but it still remains an alien entity. His next task, difficult and extremely dangerous, is the full assimilation of the "inner opponent," of the "archetypal figure of the adversary."

Ed's perilous ascent of the cliff "as smooth as monument stone" (141) is a version of an archetypal trial—the fairytale hero's climb up the crystal mountain to win "the treasure hard to attain." At one point the experience becomes deeply erotic: desperately fighting for a handhold on the wall, Ed loses control of his bladder, and his urine flows "with a delicious sexual voiding like a wet dream" (140). Suddenly, the "immense rock . . . spring[s] a crack" and Ed crawls inside it, where he lies motionless "as though . . . in a sideways grave." "I simply lay in nature, my pants' legs warm and sopping with my juices" (145). This episode symbolizes Ed's penetration into the tomb-womb of the great Earth Mother and is an instance of what Jungians call "heroic" or "regenerative" incest: the act of entering into "the Mother"—the maternal unconscious—in order to be reborn through her.[30] That Ed's "heroic incest" with *Magna Mater* does indeed bring him closer to self-realization is indicated by the appearance, at this point in the novel, of the mandala symbol—the magic circle, the archetypal symbol of the Self. As he begins to "inch upward again," he finds himself "moving with the most intimate motions of my body, motions I had never dared use with Martha or with any other human woman. Fear and a kind of moon-blazing sexuality lifted me, millimeter by millimeter." "Fuck [ing] the cliff for an extra inch or two in the moonlight," Ed suddenly sees some holes in the rocks above him, "and in one of them was a star. . . . as I went, more stars were added until a constellation like a crown began to form" (151). This circle of light is a vision of wholeness, a prefiguration of the psychic totality which awaits him at the end of his ordeals. "The mountain," writes Marie-Louise Von Franz in her *Introduction to the Interpretation of Fairy Tales*, "marks the place . . . where the hero, after arduous effort (climbing), becomes oriented and gains steadfastness and self-knowledge, values that develop through the effort to become conscious in the process of individuation."[31]

Having conquered the mountain, Ed is prepared for the confrontation with the Enemy. His heroic "effort to become conscious" has brought him to the verge of a critical stage in the individuation process: the full realization of his shadow, of his own capacity for evil. "At a definite moment of time," writes Liliane Frey-Rohn, "the self seems to 'demand' that the personality be made complete *through the recognition of what were up until then hostile, immoral and asocial tendencies.*"[32] This recognition is commonly symbolized by the slaying of the Adversary. "The 'hostile brother' has to be faced, overcome, incorporated into one's own psyche. Only in such a way can the ego evolve from partial self-knowledge to complete assimilation of the unconscious."[33]

Even before Ed kills his enemy, however, their coalescence is nearly complete: setting up an ambush for the mountaineer, the narrator feels "our minds fuse," and imagines himself performing fellatio on the stranger—visualizes a very literal act of incorporation: "If Lewis had not shot his companion, he and I would have made a kind of love, painful and terrifying to me, in some dreadful way pleasurable to him, but we would have been together in the flesh, there on the floor of the woods, and it was strange to think of it" (154). "A peculiar kind of intimacy" has developed between them (163), and, when the mountaineer finally appears, he seems different from the utterly repulsive creature that had attacked Ed and Bobby in the forest: "He was looking up the river and standing now with both hands on the gun, but with the attitude of holding it at his waist without necessarily thinking of raising it to his shoulder. There was something relaxed and enjoying in his body position, something primally graceful; I had never seen a more beautiful element of design" (161). Ed's shadow has suddenly assumed another aspect, positive and benign. "Unassimilated, the shadow figure [is entirely] evil," observes John Halverson, "a constellation of all that is demonic in the dark side of the psyche." As the archetype is integrated, however, the shadow begins to play a constructive role—"helping to bring up to consciousness those elements of the unconscious . . . necessary to the wholeness and health of the self"—and the stranger reveals himself to be the hero's helpmate and lover.[34]

The realization of the shadow is achieved with the mountaineer's death. Shooting a razor-sharp arrow through his adversary's throat, Ed becomes fully conscious of his capacity for violence. And when the wounded man crawls off, like an animal, to die in the bush, the narrator acknowledges his own bestiality by "getting down on my hands and knees and smelling for blood"—tracking his quarry "like a dog" (168, 169). When Gentry finally locates the corpse, he even considers cannibalizing it: "I took the knife in my fist. What? Anything. This, also, is not going to be seen. It is not ever going to be known; you can do what you want to; nothing is too terrible. I can cut off the genitals he was going to use on me. Or I can cut off his head, looking straight into his open eyes. Or I can eat him. I can do anything I have a wish to do" (170). "The hero," says

Joseph Campbell, "whether god or goddess, man or woman, the figure in a myth or the dreamer of a dream, discovers and assimilates his opposite (his own unsuspected self) either by swallowing it or by being swallowed."[35] While Ed does not commit "the ultimate horror," he *does* have the sensation of "being swallowed" by his shadow, momentarily possessed by his enemy's spirit. Walking "to the edge of the bluff" to see if Bobby has made good his escape, Ed spots the canoe on the river and—furious at Bobby for doing "everything wrong"—picks up the mountaineer's rifle and draws a bead on the "soft city country-club man." "Do it, the dead man said. Do it, he's right there" (171). The incident represents the surfacing of absolute evil in Ed, of the civilized man's most malevolent impulses. But he does not yield to these impulses: "I got around the feeling just by opening my fingers, and letting the gun fall to the ground." While the narrator is now fully conscious of the existence of his shadow tendencies, he does not unconditionally surrender to them. Rather, he manages to integrate the two parts of his personality, the civilized and the bestial—succeeds, as Jung puts it, in joining the shadow to the light. This psychological condition is symbolized by the actual joining of Ed and the mountaineer: having lowered the dead man down the cliff on a nylon rope, Ed follows after him and, for a while, the two hang suspended in space, connected by a cord (a scene reminiscent of chapter 72 in *Moby-Dick,* where the relationship between Ishmael and Queequeg is symbolized by the "monkey-rope" which ties them together like "inseparable twin brothers").

When the cord suddenly snaps, Ed plunges headlong into the icy river:

> I yelled, a tremendous, walled-in yell, and then I felt the current thread through me, first through my head from one ear and out the other and then complicatedly through my body, up my rectum and out my mouth and also in at the side where I was hurt. . . . It had been so many years since I had really been hurt that the feeling was almost luxurious, though I knew when I tried to climb the water to the surface that I had been weakened more than I had thought. Unconsciousness went through me. I was in a room of varying shades of green beautifully graduated from light to dark, and I went toward the palest color. . . . An instant before I broke water I saw the sun, liquid and transformed, and then it exploded in my face. (177)

The "black waters of death," writes Jung, are also "the water of life, for death with its cold embrace is the maternal womb just as the sea devours the sun but brings it forth again."[36] Having suffered this ritual death, Ed is finally prepared for his deliverance, and gradually makes his way out of the valley. His reintegration into society completes the mythic pattern which structures his story: separation-initiation-return.[37] And his "trial by landscape" produces a striking transformation. Awakening in a boardinghouse room on the morning after his return, Ed examines himself in a mirror and sees an "apparition" that bears little resemblance to the respectable suburbanite who had set out for the river a few days before. Stitched and bandaged, wearing a tattered flying suit with a web belt and a hunting knife, he looks like a wild man, a barbarian—"bearded and red eyed, not able to speak" (207). This savage he sees in the mirror is, of course, his own "inmost part,"[38] the shadow side of his civilized consciousness. Having completed his night journey, Gentry now clearly recognizes the primitive aspect of his personality. More important, he is able to *accept* this side of himself, to say in effect what Prospero says of the brutish Caliban at the close of Shakespeare's *The Tempest:* "this thing of darkness I / acknowledge mine." Looking at his reflection, at the image of his violent inner self, Ed smiles "very whitely, splitting the beard" (207). By acknowledging the reality of his instinctual nature, Gentry wins the boon: the harmony he has been searching for.

That the experience in the wilderness does indeed benefit Ed by putting him in touch with an immanent power which enriches every aspect of his life is made clear near the end of the novel:

> Another odd thing happened. The river and everything I remembered about it became a possession to me, a private possession, as nothing in my life ever had. Now it ran nowhere but in my head, but there it ran as though immortally. I could feel it—I can feel it—on different places of my body. It pleases me in some curious way that the river does not exist, and that I have it. In me it still is, and will be until I die, green, rocky, deep, fast, slow, and beautiful beyond reality. I had a friend there who in a way had died for me, and my enemy was there.
>
> The river underlies in one way or another everything I do. It is always finding a way to serve me, from my archery to some of my recent ads and to the new collages I have been attempting for my friends. George Holley, my old Braque enthusiast, bought one from me . . . and it hangs in his cubicle, full of sinuous forms threading among the headlines of war and student strikes. George has become my best friend, next to Lewis, and we do a lot of serious talking about art. (234)

This activation of Ed's imaginative powers—his metamorphosis from a "mechanic of the graphic arts" into a serious artist—is evidence of his new relation to what Frey-Rohn calls "the creative sources in the psyche." The adventure on the "night river" (235) has produced a significant enlargement of Ed's personality, an "inner transformation and rebirth into another being."[39] Revitalized and self-possessed, he relates more effectively not only to the inner forces of his unconscious but to the people around him as well. "Thad and I are getting along much better than before," he says, referring to his business partner, and George Holley, the "Braque man" who had seemed so tiresome to Gentry before the trip, is now the narrator's second-best friend. Thus *Deliverance* is much more than just a simple "adventure yarn"; it is a work in the tradition of the American "dark romance," a mythopoeic novel whose action symbolizes the dangers and rewards of the descent into "the land of impossibility" (235), into the dark, unknown depths of the psyche. "To sojourn in those depths," writes Jolande Jacobi, "to withstand their dangers, is a journey to hell and 'death.' But he who comes through safe and sound, who is 'reborn,' will return, full of knowledge and wisdom, equipped for the outward and inward demands of life."[40]

NOTES

1. This advertisement, which ran in magazines in 1952, has recently been reprinted in *Popular Writing in America,* shorter alternate edition, ed. Donald McQuade and Robert Atwan (New York: Oxford University Press, 1977): 26–27.

2. J. A. Avant, *Library Journal* (1 March 1970): 912. Though Avant's remark is obviously intended as a sarcastic "put-down" of Dickey, there actually are several references to Tarzan in the novel which serve a serious thematic function. On pages 90, 91, 213, and 225 of the paperback edition of *Deliverance* (New York: Dell, 1971; all quotations in my text are from this edition), Lewis is either compared to or called Tarzan, and Ed—whose body, we are told repeatedly, is covered with "monkey fur"—is referred to as either Tarzan's son or "Bolgani the Gorilla." These passages all relate to the novel's central theme: the necessity for the civilized man (as epitomized by Ed) to rediscover the animal side of himself, to get back in touch with the instinctual roots of his nature.

3. See Walter Clemons, "James Dickey, Novelist," *New York Times Book Review,* 22 March 1970, 22.

4. Dickey didn't help matters much either when, sometime after the appearance of *Deliverance,* he published a perfectly serious article in *Esquire* on the joys of hunting rattlesnakes with a homemade blowgun.

5. 2 May 1970, 123.

6. 22 March 1970.

7. *Southern Review* 7 (1971): 947–53.

8. April 1970, 106.

9. Ibid. Geoffrey Wolf, on the other hand, felt that the characters were "limned flawlessly by a few broad strokes" (see *Newsweek,* 30 March 1970, 94).

10. *The American Novel and Its Tradition* (Garden City, N.Y.: Doubleday Anchor Books, 1957), 13.

11. *Love and Death in the American Novel,* rev. ed. (New York: Dell / A Delta Book, 1966), p. 155. *Edgar Huntly* is a book with many striking similarities to *Deliverance.* Brown's novel, like Dickey's, concerns a civilized, sensitive, very rational man who journeys into a nightmarish wilderness, where, after undergoing a series of bizarre ordeals, is temporarily transformed into a murderous savage.

12. Ibid., 156.

13. "Psychology and Literature," *Modern Man in Search of a Soul,* trans. W. S. Dell and Gary F. Baynes (New York: Harcourt, Brace and World, Harvest Books, 1933), 152–72.

14. "The journey to Hades, or the descent into the land of the dead. 'Nekyia' is a title of the 11th book of Homer's *Odyssey.*" See Jolande Jacobi, *The Way of Individuation* (New York: Harcourt, Brace and World, 1967), 154 n. 16.

15. Walter Clemons, "James Dickey, Novelist," *New York Times Book Review,* 22 March 1970, 22.

16. This introductory section of the novel is omitted from the film version of *Deliverance,* which opens with Ed and his companions on the way to the river. While the filmmakers' decision to limit themselves strictly to the adventure in the woods was undoubtedly a wise cinematic choice—the movie is very fast paced and suspenseful—it also significantly altered the meaning of the original story, as did the casting of younger men in the four lead roles and the changes made in the ending (see n. 40).

17. Frieda Fordham, *An Introduction to Jung's Psychology* (Baltimore: Penguin Books, 1970), 78.

18. C. G. Jung, *Memories, Dreams, Reflections,* ed. Aniela Jaffe, trans. Richard and Clara Winston (New York: Vintage Books, 1963), 245.

19. P. 31. This incident foreshadows the scene in the wilderness when Ed—confronting the unbridled terrors of the id directly—is threatened with castration by one of the mountaineers (98).

20. Another possible source for Ed's surname is suggested by the poem "On the Coosawattee" (from *Helmets*), which describes a canoe trip similar in certain respects to the one in *Deliverance* and features a character named Lucas Gentry.

21. C. G. Jung, *Psychology and Alchemy, Collected Works,* trans. R. F. C. Hull (Princeton: Princeton University Press, 1968, Bollingen Series XX), 12:137.

22. *Thresholds of Initiation* (Middletown, Conn.: Wesleyan University Press, 1967), 134.

23. Herman Melville, *Moby-Dick,* ed. Harrison Hayford and Hershel Parker (New York: Norton Critical Edition, 1967), 162, 104.

24. Ibid., 12, 140.

25. "Art and Immediacy: James Dickey's *Deliverance,*" *Southern Review* 7, no. 3 (1971): 951.

26. "The Harmony of Bestiality in James Dickey's *Deliverance,*" *South Carolina Review* 5, no. 1 (1972): 44–45.

27. C. G. Jung, *The Archetypes and the Collective Unconscious, Collected Works,* vol. 9, pt. 1, 21.

28. John Halverson, "The Shadow in *Moby-Dick,*" *American Quarterly* 15 (Fall 1963): 437.

29. "Evil from the Psychological Point of View," in *Evil,* ed. the Curatorium of the C. G. Jung Institute, Zurich (Evanston, Ill.: Northwestern University Press, 1967), 162.

30. C. G. Jung, *Symbols of Transformation, Collected Works,* 5:224.

31. Chapter 7, 12.

32. "Evil from the Psychological Point of View," in *Evil,* 186.

33. Alex Aronson, *Psyche and Symbol in Shakespeare* (Bloomington: Indiana University Press, 1972), 115.

34. "The Shadow in *Moby-Dick,*" 438. Cf. Leslie Fiedler's remarks about Chingachgook, Jim, and Queequeg in *Love and Death in the American Novel,* esp. 369. Ed's uncertainty about the slain man's identity reflects, I believe, the shadow's ambiguous nature. While the shadow figure appears totally evil before it is incorporated, it performs a positive function—and assumes a correspondingly positive image—once it is brought to consciousness. The fact that Ed cannot definitely identify the dead man does not mean that he has shot an innocent person but that his shadow, having been "realized,"

no longer appears as absolutely "unprepossessing" as it did earlier. Peter G. Beidler points out that "the tall rapist" has "yellow-tinged eyeballs" and a totally toothless mouth, whereas the man Ed kills on the mountain has "clear blue" eyes and only a "partial upper plate." Beidler concludes that Ed "has killed the wrong man" (" 'The Pride of Thine Heart Hath Deceived Thee': Narrative Distortion in Dickey's *Deliverance*," *South Carolina Review* 5, no. 1 [1973]:29–40.) My contention, however, is that these physical discrepancies symbolize the shift in the shadow's nature, the "humanization" of the other.

35. *Hero with a Thousand Faces* (Cleveland: World Publishing Company, Meridian Books, 1971), 108.

36. *Symbols of Transformation,* 5:218.

37. See Joseph Campbell, *Hero with a Thousand Faces,* 30.

38. William Shakespeare, *Hamlet,* act 3, scene 4, line 20: "You go not till I set you up a glass / Where you may see the inmost part of you."

39. C. G. Jung, *The Archetypes and the Collective Unconscious, Collected Works,* vol. 9, pt. 1, 131.

40. *Complex/Archetype/Symbol* (Princeton: Princeton University Press, 1959, Bollingen Series LVII), 186. The film version of *Deliverance* ends on a very different note: with Ed haunted by nightmares of the slain mountaineer. Unlike his counterpart in the novel, the hero of the movie is unable to accept his shadow. The film's penultimate image—of the hand of the dead man rising menacingly out of the river—suggests that Ed has only repressed his aggressive side again and that it will reemerge from the depths of the unconscious, a continuing source of trouble. (I should add, however, that in cinematic terms, the shot is very effective, very chilling, and that, had the ending of the movie been as serene as that of the book, it probably would have seemed anticlimactic. So once again—as with the omission of the prologue—the filmmaker's alteration of the original story, while drastically changing its meaning, was valid and perhaps wise, given their decision to make a simple, straightforward thriller.)

Narration, Text, Intertext:
The Two Versions of *Deliverance*

R. BARTON PALMER

More than a decade has now passed since both the publication of James Dickey's novel *Deliverance* (1970) and the appearance of a film version (1972) by John Boorman and based on a screenplay by Dickey himself. In both its forms *Deliverance* achieved a popularity (and, in some quarters, notoriety) that surprised many, including the author. Dickey felt (and perhaps rightly so) that critics and public alike were overvaluing his initial foray into fiction and neglecting his substantial corpus of poetry. *Deliverance* expresses the same post-industrial malaise and urge for individual renewal that marks the best of Dickey's neo-Romantic poems, such as "On the Coosawattee." The arch-realism of the novel, however, insured a wider and more appreciative audience. In particular, its easily accessible first-person narration and an emphasis on violent action—features which resulted, according to Dickey, from a revision that saw the novel change from an "introverted" form like his poetry into something resembling the classic adventure tale—made the novel more commercial. It is easy to see now, however, that the initial popularity of *Deliverance* had much to do also with the ways in which it connected to certain preoccupations of and ongoing changes within both American society and art during the turbulent early 1970s.

The novel's thematizing of the mid-life crises of its two principal characters, Lewis and Ed, echoed both a widespread and acknowledged dissatisfaction with the banal everyday and the secret—if just as potent—apocalyptic yearnings or fears of those who envisioned the demise of consumerist society, a demise to be followed by a return to more primitive forms of existence. At the same time the film's shocking violence, especially its homosexual rape—this a scene with no antecedents in the American cinema—was received as yet another instance of the way in which Hollywood was redefining its canons of representation, a trend which had begun some five years before with *Bonnie and Clyde* and which had continued into the 1970s with (among other innovations) the slow-motion death scenes in Sam Peckinpah's films. Like *The Wild*

Originally published in the *James Dickey Newsletter* 2 (Spring 1986): 2–10. Reprinted by permission.

Bunch and *The Getaway,* therefore, *Deliverance* was often viewed as an exploration of the potential for violence concealed by the comfortable surfaces of American life, as yet another manifestation of that national obsession with "regeneration through violence" that Richard Slotkin has traced as a central theme in American fiction.[1]

In the middle 1980s, however, the radical thrust of the Hollywood Renaissance has long been blunted by a cultural swing to the right, while the yearning of Dickey's middle-aged heroes for a transcendence of dissatisfying routines has been transformed into a multimillion dollar business. Lewis's mania for physical conditioning as well as his compulsion to shoot the white waters of a fast-vanishing wilderness have equally been accommodated within the structures of mainstream culture, an indication, surely, of the extent to which an unhappiness with unrewarding living can be recuperated by the notion of "recreation." *Deliverance* played a not insignificant role in these trends (one has only to remember Dickey's consternation at the appalling number of whitewater fatalities incurred by those attempting to imitate the voyage of his bored suburbanites). But the novel's rhetorical effect, its imbrication within cultural change has paradoxically relieved the text of its ability to shock by offering a protest, however easily co-opted, against the discontents engendered by consumer society. It is thus easy now to misread *Deliverance* as an adventure tale in the tradition of H. Rider Haggard or Edgar Rice Burroughs (the latter's Tarzan stories do, of course, furnish a subtext in the novel which is exploited ironically by Dickey). Similarly, the graphic violence of early 1970s film, with its revelation of the dark sides of American culture, has become largely aestheticized in the contemporary cinema. Now an accepted part of Hollywood realism, such violence has recently figured as a conservative element of films, not a radical one. The result is that Boorman's film is often misread as an early example of the growing tradition of right-wing revenge fantasy even though it shares little in common with, say, *Death Wish* or *Dirty Harry* beyond a rhetorical use of violence. In these ways the more than ten years that separate us from the initial appearance of *Deliverance* in both its forms do problematize any evaluation of the story's cultural significance. This social distance, however, does make it easier to see how *Deliverance* connects to certain vital traditions within American fiction and not simply to ephemeral trends. The time is now right, in short, for a re-evaluation of the literary importance of the novel and the cinematic importance of the film. But this re-evaluation can only be meaningful if it is based on a simple truth, one which I will explore in the remainder of this essay, namely that the dynamics of the adaptation process have made the film a very different kind of fictional experience from that offered in the novel.

In the years immediately following publication, *Deliverance* received a good deal of scholarly attention, particularly from those academics who felt that its formal qualities and transcendental theme had been slighted by a number of reviewers, particularly Benjamin DeMott. This scholarship has demonstrated rather convincingly that *Deliverance* is not, in DeMott's phrase, an "emptily rhetorical horse-opera played in canoes."[2] Of late, however, scholarly interest in the novel has waned; this is certainly an index of Dickey's decision not to follow up his initial success with another novel in the same vein. The film has suffered a similar fate. Upon release it predictably attracted a good deal of critical interest, especially from those intrigued by its relationship to the Dickey novel. Recently, neither Boorman nor his film has been seen as having played an important role within the Hollywood Renaissance by those writing about the period. The result has been that *Deliverance,* considered now to have broken no new cinematic ground, has received little scholarly attention since the middle 1970s.

As I have suggested, however, both novel and film connect to larger and more enduring trends within the context of American fiction, and these connections have only been touched upon in earlier scholarship. Even more interesting is the fact, mentioned in passing by some critics of the film, that the adaptation process has transformed Dickey's story of the relationship between the experiencing consciousness and the world that confronts it (a tale with its roots equally in the fiction of Henry James and Joseph Conrad) into a naturalistic exploration of the struggle of man as actor with a hostile, but potentially renewing nature. This transformation cannot be explained (as it usually is) by recourse only to conventional notions, derived from Romantic literary theory, about the control exercised by the creative artist over the products of his imagination. It must also be accounted for by the different models of narration employed in novel and film. Before proceeding to an analysis of these, however, one more important point must be made. The choice of narrative models is to some extent a matter of artistic choice, but it is also much influenced by intertextuality, by the different series of texts into which novel and film were separately inserted. To discuss narration, then, is inevitably to broach the question of tradition, to see the "anxiety of influence" (in Harold Bloom's apt phrase) as a pressure that structures the individual work of art.

In his article "*Deliverance* from Novel to Film: Where Is Our Hero?" Robert F. Willson Jr. calls attention to the principal way in which the film version defeats the expectations of its audience for a certain kind of fictional experience. Willson charges that Dickey and Boorman have eliminated the novel's most important feature: the focusing of the adventure downriver through Ed. The belated publication of the screenplay (it finally appeared in 1982) certainly exculpates Dickey in the matter, for he adapted the novel's privileging of Ed's consciousness as best he could to the requirements of screen presentation. In any case, Willson raises an issue here that is more important for the analysis of the film version than its evaluation. His view that the film is a "gruesome but hardly thought-provoking adventure story in which Ed's anxieties are lost in the scenery, in the gore" certainly speaks to the institutional pressures of Hollywood filmmaking, particularly the need to privilege exterior reality over interior, to produce excitement rather than provoke thought. But it is also true, as he suggests, that the consumer of mainstream fiction and film expects that the "realism" of these forms will be an "expressive" one, that it will depend, in other words, on the evocation of the real through a privileging of the main character's experience. Such an expectation, moreover, involves not only the desire for a certain vector of presentation (one that, as Gérard Genette suggests, has no necessary connection with linguistic point of view as manifested in the different persons of narrative address). It also involves the desire for certain forms of meaning, particularly as these are derived from that complex of textual and psychological movements termed "recognition." Willson's closing remarks illustrate this neatly: "Since man is flawed and his life is tenuous, he can find only momentary release from his fears, never sure that repressed thoughts will not return to plague him. This fact underscores the irony of the word 'deliverance' itself. Here in particular the movie fails us; it has concentrated only on the river peril and its more obvious threat to the men from the city."[3] The assumption here is that "river peril"—the most obvious exterior action in the film—can be meaningful only insofar as it contributes to the recognition of a universal law of human nature, one that is revealed to us and to the main character through the dynamics of consciousness, through the isolation of the exterior, public, natural world within the private realm of individual thought.

Recognition, so defined, does constitute the principal movement of the novel—but not the film. The dependence on an "introversion" of experience means that the dynamic of character development closely resembles the aesthetic of poeticization that is revealed by the voice of works such as "On the Coosawattee." Ed, in other words, becomes the text's self-reflexive center, an embodiment of the creative sensibility from which the fiction as a whole derives its artistic form. The adventures in which he is involved thus become stages in a phenomenological awakening. The first stage consists in the opening up of his consciousness to the brute data of existence, a psychological process which is facilitated by the fact that Ed, his life threatened in the wilderness, must deal intensely with the physical (as Lewis had told him, it would all come down to the body, the one thing that can't be faked). As a result, Ed experiences a perceptual re-orientation in which the phenomenal world is no longer conceived as an estranged "objectness" but as something engaged in a dialogue with his own inner being. As he describes: "The river was blank and mindless with beauty. It was the most glorious thing I have ever seen. But it was not seeing, really. For once it was not just seeing. It was beholding. . . . The rock quivered like a coal, because I wanted it to quiver, held in its pulsing border, and what it was pulsing with was me.[4]

The mountain man waiting to kill him and his companions thus becomes someone with whom he experiences an intense sense of communion: "I had thought so long and hard about him that to this day I still believe I felt, in the moonlight, our minds fuse. It was not that I felt myself turning evil, but that an enormous physical indifference, as vast as the whole abyss of light at my feet, came to me: an indifference not only to the other man's body scrambling and kicking on the ground with an arrow through it, but also to mine" (154). This indifference, however, constitutes only the initial preparation for a plenitude of consciousness. At adventure's end, the process of introversion completes itself as Ed becomes one with the objects of his experience: "The river and everything I remember about it became a possession to me, a personal, private possession, as nothing else in my life ever had. Now it ran nowhere but in my head, but there it ran as though immortally. . . . The river underlies, in one way or another, everything I do" (233–34).

In this still moment of narration time, the Melvillean urge for unity (embodied in Lewis's desire for a confrontation with nature) and the drive toward a transcendence of the everyday, toward a Romantic communion (embodied in Ed's dissatisfaction with an unconscious "sliding" through life) equally find their satisfaction. The full passage from the experiencing-I to the narrating-I signifies the end of "adventure" and its interiorization not only as an object of consciousness but as the very focus of consciousness. At this point we can understand the full effect of the novel's use of first-person narration. For it is precisely not in heightening narrative vividness that its effect lies. Rather such narration controls the continuing passage from phenomena to a psychological transformation which is the objective correlative of artistic creation (a process that finds its source in experience just as Ed discovers that the river "underlies" all that he does). In an otherwise brilliant analysis of the novel, Fredric Jameson misjudges the ultimate goal or point of Dickey's expressive realism: "James Dickey's novel is thus a fantasy about class struggle in which the middle-class American property owner wins through to a happy ending and is able, by reconquering his self-respect, to think of himself as bathing in the legendary glow of a moderate heroism."[5] Jameson reads *Deliverance* as a Cooperian projection of ambivalent attitudes toward progress in which a more primitive state of existence (and a more savage one) is the object not only of a profound yearning but of fear. Dickey's characters, then, would be social types acting out the tragic, American drama with the wild and primitive. But this is surely to misrepresent the novel's ideological thrust, which is not directed toward the renewal of dissatisfying social relations; the novel's finale sketches not the reconquest of the primitive by the civilized, but the incorporation of the primitive, of the natural within the individual consciousness, thus precluding forever any return to the phenomenal encounter between culture and nature.

The effect of the novel's opening section, which outlines the differing dissatisfaction of Ed and Lewis with their lives, is to thematize the journey downriver as therapeutic, as the acting out of repressed desires. It is hardly surprising, therefore, that the adventure which follows not only succeeds in curing both Lewis and Ed (as Lewis confesses after their safe arrival, "I know something I didn't know before" [194]) but is in its very form a kind of wish fulfillment. Consider, for example, the relationship between the homosexual attack on Ed and Bobby and Ed's attraction to Lewis. The attack comes immediately after a scene in which the homoeroticism that characterizes the friend-ship of Lewis and Ed is most obviously acknowledged. Bathing together in the stream, Ed is struck by the beauty of his companion's body: "Everything he had done for himself for years paid off as he stood there in his tracks, in the water. I could tell by the way he glanced at me; the payoff was in my eyes. I had never seen such a male body in my life" (90).

In a complex gesture of affirmation and denial Lewis's penetrating arrow saves Ed from having to act out any repressed desire for male love (and this is a gesture he himself later reciprocates). The adventure, in short, traces move-ments of consciousness more than it offers a socially typical drama which, in the complex manner of fiction, is meant to reference events in the "real world." Its real theme has little to do with social issues—these constitute the form of the events rather than their true content. Instead, it offers both in the textual co-presence of the experiencing and narrating "I's" and in its illustration of the process that carries the "I" from experiencing to narrating, from event to consciousness, an understanding of the poeticizing introversion that has cre-ated the text. The novel's paradigm of narration, then, is not one chosen van-tage point from which the story might be told. Without access to the consciousness that gives it meaning (apparently in an act of self-explanation, for Ed offers no reasons for his tale-telling, addresses no readers), *Deliverance* would simply be a pattern of events lacking true content.

The introversion of the novel, then, is so central to its effect that the text is rendered uncinematic (for the cinema has not the same access as fiction to subjective discourse). Dickey's screenplay, however, attempts to salvage much of the novel's effect by retaining the focus on Ed in the opening and closing segments (which frame the canoe trip) and dramatizing through extended dia-logue Ed's attitudes and feelings. These features of the screenplay do create more problems than they solve. Not only are the long passages of dialogue essentially uncinematic, but a structural difficulty arises because Ed is not the focused character throughout the whole journey although he is in the segments devoted to suburban life. As written, Dickey's screenplay would make an inter-esting—if overlong and stagey—film; but it would fail, as does Boorman's ver-sion, to reproduce the fictional experience of the original. Boorman's solution to the problem may be simply put. He cut out the opening section almost entirely (all that remains in the release print is some voice-over conversation among the four men about their trip plans); of Dickey's closing only one scene remains, the disquieting re-union of Ed with his wife (Boorman has made an important addition here, a nightmare about his experiences from which Ed awakes in stark terror). During the journey itself Ed is privileged only when he emerges dramatically as an important character; as Willson suggests, this part of the film lacks a protagonist through whom the experiences of the group are filtered and understood. In short, the expressive realism of the novel is dis-carded; narration, instead of being assigned to Ed, is truly extradiegetic, a func-tion of that dramatic intelligence which can conveniently be called Boorman.

It would be incorrect, however, to think of Boorman's changes as adding up to simply an altered vector of storytelling, one that, rather in the manner of New Hollywood directors such as Robert Altman or Francis Coppola, refuses to hide the intentionality of narration behind a main character (whose desire and movements may be thought of as motivating the camera and thus mystifying the director's role). As I have maintained, the tale is (in some important senses) its telling. The principal effect of Boorman's changes, in fact, is more ideological than narratological. For the adaptation process, as it were, deconstructs the ways in which the novel contains and processes its social raw materials. We have seen that Dickey achieves closure through a retreat from the historical or phenomenal into a privatized and individual consciousness; this retreat is imaged by the river becoming a lake, a development that is no synthesis of the opposition of nature to culture but a masking of that contradiction (it hides, we remember, the evidence of the crime, the traces which prove that the society which emerges from the struggle ever had a history). Ed's internalization of the wilderness is said to have effected a transformation of his psyche—"the river underlies . . . all that I do"—but the text denies this anagnoresis by showing that he had resumed his previous life. The descent into the hidden horror and wonder of the national past finally yields a reaffirmation of consumerism in which elemental thing-ness is commodified (the river of adventure becomes a lake for recreation). Here, once again, the novel's privileging of the individual character is revealing. For it not only, as we have seen, exemplifies the process that brings the text into being; it also eloquently describes the asociality and ahistoricity of the post-industrial society to which it is addressed.

In the film the conflict repressed in the novel is released, its closure problematized. The allegoresis of the adventure downriver, achieved by the relationship established between the desires of Ed and Lewis and what subsequently happens to them, is discarded, with the result that the conflict between man and Nature (or natural society) is restored to its full historical value; since textual closure is achieved by the "introversion" of the wilderness in the novel, this structural feature likewise falls away in the adaptation process. In its original form the story is a Hawthornian romance; on film it becomes a wilderness tale in the tradition of Fenimore Cooper and, even more obviously, the naturalist writer Jack London. We can see this change quite clearly in the opening segments, which are, almost entirely, added by Boorman. Over the title we hear the voices of four men discussing a canoe trip down a river; the dominant voice, which turns out to be that of Lewis, says that they (the conspiratorial forces of encroaching civilization) intend to "drown" this river, which is the "last, wild, untamed, unfucked-up river in the South." The purpose of the trip is thus defined as "adventure" (the last possible journey into a vanishing wilderness) rather than "therapy" (the cure for urban discontent). As the conversation continues, the title is replaced by a moving camera shot (at the level of the water) of a wild river, and this is followed by shots of large trucks moving

earth and of dynamiting operations. We read these shots through the conversation we hear, assuming that the river and the dam being discussed are what we
see. The sequence, up to this point, is motivated by the principle of "illustration," and is thus closely tied to the actions—in this case purely verbal
ones—of the unseen characters. Narration here, in short, is expressive in the
usual Hollywood sense of the term, that is, it is "tied" to dramatic action in
such a way as to obscure its location in the complex agency—that institutional
narrator—which is the film's true source, the "voice" that really speaks it. At
this point, however, the institutional narrator announces his presence in a
startling fashion. The shots of dynamiting operations make way for a long,
descriptive shot of a misty mountain forest where the loud crack of thunder
"answers" to the sounds of blasting. This shot is not motivated by the dialogue,
not in any sense an illustration; instead it effects a visual and aural metaphor
(what Eisenstein would call intellectual montage), and its purpose is to thematize the adventure by suggesting that the nature about to be overcome by
human purpose retains its own strengths and presence. The relationship between man and the wilderness, in other words, is defined by struggle. The
sequence closes with another view of the same mountain range, framed in such
a way as to allow the car full of canoers to travel along the lower edge, domi-
nated by the wilderness they are passing through. The film, in this way, under-
cuts the expressiveness it begins with; the woods and river are more than
projections of human purpose, more than objects to be put to human uses,
whether damming or recreation. The wild has its own powers, and these will
be discovered by those who are searching simply for unrepeatable thrills and
experiences.

In his article "*Deliverance:* Four Variations on the American Adam," Robert Armour suggests that in both the novel and film the four voyagers are
variations of the archetypal Adam, who is, in the words of R. W. B. Lewis, "an
individual emancipated from history, happily bereft of ancestry, untouched and
undefiled by the usual inheritances of family and race, an individual standing
alone . . . ready to confront whatever awaited him with the aid of his own
unique and inherent resources."[6] This is a useful perception, but, I would
argue, quite wrong in one important aspect. Dickey's characters are not Adams
at all according to Lewis's definition; they resemble more closely a later American type, the world-weary Progressive who, confronting the problems of re-
forming a world that seems hopelessly corrupt and unjust, looks back with
nostalgia toward the heroic Adams of the past (as, for example, the narrator of
Owen Wister's *The Virginian* contemplates with admiration—and with a sense
of profound loss—the "natural gentleman" of the book's title). In the film,
however, the elimination of the initial framing section means that the four
men do appear "happily bereft of ancestry" and ready for a confrontation with
the unfathomed powers of nature. Positioned by the dramatic irony of the
narrator's opening metaphor, the spectator awaits the necessary fall into experience which such a confrontation will bring.

The river, however, will not constitute the sole antagonist; the woods are home to a "natural society" that is only in a very complicated way truly primitive. It is reached quickly, without difficulty, and our initial encounter with it establishes not a distance from suburban culture (an effect intended by the screenplay's delineation of the stages by which the four arrive at the town of Oree) but rather a sense of connection. Surveying the junked cars and appliances which literally crowd the landscape of the country filling station, Bobby remarks (in a line added by Boorman) that "this is where everything winds up." What immediately follows is the dueling banjoes scene in which the albino country boy outplays Drew and refuses his offer of friendship. This scene derives from the novel but is given more importance by Boorman; the filmic narration reprises the musical theme, in altered forms, at various crucial times in the narrative (as when Ed slips from the cliff after killing the second mountain man). When the canoers start out, moreover, Boorman has them pass under a bridge where the albino boy stands, contemplating their passage but refusing once again to acknowledge an offer of friendship (this is a scene also added to the screenplay). Natural society, as the film defines it, not only embodies the discontents of modern culture—its primitiveness is a function of presence rather than lack—but also possesses superior knowledge and power that are intimately connected to deformity, itself, through the agency of inbreeding, a product of culture. Boorman's natural society, in short, is hardly a Cooperian ideal formation where the principle of community insures just social relations; the film's vision is Freudian rather than Rousseauean, describing, as it does, what is lost through the repressive work of civilization and what is better left behind. The town of Oree is in no way a lost utopia, and yet it exerts, primarily through the unlearned virtuosity of its music, a fascination over Drew and Ed in particular.

In the novel the primitive, in both its human and natural forms, forces Ed to make the phenomenological leap into communion. In the film, on the other hand, the encounter with the primitive resembles the ego's encounter with the id, presenting Ed with experiences and feelings that must be overcome if the state of civilization is to be regained. He must learn to do "wild work" (as Lewis already knows) if he is to save his own life and those of his companions. Killing the mountain man is a test rather than a source of recognition, but, as in the novel, it leads inexorably toward the interior self. The film's close presents the final result of the process of introversion. A close shot of the river—retrospectively marked as Ed's dream—reveals the sudden and dreadful appearance of a corpse's hand. Ed wakes in a cold sweat and, comforted by his wife, at last manages to fall back asleep. Here the film ends. The scene makes use of material from the novel and screenplay but utterly reverses its value. Dickey's Ed is comforted by the memories of his experiences on the river since they recall his intimate connection to brute reality, to a primitiveness that has effected a reconciliation between him and his world. Boorman's Ed is disquieted by his memories, for they represent the fall from an innocent and civilized ignorance into the sinful knowledge of human nature and culture. The journey downriver makes Ed recognize the extent to which everydayness is bought at the price of repression, for this is the price which, in lying to the police and others, he must pay to return to domestic comfort. The film's Ed has internalized the river, but his fear is that what the river covers will be exposed; internalization, in other words, can be achieved only at the cost of continuing surveillance, and it is banal—if still significant—that this frightening image returns to him in his dream, an element of the cultural unconscious that surfaces, unwilled, in his own.

From Dickey's vision of the transcendence that attends the simultaneous embrace of and retreat from the usually hidden sources of American vitality (an experience that justifies continued living in an ersatz consumer society, and even a direct role, through work in advertising, in the continuing reification of human relations), Boorman, with Dickey's largely disappointed connivance, has created a much more pessimistic image. For the film undermines the notion of "deliverance," suggesting, as it does, both the failure of subjectivity to master phenomenal experience and the uneasiness—both Ed's and our own—which necessarily results from the fall into knowledge.

NOTES

1. Richard Slotkin, *Regeneration Through Violence: The Mythology of the American Frontier* (Middletown, Conn.: Wesleyan University Press, 1973), esp. the chapters on the frontier myth in Romantic literature and on Leatherstocking.

2. The quote is from a review in the *Saturday Review* (28 March 1970), as quoted by Donald J. Greiner, "The Harmony of Bestiality in James Dickey's *Deliverance*," *South Carolina Review* 5 (1972): 43. Greiner's article is a useful source for reviewers' reactions to the novel.

3. *Literature/Film Quarterly* 2 (Winter 1974): 58.

4. I quote from the paperback edition (New York: Dell Publishing, 1971): 146–47; hereafter cited parenthetically in the text.

5. "The Great American Hunter, or Ideological Content in the Novel," *College English* 34 (November 1972): 186.

6. *Literature/Film Quarterly* 1 (Winter 1973); the quotation from Lewis is on p. 280.

Erotic Pantheism in James Dickey's "Madness"

LAURENCE LIEBERMAN

In "Madness," a work ostensibly pure animal fable, James Dickey has written one of his most personal—and, indeed, personally revealing—poems. Under the guise of the astonishing story—immediately rising to the permanence of myth or legend—of a bizarre sexual encounter between the household dog and a "rabid female fox," Dickey has enacted his most powerful allegory for the terror of human sex. Sexual terror, the turmoil of even normal ordinary sex, is his true subject, disguise it as he will with the southern gothic tall tale. To be stricken by *illicit* sexual craving is equivalent to being infected with rabies. The only cure may be death by beheading: decapitation is synonymous with the total loss of rational controls, a descent into sexual *madness*. Perhaps the only *help* for such an affliction, if you happen to be a poet of genius as well as a man-soul prey to strong sexual passions, is to write a work of utmost purgative release:

> . . . strangers
> Cut off the head and carried and held it
> Up, blazing with consequence   blazing
>   With freedom saying   bringing
>   Help   help   madness   help.

I

At the outset, "Madness" achieves with flawless consistency of tone the illusion of a household pet's point of view. The voice of the speaker captures the total innocence and naivete of the dog persona with a matchless command of nuance and an economy of style that recalls Faulkner's orchestration of the idiot Benjy in *The Sound and the Fury:*

> Lay in the house mostly living
> With children when they called   mostly

Originally published in the *South Carolina Review* 26 (Spring 1994): 72–86; reprinted in *Beyond the Muse of Memory: Essays in Contemporary American Poetry,* by Lieberman (Columbia: University of Missouri Press, 1995). Reprinted by permission.

Under the table begging for scraps lay with the head
On a family foot
Or stretched out on a side,
Firesided. Had no running
Running, ever.
Would lie relaxed, eyes dim

With appreciation, licking the pure contentment
Of long   long notched
Black lips. Would lap up milk like a cat and swim clear
In brown grateful eyes. . . .

The keynote, here, is excessive comfort, too much soft effortless pleasure. To subject a wild animal—the wild animal locked in ourselves, by inference—to a life of passivity and indulgence is unnatural, against nature. It would be to invite the lawless Dionysian side of our species to revolt, and to seek out the wild orgiastic counterpart of our neglected hot-blooded being in the world at large:

. . . it was best
To get up and wander
Out, out of sight. Help me was shouted
To the world of females   anyone will do
To the smoking leaves.

Love could be smelt. All things burned deep
In eyes that were dim from looking
At the undersides of tables   patient with being the god
Of small children.

Help me, the desperate plea for risk, for danger, is murmured by the soul of one afflicted with a sickness unto death from inactivity, any wild fate to be preferred to such enfeeblement.

The portrait of the female fox that follows is almost too transparently humanized, but Dickey's comic wit and his command of southern vernacular strike the authentic ring to our ears. His zany caricature of "a god's wild mistress" could take almost any form, creaturely or mythic: centaur, mermaid, or minotaur (I'm reminded of Yeats's poems about sexual relations between divinities and humans, "Leda and the Swan" and "News for the Delphic Oracle"— *Nymphs and satyrs copulate in the foam*), so why not a rabid lady fox?

And there

She lay, firesided, bushy-assed, her head
On the ground wide open, slopping soap:
Come   come close
She said like a god's

Wild mistress said come
On boy, I'm what you come

Out here in the bushes for. She burned alive
In her smell and the eyes she looked at burned
With gratitude, thrown a point-eared scrap
Of the world's women, hot-tailed and hunted. . . .

Like Dickey's "Sheep Child," this fox partakes of the supernatural realm, part goddess, part human. Who among us could resist the allure of her ambrosial smell? Does she burn with earthly fires, or fires of the demonic netherworld? Both, perhaps. No matter, the domestic pooch burns back, flame for flame, whatever the mystic consequences. The language of the encounter is so tactile and boldly rough-hewn, so vividly earth-laden, a reader could easily overlook the gnostic, or spiritual, overtones:

. . . she bit down
Hard on a great yell
To the house being eaten alive
By April's leaves. Bawled; they came and found.

II

A half-veiled erotic pantheism emerges here. The dog protagonist's plea, his cry for help, was "shouted" to "the world of females" *and* to "the smoking leaves," and both the fox and leaves have answered—with a vengeance. He'd been starved and hungered, equally, for sex and Nature: now both privations are resolved in the one fierce bite the fox takes into his snout.

As the drama unfolds, *firesided* evolves a startling double meaning. To begin, it suggests the light and warmth cast by the safe domestic fireplace upon the exposed sidehair of the dog lying by the hearth. Coddled and pampered by the children, he has been *firesided* into a defenseless stupor. The word, then, evokes all domestic security and placidity. But the fox lying in ambush, "firesided, bushy-assed," is on fire with her own heat, "burned alive in her smell." Now the word's overtones elicit danger, lethal risk. All the vocabulary of heat, of burning, has shifted from domestic safety, household comforts, to sexual incinerations, sexual flamings: "She burned alive / in her smell," while, in response, his eyes "burned / with gratitude," and, finally, he's "being eaten alive / by April's leaves."

Somehow, the leaves of Spring are in complicity with the rabid fox. Her rabies, not an isolated private affliction, runs rampant through Nature, and this erotic spirit is the secret pantheistic deity of this poem's cosmos. The leaves, then, by their multiplicity, are the aptest medium for this pervasive spirit. The dog shouted his yearning to the leaves, quite as intensely as to "the world of females," and hence, the leaves partake of his ravishment by the fox. This rabies can spread like *wildfire,* since the leaves themselves are secret carriers of the bacilli. At first reading, the rabid fox, alone, strikes us as being the demon who spreads the infection. But we come to know, tipped off by the luminous chain of images, that Nature hiddenly collaborates with the sex-crazed fox. In his mania, his feverish delirium, the stricken dog may dream that all the leaves are pecking at his flesh ("being eaten alive / by April's leaves"). Ultimately, they may appear to become as rapacious and all-eating as Hitchcock's birds.

The children and "friends and family," hurrying to rescue the wounded pet, seem totally oblivious to signs of the impending tragedy. Their casual aplomb intensifies the ominous feel of secret terror building, the explosion that will devastate the placid domestic order and balance of the family household:

> The children cried
>
> Helping tote to the full moon
> Of the kitchen   "I carried the head"   O full of eyes
> Heads kept coming across, and friends and family
> Hurt   hurt
> The spirit of the household, on the kitchen
> Table being thick-sewed   they saying it was barbed
> Wire looked like
> It got him, and he had no business running
>
> Off like that. . . .

Do I detect a southern drawl in these minimal snippets of local speech? The few telling phrases of dialect seem to evoke the total verbal ambiance that surrounds the scene. In their domestic malaise, the adults and kids, alike, de-flate the dog's injury, putting it down to a mere run-in with barbed wire, little guessing that the tear in his muzzle will escalate to deep lacerations in the very fabric of their well-ordered social milieu. They suppose that the dog's wounds can be explained away as mild punishment for infraction of yard rules, "they saying it was barbed / Wire looked like / It got him, and he had no business running / Off like that. . . ."

But we, who have been briefed by the momentous overtones of charged language, know that a powerful demonic ritual has been set in motion, some-thing like an ancient curse or plague upon the clan (a larger social unit than a single family comes into play, here—the whole expanded familial community of this township), from the moment that Great Nature herself commanded the dog to run astray, ". . . and it was best / To get up and wander / Out, out of sight."

Now there would be no turning back, for even the "rain had sown thick and gone / from the house where the living / was done," and no amount of *thick-sewing* of the dog's rent lips with surgical black thread could undo the fateful scenario that has been decreed and initiated by the rain deity. Likewise, the reference to "the full moon of the kitchen" alerts us to the vampirism that

has occurred, and the consequent transformation of the dog victim to werewolf
that is quietly taking place below the kitchen table following the lip-sutures, a
mere cosmetic patch-up, hiding the deeper wound:

> . . . Black lips curled as they bathed off
> Blood, bathed blood. Staggered up under
> The table making loud
> A low-born sound, and went feeling
>
> For the outer limits
> Of the woods   felt them break and take in
> The world . . .

III

Though the drama in "Madness" is ascribed to a Deep-South, American
setting, we now catch the expansive nuance of an international and timeless
sweep of voice ("take in the world"). James Dickey, once again, starting from
a narrowly localized episode, sets limitless vortices in motion. If we have moved
beyond the "outer limits of the woods," we have been carried along by the
synchronicities of the countless leaves acting in concert:

> Fireheaded   formed a thought
> Of Spring   of trees in wildfire
> Of the mind speeded up   and put all thirst
>
> Into the leaves. They grew
> Unlimited. Soap boiled
> Between black lips. . . .

A reader senses that all reckless unbounded possibility looms here—the
spirit of wild abandon is in the air. Like the marvelous psychic adventures, the
out-of-body travels of the stewardess in Dickey's earlier poem "Falling," the
dog's "mind speeded up" will crash through all barriers. We now perceive this
to be a poem about mental capacities racing beyond the lawful, normal, domestic boundaries. The mentality is so radically new that it threatens to transform
everything and everyone outside it into its own new reality. Hence, the terror
of all other creatures that soon follows. Their very cosmos is intimidated by this
totally unfamiliar alien force, which sends them all into panic, a community of
repression. They, too, will rage "beyond their limits," mobilizing a power to
match and contain the power of insurrection unleashed, as revealed by the
rabid dog's scary "low-born sound":

> . . . the spirit ran
> Ran with house-hair
> Burr-picking madly   and after came

<blockquote>
Men   horses   spirits
Of households leaping crazily beyond
Their limits dragging their bodies by the foaming throat through grass
And beggar-lice and by the red dust
Road where men blazed and roared
With their shoulders   blew it down and apart where it ran
And lay down on the earth of God's
One foot and the foot beneath the table kicked
The white mouth shut: this was something

In Spring in mild brown eyes   as strangers
Cut off the head and carried and held it
Up, blazing with consequence   blazing
With freedom saying   bringing
Help   help   madness   help
</blockquote>

Where does all the access of power and intensity spring from, we might ask? The emotional *seizure* that erupts, here, recalls the chaotic upheaval in the social order of a southern family triggered by incest in Faulkner's *Sound and the Fury,* The violation of forbidden taboos, as in Dickey's earlier poem "The Sheep Child," unleashes a primitive brute energy. And there is no stopping this titanic flood of lawless passions until the violence and tragedy have run their course.

IV

I'm awed, afresh, by the celerity of syntax in "Madness." The speed of delivery in this poem, from first strophe to last, strikes me as unique in Dickey's entire oeuvre. The principal action could easily have sustained a poem two or three times this length. Merely to say that the work has pared away all excess is to miss the point. Dickey's technique advances to a bold thrust of delivery, a mastery of ellipsis in grammar and syntax, a control of elisions that surpasses any of his previous work. His technique, as the poem unfolds, achieves progressively a tempo—a pacing, so to say—of *breathlessness.* And this crescendo peaks in a passage near the finish in which the active verbs seem to multiply, incrementally, without strain or imbalance—there's so much raw lively intense happening, we don't think to question the quantitative proportions of style, parts of speech, or the like: "flaming . . . ran / Ran . . . burr-picking madly . . . leaping crazily . . . dragging . . . foaming . . . blazed and roared . . . blew it down and apart where it ran / And lay down . . . ."

I include a few adverbs in my linkage, since they are so closely tied to the verbs they amplify—never merely modifiers—in these marvelously condensed lines just preceding the poem's final coda. The passage from which I extracted, above, is the closest approach to pure streamlined action I can recall in any contemporary poetry. This verse measure and medium are the Ferrari or Maserati speedster on the verse race track, the full velocity achieved—as in the case of the auto-czars invoked—with no loss of elegance or classy verve of meters.

Then, I'm equivalently struck by the magical deft pullback of the denouement:

> . . . blew it down and apart where it ran
> And lay down on the earth of God's
> One foot and the foot beneath the table kicked
> The white mouth shut . . .

Serenity, quiescence! Why aren't our hearts still pounding after the violent *effort*-ful gallop by all the players? How, indeed, does Dickey manage to scale down the feral syntactic hopscotch by so few jaunty shifts, all ease and lightness of modulation? I note that we have swung full circle in the color spectrum as well, moving from "black lips curled as they bathed off / Blood, bathed blood" to "kicked / The white mouth shut." How do *black lips* come together in a *white mouth?* Is it simply the bloodless paleness of death? Or more soapy rabies foam bubbling out between the lips? So attentive Dickey is to the least detail of accurate anatomy, whatever the symbolic overtones to be sought, we feel that he must have witnessed a dying dog's black lips close on a final whiteness, whiteness blazing with all its inexplicable mystery. Plain honest observation, rather than bold invention, seems to have been the guiding principle behind Dickey's imagery here. In any case, the sudden color reversion from black to white seems a perfectly apt visual counterpart to the abrupt deceleration of the action, the calming of tone and metrical pulse just prior to the poem's closing stanza.

The stanza form that Dickey has improvised for "Madness" resembles a gyroscope, a freely variable spinning top. Most stanzas whirl and interweave very long lines with short, the voice bridging the gap between one unit and another in mid-sentence, the spun top rarely falling to rest before the very last line, which is not a conventional line, after all, but four naked words waved like flags, or pennants, between blank spaces:

> Help   help   madness   help

In mid-line, throughout the poem, spaces usually stand in for punctuation marks. Dickey gets more than the usual vigor of swerve or tilt from surprise line endings. Often, one, two, or three word units take a measure of breath-space to themselves. Several short units, in succession, as in the last line quoted above, may capture a rhythm all their own, which we can ponder as singular moments, fascinating entities of style, apart from their contexts.

V

The great pivot in "Madness," the irreversible shift in its scope from one family household to the full-blown pastoral community, is the moment when the now-rabid dog runs amok and bites "the youngest child":

> . . . the house
> Spirit jumped up beyond   began to run shot
> Through the yard and bit down
> On the youngest child. And when it sprang down
> And out across the pasture, the grains of its footprints leapt
> Free, where horses that shied from its low
>
> New sound were gathered, and men swung themselves
> Up to learn what Spring
> Had a new way to tell, by bringing up
> And out the speed of the fields. A long horn blew . . .

Immediately, we know that this second bite-down shall have far-reaching repercussions; it is more horrific than the first love bite, for it shall wreak havoc on all sectors of the rural society. Once the human child has been assaulted, the poem's equation tilts, inverts, all craziness redoubled, leaving no child, adult, dog or horse untouched. One moment, the entire farm municipality lay dormant, unsuspecting, as the dog's rabies slowly incubated; the next, "long horn blew," summoning all souls—humans and animals of the hunt, in tandem—to assemble into an army of resistance.

Simultaneously, too, warring factions in nature—opposed divinities, say— may be perceived to choose up sides in the battle that follows. Pantheistic spirits may be at odds and come to blows, as enacted by the players they each inhabit in the drama. If the rabid dog and fox draw their superabundant energy from the leaves, from "trees in wildfire," and even wild burrs snatched from the weeds as the dog runs across the pasture ("house-hair / burr-picking madly"), the men and horses draw their fiery power of the chase from the turf of pastureland itself ("to learn what Spring / Had a new way to tell by bringing up / And out, of the fields").

Their sole antagonist, the enemy that rouses them to unified battle, is the dog's "mad head," which rages with a boundless supernatural force, a surge of erotic energy that we are reminded was conceived in one frenzied chomp of "the weather of love running wild":

> . . . the mad head sang
> Along the furrows   bouncing and echoing from earth
> To earth through the body
> Turning   doubling back
> Through the weather of love running wild and the horses full
>
> Of strangers coming after. . . .

The head seems to have become an autonomous entity, whirling in its own orbit, self-hurtled, as if disengaged already from the dog's trunk, prophesying the actual decapitation soon to follow. This passage, more than any other perhaps, suggests that the infection in the dog's blood forms a tributary with the intense love currents rivering through Nature. The head sings in its passionate streaming, its juices reverberating with the "furrows" of just-tilled farmland, a life-flow passing to and fro between the patches of earth it courses over; "doubling back," the head keeps drawing fire from the poison of the original love bite, and that fount is "running wild" through its blood vessels.

Finally, the currents surging through the dog and Nature seem to overspill into an electro-magnetic field, picked up by even the long segments of fence wire:

> Fence wire fell and rose
> Flaming with messages as the spirit ran
> Ran with house-hair
> Burr-picking madly . . .

Not the mistaken "barbed wire," this, which the deluded family has supposed gave the dog its slash. No, this "fence wire" seems to be everywhere continuous in the fields and, as such, it picks up the charge of the various creatures rocketing past. This mystic fence wire, like the wire in Dickey's early short poem named after it, serves as a secret conduit for fevers or passions coursing through the living creatures that grasp it, or zoom near:

> . . . a man who holds
> His palm on the top tense strand
> With the whole farm feeding slowly
> And nervously into his hand.
>
> If the wire were cut anywhere
> All his blood would fall to the ground
> And leave him standing and staring
> With a face as white as a Hereford's.

("Fence Wire")

A force like lightning that can surge, alike, through animal flesh, metal fence wire, and tree trunks, this fierce charge of rabies—emanating from "the weather of love"—finally becomes a pervasive interconnecting effluence in the cosmology of "Madness." It is a wave pulse that easily leaps the usual genetic hurdles between animal species, or the atomic barriers between flesh and metal and wood and leaf cells. This effluence partakes of all beings and atomic structures in the cosmos of the fields. As the rabies of love grows even stronger, it pulls more and more of the energies of the very atmosphere, earth and air and fire commingled, into its vortex.

In counter-reaction, all humans and creatures in pursuit have been yanked into modes "beyond their limits," stretching their skins or hides to constrain the dog's dangerous new identity:

> And when it sprang down
> And out across the pasture, the grains of its footprints leapt
> Free, where horses that shied from its low

> New sound were gathered, and men swung themselves
>   Up to learn what Spring
>   Had a new way to tell, by bringing up
>   And out the speed of the fields. A long horn blew. . . .
>
>   Men   horses   spirits
>   Of households leaping crazily beyond
> Their limits, dragging their bodies by the foaming throat through grass
>   And beggar-lice and by the red dust
>   Road where men blazed and roared
> With their shoulders   blew it down and apart where it ran . . .

The new reality, the revolutionary new element in this smug selfcomplacent backwoods culture, is heralded by the dog's "low new sound," which is scary and threatening. It is the voice of rebellion, the spirit of raw sexual freedom ("the weather of love running wild"). Even the horses *shied* away from it, at first. It is recognized to be a power so strong, it must either be vanquished and suppressed, or it may convert all things, all other beings and entities, into its radical new essence. And by a stunning irony, implicit in the language and imagery of this passage, the various repressive agents mobilized and assembled to destroy the dog-carrier of this plague of love bacilli seem to be infected already by a rabies-like fever themselves, when they are just on the verge of catching up with the fugitive runaway hound and blowing him "down and apart" with their rifles: "leaping crazily beyond / Their limits, dragging their bodies by the foaming throat through grass . . ."

Their throats, too, are *foaming,* whether from rabies or some equally abnormal fever and brain-twisting passion, the counterfever of resistance, say, putting down the erotic uprising. Such *madness,* it would seem, can only be countered and defused by an equal and opposing madness.

VI

James Dickey's imagery in "Madness" compels the reader's ear to accept the amazing claim that inanimate things can become the vehicle and medium for ghostly spirits sweeping across the poem's landscape. Doubtless, this is a poem about the miracle world that lurks, always, within normal everyday happenings. It is the Other world of Holy Specters crying out for momentary rest stops in the world of matter, flesh or inanimate forms, interchangeably:

>   Staggered up under
>   The table making loud
>   A low-born sound, and went feeling
>
>   For the outer limits
>   Of the woods   felt them break and take in
> The world   the frame turn loose and the house
> Not mean what it said it was.

To state this unique mode of happening in the universe in terms of the house inscrutably hatching into a new form, an utterly novel identity: what a marvelous way to articulate the total annulment of domestic safety, all normal stability and expectation gone awry. A fantastic new species of event has taken over the scheme of things. The house, itself, speaks with a new voice—its speech, like the woods' speech, threatens to alter, permanently, the world around it.

The specter, the message carrier, inhabits one host after another: the dog's larynx, the woods, the house frame, the "grains" of the dog's "footprints," which "leapt free" of his doggy paws, the fence wire which "fell and rose / flaming with messages." That disembodied spirit, perhaps, is the real persona in this enchanting fantasia that, like Shakespeare's *Ariel,* can inhabit a wide succession of beings and entities as it works its way across the poem's wildly expansive spiritual trajectory.

As I said at the outset, sexual terror is the central motif. The spirit of eros lurks everywhere: it takes possession of the fox, passes to the domestic dog, and finally, is unleashed upon us all. The demonic possession becomes all-encompassing, and only an act of uttermost purgation, like the lancing of a great pus-swollen boil, can set things aright. Hence, the ritual beheading of the dog.

Polarities abound, everyplace, in the poem's imagery. Many key images, double-edged, cut two ways. Towards the last, two feet are mentioned separately, in the same line: "And lay down on the earth of God's / One foot and the foot beneath the table kicked / The white mouth shut."

"God's / One foot," the final resting place for the dog's head, is earth itself, while the "foot beneath the table" belongs to the master of the household, tapping the family dog's head for the last time. The dog, himself, was repeatedly designated the "god of small children," always printed with lower case *g,* his head by the fireplace reclining on "God's foot," differentiated by capital G. The "barbed wire," early on, signifies a mundane boundary, lacking all resonance or overtones. It gives place to the "fence wire," which "fell and rose / Flaming with messages," a luminous conveyer of truth or vision. "The smoking leaves," lying dormant after the leaf bonfire by the yard, are supplanted by the leaves of "trees in wildfire" that "grew unlimited," these the direct recipient of the rabid waking dog's new expanded consciousness ("the mind speeded up"). The dog himself who, prior to the central action, "had no running / Running, ever," compresses a whole lifetime's running into an unstoppable mad dash to his gundown death.

And finally, the dog's *head,* forever lying by the fireside or petted and tapped into lassitude under the kitchen table, by a single blast of love-sickness, is sent into violent oscillations between furrows of farmland, "bouncing and echoing from earth to earth." Then, hacked from its body by vigilantes, the head is held aloft for all to see in the passing procession of countryfolk, paraded as a trophy of the hunt, then foisted into the air as a warning to future transgressors of the civil order (not unlike the historic southern lynchings of blacks accused of rape, burglary, or lesser offenses):

as strangers
Cut off the head and carried and held it
Up, blazing with consequence.

VII

We are briefed, repeatedly, that Spring, "the weather of love," is the secret impresario, the mover and shaker behind the scenes of "Madness:"

(1)

That was then, before the Spring
Lay down and out
Under a tree, not far but a little far and out
Of sight of the house.

(2)

The head, lying on God's foot firesided
Fireheaded   formed a thought
Of Spring   of trees in wildfire
Of the mind speeded up. . . .

(3)

. . . men swung themselves
Up to learn what Spring
Had a new way to tell. . . .

(4)

. . . this was something

In Spring in mild brown eyes   as strangers
Cut off the head and carried and held it
Up, blazing with consequence   blazing
With freedom saying   bringing
Help   help   madness   help.

The last reference to spring, which closes the poem, is the quietest. But it's the most spooky, premonitory, in its warning that even the least aggressive being in the safe domestic household can become, instantaneously and unwittingly, the agent of immense destructive passions. Don't be fooled by those "mild brown eyes"; they, too, can become limitlessly love crazed.

James Dickey: Southern Visionary as Celestial Navigator

MONROE SPEARS

Some years ago James Dickey responded to an interviewer's question about the sense in which he was a southern writer with the ringing declaration that "the best thing that ever happened to me was to have been born a Southerner. First as a man and then as a writer." He would not want to feel that he was limited in any way by being a southerner or was expected to "indulge in the kind of regional chauvinism that has sometimes been indulged in by southern writers," he said, but the tragic history of the South gave him a set of values, "some of which are deplorable, obviously, but also some of which are the best things that I have ever had as a human being." Southerners, he suggested, let their ancestors help: "I have only run-of-the-mill ancestors but they knew that one was supposed to do certain things. Even the sense of evil, which is very strong with me, would not exist if I had no sense of what evil was."[1]

Dickey is convinced, then, that being southern is central to the way he thinks and feels, but he does not want to be thought of as *merely* regional; he suggests that the most valuable southern quality is a special awareness of the personal past in the sense of inheriting traditions and codes of values from one's ancestors, and a special awareness of the regional past in its full tragic meaning, including the sense of evil. But rather than continue to depend on Dickey's own statements, now that I have used him to run interference for me, let me try to define more specifically just what kind of southern writer he is and how he is related to other southern writers.

The obvious starting point is his relation to the Fugitive-Agrarian groups. Except for Donald Davidson, all of the Fugitives and most of the Agrarians had left Vanderbilt long before Dickey arrived; thus, there was no possibility of personal influence. But Ransom, Tate, and Warren had become major figures in the literary world, and Brooks, Jarrell, and others were establishing high reputations. Vanderbilt students and faculty—most of them—were proud of the connection, and the campus was alive with legends of the days when giants

Originally published in *American Ambitions: Selected Essays on Literary and Cultural Themes,* by Spears (Baltimore and London: Johns Hopkins University Press, (1987), 69–86. Reprinted by permission of the Johns Hopkins University Press.

had walked that very earth. In this context creative writing seemed exciting and important to a good many students, and so did being a southerner. It seems plain enough that Dickey's commitment to poetry and his awareness of his identity as a southerner owed much both to his reading of the Fugitive-Agrarian writers and to the Vanderbilt tradition of respect for serious writing. R. V. Cassill is amusing but quite wrong when he portrays Dickey as a rebel-lious Young Turk who refused to conform to the southern ruling circles by speaking "smartly about Miss Eudora and Mr. Ransom" and being "reverent about Traveler" while snickering down Whitman and the midwesterners.[2] In the first place, the southern literary establishment, insofar as there ever was one, was not reverential about Traveler; Tate abandoned his biography of Lee because he had ceased to believe in him, and the *Fugitive* announced early that it fled nothing so much as the genteel pieties of the Old South. In the second place, Dickey was recognized early by the southerners and usually given what-ever awards they had to offer. Although he never had the rare good luck that the Fugitives did of close association with a group of like-minded peers, the fact that the tradition of serious writing was still alive at Vanderbilt kept him from the near-total isolation of a writer such as Faulkner. Tate has gone on record with the opinion that Dickey is the best poet the South has produced since the heyday of the Fugitives, and Warren has said in the *South Carolina Review* that he is "among Jim's greatest admirers"[3] and in the *New York Times Book Review* that *The Zodiac* is a major achievement, worthy of comparison to Hart Crane's *The Bridge*.

In recent years some nostalgic epigones of the Fugitive-Agrarians at Van-derbilt have written requiems for the Southern Literary Renascence, maintain-ing that it has suffered death by melancholy. Their thesis is that southern literature has been dying since World War II, when modernism triumphed over the South, and any hope is illusory. I have never quite believed in the Southern Renascence, suspecting that it was created artificially, like Frankenstein's mon-ster, in the laboratories of academic critics, and reports of the loss of such artificial life need not disturb us. At any rate, Dickey, thank God, like Madison Jones and others of his contemporaries at Vanderbilt, and like such older south-ern writers as Robert Penn Warren, Walker Percy, and Eudora Welty, does not know he is dead and refuses to lie down. As stubbornly as the astronomical phenomena that Galileo saw through his telescope in spite of the irrefutable arguments of his learned opponents that they could not possibly be there, the works of these writers continue to exist and to grow, unquestionably alive. Most of us, however we may feel about the modern world, would rather have the poems and novels than have a thesis about it demonstrated; and our own Poe has taught us to beware of premature burial. So we will be grateful that some of our writers flourish and we will refuse to abandon hope.

While Dickey seems to have no interest in Agrarianism as a political or economic program, he shares with the Agrarians a deep concern about man's relation to nature and the distortions produced in this relation by the increasing urbanism and commercialism of our society. Dickey's true subject, however, is neither rural nor urban, but *suburban*. Because southern cities are smaller, their suburbs are not wholly distinct from nearby small towns, and both maintain more connection with the country than their northern counterparts. Compare, in this respect, those Dickey represents with John Cheever's dormitory suburbs around New York, with swimming pools linked in one giant fantasy. But both writers describe the modern nuclear family—nuclear both in being small and without the connections families used to have and in being under the threat of nuclear war. In these respects there is little difference between North and South, though the South may be slightly less nuclear simply because it is less urban.

Dickey's remarkable achievement is that he has taken his subject seriously and redeemed the word *suburban* from its comic or pejorative overtones. Instead of describing bored wives at the country club, adulteries in commuterdom, hysteria and desperation breaking out from the pressures of enforced uniformity, or the absurdities of Little League baseball, he shows us a suburban world that is still in touch with a nature that remains wild, not tamed or prettified. Dickey's suburbs have no cute ceramic animals, no dear little Bambis or gnomes on the lawns, but the call of the real wild, and inner nature answering to outer. *Deliverance* is the most extended example, with its gradual revelation that the wilderness has always been present in the suburbs, whose security is an illusion. On the other hand, "The Firebombing" treats the homeowner's longing for security sympathetically because of his vivid awareness of its precariousness in view of what he did to his Japanese counterparts. "Dark Ones" transmutes into poetry the eventing ritual of the arrival home of the commuters.

To say that Dickey is a visionary poet is a paralyzingly obvious assertion. Almost every poem he has written describes a vision of one kind or another, and in recent years he has dealt explicitly with the loss of physical vision in works such as the unfinished novel "Cahill Is Blind." Perhaps he will become the patron or mascot of ophthalmologists, as Wallace Stevens was adopted by ice-cream manufacturers after writing "The Emperor of Ice-Cream." Yet the truism is worth repeating, for it says something about his relation to southern literature. Dickey belongs to the line of visionaries running from Blake through Rimbaud and Whitman to such modern exemplars as Hart Crane, George Barker, Dylan Thomas, and Theodore Roethke. It is noteworthy that there are no southern names on this list, since as far as I know there are few southern poets who could be called visionary. Tate and Warren, for example, are in their different ways primarily concerned with history, with attempting to relate the past to the present. Perhaps one reason good southern poets have shied away from the visionary mode is that they remember how much older southern poetry was emasculated by the necessity of avoiding politics and, hence, driven from reality into fake vision. The old southern tradition of escapism and sentimentality—of "gutless swooning," to borrow a phrase from Faulkner—was certainly one thing the Fugitives were fleeing. I am afraid Henry Timrod often exemplified this tradition, and Tate surely intended a contrast with Timrod's "Ode Sung at the Decoration of the Graves of the Confederate Dead at Magnolia Cemetery" when he wrote his own ironic "Ode to the Confederate Dead." Timrod's "Ethnogenesis" is a kind of vision, it is true, but appallingly detached from any sense of reality: In it the new Confederacy, with its economy based on cotton and slavery, is seen as bringing wealth, moral improvement, and a better climate to the whole world.

Before Dickey, the only southern poet who was a true visionary was Poe; and his visions, as every schoolchild knows, were very peculiar indeed. Although one might argue that Dickey's poetic rhythms are often incantory, and intended to put the reader into a kind of trance state, they are far more subtle than Poe's blatantly hypnagogic music; and, though both poets are most interested in states of consciousness beyond normal waking life, they are not interested in the same states. Much as I would like to, I do not see how I can make a case for any resemblance beyond the fact that they are both visionaries. Dickey has none of Poe's morbid preoccupation with death, his concern being rather with new and different modes of life; you cannot imagine him saying that the ideal poetic subject is the *death* of a beautiful woman. Poe strives obsessively to make the reader feel the horror of being a living soul in a dead body, of an irreparable crack or split in the edifice of the mind, of long-ago irremediable losses. Dickey, in contrast, produces in the reader a new awareness of nonhuman forms of life, from dogs on the feet to owls in the woods and panthers in the zoo; the poems seek new forms of union, wider possibilities of consciousness. Mind and body are not separated as they are in Poe, but totally fused. Finally, Dickey gets into his poems a solid feeling of everyday reality and normal experience before moving to transcend them. It is this feeling or rendering that distinguishes him not only from Poe but also from the kind of fantasy that is now so enormously popular in movies and cheap fiction. Dickey's visions have nothing in common with these self-indulgent daydreams unrelated to any kind of reality.

Dickey's most ambitious visionary poem is certainly *The Zodiac* (1976). It is, I may concede to begin with, impossibly ambitious and hence foredoomed to failure. Dickey has said (in unpublished interviews) that he knew it would be a failure but is glad he did it and has a special affection for it because it explores that part of creativity that depends on being drunk. Robert Penn Warren observed that no poem since Hart Crane's *The Bridge* has been "so stylistically ambitious and has aimed to stir such depths of emotion," and that *The Zodiac* "can be said to be about the over-ambitiousness of poetry—even as it celebrates its ambitiousness." But, mentioning some of its limitations and defects, he finds that "the audacity of imagery, assemblage of rhythms, the power of language redeems all."[4]

To write a long poem that will rival the epics of the ancient world is still, as it has been since the Renaissance, the ultimate challenge for modern poets.

(The shores of literary history are littered with the massive and curious wreckage of their attempts, from Ronsard's *Françiade* through Cowley's *Davideis,* Davenant's *Gondibert,* Chamberlayne's *Pharonnida,* and Blackmore's *The Creation* to Pound's *Cantos* and Williams's *Paterson.* Only *Paradise Lost* is still afloat, with the comic epics in verse from *The Rape of the Lock* to *Don Juan,* and in prose from *Tom Jones* to *Ulysses.*) Because James Dickey is a poet who has always sought out challenges, scorned the safe and prudent way, and aimed unblushingly at the sublime, accepting the roles of Icarus and Prometheus with full awareness of their risks, it is not at all surprising that he should attempt a long poem. (Long, that is, for a modern poem: more than twice the length of *The Waste Land.*) Nor is it surprising that *The Zodiac* should deal with nothing less than the meaning of the visible universe. What is surprising is that *The Zodiac* should be neither southern nor even American in subject, but based on a Dutch poem with a Dutch protagonist whose experiences are distinctively European.

According to the dust jacket of *The Zodiac,* Dickey "finds inspiration in the experiences of a real-life Dutch sailor, Hendrik Marsman, who during a lifetime at sea was bedazzled by the constellations and possessed by the mysteries of the zodiac. On the verge of madness he wrote bits of poetry, and it is from these fragments of Marsman's verse that Dickey has fashioned" his poem. This statement is staggeringly inaccurate and misleading, even for a jacket blurb. Marsman (1899–1940) was a well-known poet in real life, not a mad sailor. The publication of his *Verzen* in 1923 was a major event in Dutch literary history and established the Vitalist movement. After this he wrote mainly critical and narrative prose, editing an influential magazine, *Vrije Bladen,* beginning in 1925. After traveling for some years, he returned home to fight totalitarianism. His last great poem, *Tempel en Kruis (Temple and Cross),* a kind of poetic autobiography, appeared in 1939. *The Zodiac* is a part of this work. It is not a collection of bits or fragments, but a carefully wrought long poem in twelve sections.

Dickey's own statement in his headnote that his poem is "based on" Marsman's poem but is "in no sense a translation" is accurate and generous, with its concluding "homage to Hendrik Marsman, lost at sea, 1940–," but it does not convey a full sense of the relationship. While Dickey's poem is not a translation, it is an "imitation" in the sense popularized by Robert Lowell. Because Dickey reproduces Marsman's situation, protagonist, narrative, and principal images, each of his twelve sections corresponding in detail to its original, his poem is rather closer to its source than are many of Lowell's "imitations." Though naturally enough, Dickey, like Lowell, wants the reader to see his work primarily as a contemporary poem, its relation to its original constitutes a significant dimension of its meaning.

Where did Dickey discover Marsman's poem—which is, to say the least, not well known in America? Probably in the *Sewanee Review,* where it appeared in 1947.[5] A. J. Barnouw, the translator, reprinted it in an anthology, *Coming*

After, the following year; but because Dickey was certainly reading the magazine in those years at Vanderbilt (his first published poem appeared in it), it seems likely that he encountered it there. Whether it lay fallow in his imagination for nearly thirty years, or was discovered—or rediscovered—by him at some later date is a question of some interest that Dickey does not seem to have answered in any of his subsequent interviews or essays.

The most interesting question, however, is why Dickey chose this poem—certainly unfamiliar to most of his readers—to imitate. My guess is that the Marsman persona was attractive because it provided him with an alternative to his own established role. Writing as Marsman, Dickey has a different mask of the self and different memories. Instead of writing about the South or the wartime Pacific, he writes as a man of an earlier European generation about Amsterdam; instead of writing as a survivor, he is now one who died early in the same war. Even the name *Marsman* may have reinforced this appeal: an author with a message from outer space. But on a deeper level Marsman's poem expresses interests and beliefs that Dickey shares. He has been fascinated by astronomy since he studied it at Vanderbilt and has kept up his interest; a few years ago he completed a correspondence course in celestial navigation and is now a certified marine navigator. His primary religious sense is of "how wild, inexplicable, marvelous, and endless creation is," and religion, he says, "to me involves myself and the universe, and it does not admit of any kind of interme-diary, such as Jesus or the Bible."[6] He would like to be reincarnated as a migra-tory sea bird like a tern or a wandering albatross, he says, and "Reincarnations II" is a vivid imagining of just this possibility. The themes of the aging wan-derer returning home and so finding his own identity, and of the poet's reexam-ination and reaffirmation of his poetic faith and vocation, must also have appealed to Dickey with peculiar force in this poem. "Imitating," then, frees Dickey from his public self and gives him a fresh start at the same time that it provides him with a way of expressing some of his most deeply felt convictions from a different perspective.

Marsman's poem, as translated by Barnouw, is relatively conventional in language and versification. The first section, for example, is in regular blank verse. It begins:

> The man of whom I tell this narrative
> Returned, some time ago, to his native land.
> He has since lived, for nearly a full year,
> Over the peaceful broker's offices. . . .
> The square lies, like an empty crater bowl,
> Amid the agonized obscurity
> Of the dead city's hellish neon light.

(238)

Dickey shatters and transforms this:

> The man I'm telling you about brought himself back alive
> A couple of years ago. He's here,

> Making no trouble
> > over the broker's peaceful. . . .
> The town square below, deserted as a Siberian crater, lies in the middle
> Of his white-writing darkness   stroboscoped   red-stopped by the
> > stammering mess
> > Of the City's unbombed neon, sent through river and many cities
> > > By fourth-class mail from Hell.
>
> > > > > > (9–10)

It is by this transformation of language that Dickey makes the poem his own. He makes it emphatically contemporary and personal, with a tone quite different from Marsman's and with far more dramatic power and variety. In the process of expanding and loosening the language, and through adding new material, Dickey makes his poem about twice the length of Marsman's.

The protagonist (who is never named) is neither Marsman nor Dickey but a dramatic character, given distance and universality by his anonymous condition. As the passage quoted indicates, he is technically not the speaker of the poem, but when he does speak directly the language does not change. The situation and narrative remain exactly what they were in Marsman's poem: The scene is Amsterdam in 1938–39, and, insofar as the protagonist's self-doubt and near-despair have historical referents, they relate to the coming of World War II: "The gods are in pieces / All over Europe"; "What does his soul matter, saved like a Caesar-headed goldpiece, / When the world's dying?"[7]

The central fact about the protagonist is that he is a poet dedicated to the belief that poetry reveals ultimate truth and that it comes from sources above or beyond the rational intellect. Under the pressures of impending catastrophe, both personal and collective, this "drunken and perhaps dying Dutch poet" (to quote Dickey's headnote) reexamines his visionary faith. He feels that he has misused and wasted his life, and he sees his world moving swiftly to destruction. Returning to his home in Amsterdam, he "tried desperately to relate himself, by means of stars, to the universe." He seeks the answer in the stars partly because his father was an amateur astronomer, partly because he has spent much time at sea, and partly because of the ancient and widespread beliefs embodied in the symbolism of the zodiac.

A final word about the relation of Dickey's poem to Marsman's. Perhaps the most important change Dickey makes is to have the protagonist drunk throughout the poem. (Belief in intoxication as a cognitive mode, drunkenness as a way of knowing, has of course always been central to the Dionysiac tradition, in poetry as elsewhere; Dickey is merely making the case an extreme one.) The protagonist becomes more dramatic: His moods change abruptly and are exaggerated by the drink; his rhetoric is unshackled, and his inhibitions and pretenses are gone; we feel that he speaks truth, or tries to. Dickey provides him with a richly symbolic drink, *aquavit:* In Marsman he drinks only on one occasion, and plain gin at that. Dickey also gives him, as the single ornament in his bedroom, a crude mobile made from coat hangers and a shattered whiskey bottle. This is developed from a hint in Marsman, but becomes far more important in Dickey: It comes to represent a little man-made universe and hence the world of Art, a microcosmic counterpart to the zodiac. (Other central features of the poem's symbolism, such as Orion and Pythagoras, have no basis at all in Marsman.)

The essential theme is, in the largest terms, the same as Crane's: the nature of the poetic imagination and its relation to reality. The drama, as by implication in *The Bridge* and more explicitly in such other poems of Crane's as "The Broken Tower," consists in the protagonist's struggle to clarify and reaffirm his faith that poetry is vision and that what it reveals is the deepest truth. Except for walks around Amsterdam, Dickey's protagonist travels only in memory, but his quest is the same as that of countless poet-voyagers from the Ancient Mariner to Crane's Columbus. Like almost all poets who conceive of their art as lamp rather than mirror, he worries that the light will die with the guttering lamp and he vacillates about the reality of what it reveals; but he has the additional problems of distinguishing the hallucinations produced by delirium tremens from reality and of reconciling an awareness of modern astronomy with belief in the significance of the zodiac. There is some dramatic suspense: Will he be able to retain and affirm his faith that poetry can decipher the meaning of the universe through the stars? The zodiac may seem at first a curiously archaic and arbitrary locus of poetic faith, but it is this archaism and richness of mythological association that make it the supreme test case of the relation between man's imagination and God's. To believe in its significance is to bear witness that the universe is not meaningless, that there is a connection between the little world of man and the great world of the stars, between the world inside and that outside.

Waking with a hangover, the protagonist surveys the desolate city from his empty room and reflects on his futile, drunken life:

> He moves among stars.
>   Sure. We all do, but he is star-*crazed*, mad
> With *Einfühling*, with connecting and joining things that lay their
>   meanings
>   Over billions of light years
>   eons of time—Ah,
>   Years of light: billions of them: they are pictures
>   Of some sort of meaning.   He thinks the secret
>   Can be read.   But human faces swim through[8]

and a "young face comes on" like the "faint, structural light / Of Alnilam, without which Orion / would have no center   the Hunter / Could not hunt, in the winter clouds." She "is eternal / As long as *he* lives—the stars and his balls meet." The zodiac is his only way beyond the room: "He must solve

it   must believe it   learn to read it." Seasick and airsick, he looks at the little
mobile he has set spinning like a model of the universe:

> Even drunk
> Even in the white, whiskey-struck, splintered star of a bottle-room
>   dancing
>   He knows he's not fooling himself   he knows
>   Not a damn thing of stars   of God   of space
> Of time   love night death sex fire numbers signs words,
> Not much of poetry.   But by God, we've got a *universe*
> Here
>   Those designs of time are saying *some*thing

>   (17)

He tries to write, but "he can't get rid of himself enough / To write
poetry." But then, in a dawn flash of inspiration, he realizes that "Everybody
writes / With blackness" and that whiteness alone is death; it "is dying / For
human words to raise it from purity   from the grave / Of too much light."
"The secret is that on whiteness you can release / The blackness, / The night
sky." Getting drunker, he imagines himself creating a new beast for the zodiac:
a healing Lobster to replace Cancer. But he cannot sustain the illusion: "I've
failed again. My lobster can't make it / To Heaven." In a brilliant passage, he
reproaches his "old lyre-picking buddy" Pythagoras, but reaffirms allegiance to
him:

> By GOD the poem is *in* there   out there
> Somewhere   the lines that will change
> Everything, like your squares and square roots
>   Creating the heavenly music.
>   It's somewhere,
>   Old great crazy thinker
>   ah
>   farther down
>   In the abyss.   It takes triangular eyes
>   To see Heaven.   I got 'em from you.

>   (25)

He decides to put his favorite constellation, Orion, in the zodiac. The
stars, he says, are gasping for understanding; they have had Ptolemy and Baby-
lon, and now they want Hubbell, Fred Hoyle, and the steady state. "But what
they really want   need / Is a poet and / I'm going to have to be it." The sight
of birds brings him back to earth, and he says

>   . . . . I can always come back to earth.
> But I want to come back with the secret
>   with the poem

That links up my balls and the strange, silent words
      Of God   his scrambled zoo   and my own words
                            and includes the earth
  Among the symbols.

                                    (29)

    The rest of the poem can be quickly summarized. The poet goes out into the neon hell of the city, meditates on a black church, and comes back to nightmares of the one-eyed animals of light:

  . . . Is all this nothing but the clock-stunned light
Of my mind, or a kind of river-reflection of my basic sleep
Breaking down   sleeping down into reprisal-fear of God:
    The Zodiac standing over, pouring into
      The dreams that are killing me?

                                    (45)

He vacillates between spirit and flesh, his star-obsession and ordinary life. He adjures himself to give up this poetry "that's draining your bones / Of marrow"; leave it, and get out. "Go back to the life of a man. / Leave the stars. They're not saying what you think." Daylight comes, and he walks around the city, free for twelve hours from his obsession; he returns to the house in which he spent his childhood and remembers his parents and early sweetheart, but imagines his mother telling him not to come back, not to be a memory-animal like the lizard on the wall (Scorpio?). He spends the night with a young girl, but "knows that nothing, / Even love, can kill off his lonesomeness." A party with friends thaws him out; he "shakes free of two years of wandering / Like melting-off European snows," and he is "back home." But that night he is once more in the grip of his obsession:

      A day like that. But afterwards the fire
  Comes straight down through the roof, white-lightning nightfall,
  A face-up flash. Poetry. Triangular eyesight. It draws his
  fingers together at the edge
  Around a pencil.   He crouches bestially,
      The darkness stretched out on the waters
    Pulls back, humming Genesis. From wave-stars lifts
      A single island wild with sunlight,
    The white sheet of paper in the room.

                                    (60)

    The whole last section, of which this passage is the beginning, is a triumph in which Dickey recapitulates the main themes of the poem and brings it to a magnificent close. Perhaps in part because of the translation, Marsman's conclusion is rather awkward and anticlimactic. For the sake of one last comparison with Dickey, I will quote it:

I pray thee, spirit, grant to this small hand
The quiet and the still tenacity
To steer the ship onto the morning land
That slumbering in each horizon waits.
And grant the man who listens to the note
That hums along the dancing of the planets
And through the seething of the emerald sea
To tune the instrument upon the fork
Which, at the touch, reveals the structural form
Of the immemorial European song
That sounded at the dawn of culture when
It started on its course in the azure sea,
And will resound throughout the western world
As long as exaltation spans around space
A firmament of intellect and dream.

(251)

Here is Dickey's version:

Oh my own soul, put me in a solar boat.
        Come into one of these hands
        Bringing quietness and the rare belief
    That I can steer this strange craft to the morning
Land that sleeps   in the universe on all horizons
    And give his home-come man who listens in his room

    To the rush and flare of his father
Drawn at the speed of light to Heaven
Through the wrong end of his telescope, expanding the universe,
    The instrument   the tuning-fork—
He'll flick it with his bandless wedding-finger—
    Which at a touch reveals the form
    Of the time-loaded European music
    That poetry has never really found
Undecipherable as God's bad, Heavenly sketches,
Involving fortress and flower, vine and wine and bone,

    And shall vibrate through the western world
So long as the hand can hold its island
    Of blazing paper, and bleed for its images:
    Make what it can of what is:

        So long as the spirit hurls on space
The star-beasts of intellect and madness.

(61–62)

Dickey's essential affirmation is the same one made by his predecessors in
the visionary line, from Blake through Hart Crane and the Dylan Thomas of

Altarwise by Owllight: the analogy, or identity, of the poetic imagination and the divine power that created the stars. (For this symbolic affirmation, the little mobile in the protagonist's room, which is counterpart to the universe outside, seems more plausible than Brooklyn Bridge—though of course I am not suggesting that Dickey's poem is therefore better than Crane's.) The subject of *The Zodiac,* then, is not astrology but the nature of reality and its relation to the poet's creative imagination, treated not in post-Kantian philosophical terms but dramatically and mythologically.

Dickey's poet, as we have seen, tries to change the zodiac through his own creative powers. He makes Cancer into a Lobster, and he adds his favorite constellation, Orion. Of course, he fails in both attempts. (If we recall the story of Orion, it is easy to see why the myth, as well as the constellation itself, would be Dickey's own favorite: The great hunter was blinded while drunk—Merope's vengeful father did this to him—and regained his eyesight by walking on water until he reached the east; he was killed at last by Scorpio. Dickey's preoccupation with vision and blindness, both literal and symbolic, is well known, from his time as a night-fighter pilot to his novel-in-progress with its temporarily blinded hero.)

The question, then, is not whether or not *The Zodiac* fails, since all such poems inevitably fail, but how and how badly. As Warren remarked, there are some flaws in the "dramatic pivots": the dramatic logic of the protagonist's movements and shifts of moods is not always clear. Although the language is always dramatically appropriate, the protagonist's drunken ranting sometimes becomes a little insistent and hectoring, so that the reader feels trapped as if by a real drunk; and his assertions of the connection between the stars and his balls seem crude by comparison to, say, Eliot's subtle intimation of the link between the dance along the artery, the circulation of the lymph, and the drift of stars, or his tapestried boarhound and boar reconciled among the stars. But the power is there when needed at dramatic high points of the poem, and abundantly in the whole last section.

The Zodiac belongs in some respects with that galaxy of poems produced during World War II, of which the most notable are *Four Quartets, Notes toward a Supreme Fiction, Seasons of the Soul, For the Time Being,* and *The Sea and the Mirror.* In all these poems, an action that is essentially subjective has been successfully embodied in a traditional objective form: most obviously, the string quartet in Eliot, the oratorio and closet-drama in Auden. For Dickey, the same function is performed through Marsman's poem, with its traditional symbolism and structure. The poem is at once fixed in time and space (in these respects another poem of World War II) and made universal, since the voice is so clearly that of Dickey, a survivor of that war and a contemporary, speaking through the mask of Marsman, who died early in it.

Poets of other persuasions do not seek meaning in the stars. Auden could say cheerfully, "Looking up at the stars, I know quite well / That for all they care, I can go to hell," and Warren that the stars "are only a backdrop for /

The human condition" and the sky "has murder in the eye, and I / Have murder in the heart, for I / Am only human. We look at each other, the sky and I. / We understand each other."⁹ Visionary poets, however, affirm that there is a relation, that the stars are saying something to man. Just what they say is, naturally, impossible to state in cool discursive prose. But Dickey, like his visionary predecessors, affirms the ultimate analogy, or identity, of the poetic imagination and the divine power that created the stars. For this symbolic affirmation, the zodiac works better than the Brooklyn Bridge.

To say that visionary poets do not age well is an academic understatement, or litotes. Rimbaud gave up poetry for gunrunning at the age of nineteen, and Hart Crane leaped into the sea at thirty; Dylan Thomas drank himself to death at thirty-nine, and Roethke, after increasingly harrowing bouts of mania and depression, in his fifties. Blake and Smart, under cover of madness, made it into their fifties. But except for Whitman, who was only in one sense a visionary poet, it is hard to think of any who attained the age of sixty. Dickey's achievement in surviving not only two wars but the special hazards that beset his kind of poet is, then, a notable one: Like Faulkner's Dilsey, he has endured.

Dickey has not only remained very much alive, but he has continued to grow and develop. *Puella* (1982) marks his entrance into a distinctive new stage. In *Puella* there is a shift from the cosmic vision of *The Zodiac* to a very different kind of vision that might be called domestic. The poet is not tamed but gentled as he lovingly describes what Hopkins called the *mundus muliebris*, the woman's world inhabited by the daughter-wife figure whose girlhood he relives. At the risk of embarrassing Dickey, I might suggest a large and vague parallel with the change in Shakespeare's career from tragedies such as *Lear* to romances such as *Cymbeline, The Winter's Tale,* and *The Tempest* with their themes of reconciliation, fulfillment, the joy of recovering what was thought to be lost forever. Deborah in these poems has something in common with Marina, Perdita, Miranda, and other such young girls in these plays; with Yeats's Dancers and the daughter for whom he wrote the great prayer; and with the young girls in Hopkins—in "Margaret, are you grieving" and the "Echo" poems, for example. (I am beginning to sound like those nineteenth-century studies of the girlhood of Shakespeare's heroines; but that is the mood of the book, with its charming epitaph from T. Sturge Moore: "I lived in thee, and dreamed, and waked / Twice what I had been." If the word *mellow* had not been preempted by the Californians of "Doonesbury," it would be hard to avoid using it here. There is also the first time the word *charming* has been conceivable as a description of Dickey's poetry.)

The girl in the poems is intensely herself, yet she is also representative of all young girls, as the title *Puella* suggests. She is pictured in scenes that are archetypal, sometimes *rites de passage,* sometimes with mythical or historical contexts; sometimes heraldic as if in medieval tapestry, sometimes playfully absurd as if in a modern folk-naive painting. While the poems are obviously very personal, they exhibit a new kind of formality, both in the speaker's atti-

tude toward his subject—affection tinged with gentle humor, folk ceremoni-
ousness, a degree of detachment making possible fresh appreciation of physical
beauty—and in the verse itself. Dickey has always treasured the "wildness"
aspect of Hopkins, as did Roethke—"long live the weeds and the wildness
yet!"—but these poems show a new sense of the beauty of formal sound patterns that is often reminiscent of Hopkins. There is a tenderness, a delicacy, a
fresh appreciation of the beauty of the visible universe that seem to owe something to Hopkins while being also strongly individual.

The beginning of "Heraldic: Deborah and Horse in Morning Forest" has
an epigraph from Hopkins and is a kind of homage to that poet:

> It could be that nothing you could do
> Could keep you from stepping out and blooding-in
> An all-out blinding heraldry for this:
> A blurred momentum-flag
> That must be seen sleep-weathered and six-legged,
> Brindling and throwing off limbo-light
>
> Of barns. . . .[10]

In another, Hopkins's verse techniques are used to describe Deborah's piano-
playing:

> With a fresh, gangling resonance
> Truing handsomely, I draw on left-handed space
> For a brave ballast shelving and bracing, and from it,
>   then, the light
> Prowling lift-off, the treble's strewn search and
>   wide-angle glitter.
>
> (39)

As for playful folk-ceremony poems—a world apart from what one critic calls
the "country surrealism" of "May Day Sermon"—there are "Deborah and
Deirdre as Drunk Bridesmaids Foot-Racing at Daybreak" and "Veer-Voices:
Two Sisters under Crows," in both of which the titles are enough for present
purposes. But I cannot resist quoting the end of my favorite poem in the book,
"Deborah in Ancient Lingerie, in Thin Oak over Creek." This is both a vision,
at once tender and absurd, of Deborah in her "album bloomers" diving into
the creek, and a ritual acted out in the poem itself:

>   . . . snake-screaming,
>   Withering, foster-parenting for animals
>   I can do
>   very gently from just about
>   Right over you, I can do
>   at no great height I can do
>   and bear

And counter-balance and do
         and half-sway and do
                and sway
                      and outsway and
                          do.
                              (22)

The poems move from the realism of "Deborah and Scion," where she is seen "In Lace and Whalebone" thinking of the kind of looks she has inherited—"Bull-headed, big-busted . . . I am totally them in the / eyebrows, / Breasts, breath and butt" (32)—to the visionary heights of "The Lyric Beasts," where she speaks as "Dancer to Audience" and becomes a kind of goddess challenging the audience to "Rise and on faith / Follow" (35). In a sense I suppose the book is Dickey's reply to the radical feminists, for Deborah in it is both herself and Dickey's ideal modern woman, enacting her archetypal feminine role in full mythic resonance, but not enslaved or swallowed up by it. If so, Kate Millett and Adrienne Rich may eat their hearts out!

I have not mentioned many qualities in Dickey that might be called distinctively southern, on the ground that they are large, vague, and obvious—more obvious in the novel *Deliverance* and the two books about the South, *Jericho* and *God's Images,* than in the poetry—but perhaps they should be summed up briefly. A strong sense of place is the first, as in the poems about Cherrylog Road, kudzu, chenille, the Buckhead boys, the woman preacher, and the lawyer's daughter whose dive from the Eugene Talmadge Bridge brought revelation from the burning bush. Love of storytelling, and hence of communal myth, is important, and from this it is a short step to love of ceremony and ritual both within the family and with other life-forms, from the Owl King to *Puella.* Dickey's humor is more frequently present than most people seem to realize, but its most characteristic form is the preposterous lie or grotesquely implausible vision that outrages the reader but then turns out to be, in a deeper sense, true. Like most southerners, he has a strong religious sense: His poems are often sermons or prayers or invocations. But his creed might be called natural supernaturalism, or fundamentalism so fundamental that it concerns man's relation to all other life forms.

As we have seen, Dickey has little significant relation to earlier southern writing; it would take a truly ingenious academic to show how he was influenced by Sidney Lanier! Poe seems to be his only southern predecessor in being a genuine visionary; but he was a very different kind: Whereas Poe's visions are of horror and death-in-life, Dickey's are of larger modes of life. Dickey is so far from being a regionalist in any exclusive sense that the spiritual ancestors most prominent in his recent poetry are that New Englander of the New Englanders, Joseph Trumbull Stickney, who lies behind the wonderful poem "Exchanges"; the Dutch poet and sailor Hendrik Marsman, who lies behind *The Zodiac;* and the English Jesuit Gerard Manley Hopkins, who lies behind *Puella.*

In contrast to more recent southern poets such as Tate and Warren, Dickey has not been interested in communion with other humans through acceptance of the human condition but in getting beyond ordinary humanity to participate in the life of nonhuman creatures and in more-than-human forces. His essential subject has been exchange or metamorphosis or *participation mystique* between man and wild animals, fish, or birds; or, in *Zodiac,* stars and the mysterious universe in general. Since the rational mind is a hindrance, or at best irrelevant, to this quest, his poems represent extreme states of consciousness: intoxication, terror, rage, lust, hallucination, somnambulism, or mystical exaltation. His concern is not the limitations but the possibilities of human and nonhuman nature, not history but vision.

As I have tried to suggest, *Puella* constitutes a new kind of vision, back from the cosmic extremities of *The Zodiac* to the human and domestic world. The figure of the daughter-wife is suffused with a new tenderness, gentleness, and humor, and the verse takes on a new formal musicality. A Jungian would say that the girl in these poems is an anima figure; but whether the sense of fulfillment and joy in these poems comes from integration of the personality or from some deeper cause, I will not attempt to decide. Nor will I comment on the fact that Deborah is not only southern but South Carolinian; southern chivalry toward ladies who have the misfortune to be born elsewhere forbids it. But I will risk the charge of southern chauvinism by saying that the book is a most notable contribution to southern letters.

NOTES

1. James Dickey, in *The Expansive Imagination: A Collection of Critical Essays,* ed. Richard J. Calhoun (DeLand, Fl.: Everett/Edwards, 1973), 17.

2. R. V. Cassill, "The Most Dangerous Game of the Poet James Dickey," *South Carolina Review* 10 (1978): 7.

3. Both quoted by Robert W. Hill, "Editorial," in *South Carolina Review* 10 (1978): 3.

4. Robert Penn Warren, "A Poem about the Ambition of Poetry: *The Zodiac,*" *New York Times Book Review,* 14 November 1976, 8.

5. Hendrik Marsman, "The Zodiac," from *Tempel en Kruis,* trans. from the Dutch by A. J. Barnouw, *Sewanee Review* 55 (1947): 238–51; hereafter cited by page number in the text.

6. James Dickey, *Self-Interviews* (New York: Dell, 1970), 78.

7. But some references, like that to the present Astronomer-royal ("Fred Hoyle and the steady-state" [28]), are emphatically postwar.

8. James Dickey, *The Zodiac* (Garden City, N.Y.: Doubleday, 1976), 12; hereafter cited by page number in the text.

9. W. H. Auden, *Collected Poems,* ed. Edward Mendelson (New York: Random House, 1976), 445 (from "The More Loving One," [957]); Robert Penn Warren, *Selected Poems, 1923–75* (New York, 1977), 17 (from "The Nature of a Mirror," *Or Else-Poem/Poems* [1968–74]).

10. James Dickey, *Puella* (Garden City, N.Y.: Doubleday, 1982), 23; hereafter cited by page number in the text.

James Dickey's *Puella* in Flight

PATRICIA LAURENCE

James Dickey's collection of poems, *Puella,* begins with the dedication, "To Deborah—her girlhood, male-imagined." The nineteen difficult poems published in only one edition by Doubleday in 1982, and a small private printing by Pyracantha Press in 1985, limn a poet's changing imaginings of his young wife as a girl coming of age. The poems illumine Dickey's epigraph:

> I lived in thee, and dreamed, and waked
> Twice what I had been.
>
> —T. Sturge Moore

Coming to these poems from the masculine wilds of Dickey's novel, *Deliverance,* the work that looms largest in the American imagination, we veer in this collection into another kind of male voyage, this time into womanhood. Male imaginings of women have been under review since Virginia Woolf in her graceful polemic, *A Room of One's Own,* attempted to explain, in part, the imaginative necessity that women so often are to men. She describes "the looking glass vision," how "women have served all these centuries as looking-glasses possessing the magic and delicious power of reflecting the figure of man at twice its natural size."[1] Dickey is no exception: he awakes from his imagined encounter with Deborah's girlhood at least "twice" what he had been.

Feminist critics continue in the spirit of Virginia Woolf to observe the male voicing of womanhood as they take new critical turns into the historical and social inscriptions of language that bind women to certain roles or images. Amidst this scholarly activity, however, women continue to wonder why women poets do not write collections of poems about the boyhood of their lovers or husbands, and why male poets and novelists are so intrigued by the idea of possessing with the pen, the girlhoods or womanhoods of the women with whom they are engaged. The obsession to recover her past, particularly her sexual relationships, and to know and record them jealously leads to a terrifying conclusion. What such works share with Dickey's more innocent *Puella* is the author's desire to possess his woman, "before she met him."

Through the centuries, a reader might identify this impulse to "possess"

Originally published in the *South Carolina Review* 26 (Spring 1994): 61–71. Reprinted by permission.

as peculiarly male; women more often are "possessed" than "possessing." As
Emily Dickinson states:

> I am afraid to own a Body
> I am afraid to own a soul
> Profound-precarious property
> Possession.[2]

Women are often afraid to own their own souls, bodies, and voices, let alone
anyone else's. And when they do seek to possess, as does the energetic Maud
Bailey in A. S. Byatt's recent novel *Possession,* it is, astonishingly, Victorian love
letters. Since this critical consideration of Dickey takes place at a time when
such social paradigms are being questioned—when women are less patient with
male fictionalization of women's experience and are struggling to possess their
own voices in literature   we pause. . . . Dickey has, after all, presented us, in
his previous works, with a certain vision of the "masculine."

Acknowledging then that "possession" is Dickey's drive in these poems,
"lightness" is the quality that holds. "Puellae" in various kinds of personal and
cultural flight are, somehow, levitated by the quality of Dickey's writing. He
breathes what he has lived and dreamed of the sensuous life of his "puella"—in
her southern landscape—into her voice in these poems. We, in the meantime,
rehearse in our heads the current declension of "correctness." Puella: We must
remain in our own skins. Puellae: We must remain in our own bodies. Puellae:
We must remain in our own gender. Fixed identities. Dickey, despite his glori-
fication of male initiations and macho stances—the hunter, the ex-combat
pilot—resists such fixity of identity and admirably pits his imagination against
social naming. As James Applewhite perceptively says of the poem, Dickey seeks
"to feel through her senses, wake in her psyche."[3] I would broaden the field of
"being" or "non-being" even further to suggest that he also attempts to
awaken the consciousness of a doll, trees, rain, a whale, an environment, or the
sounds of crows. Dickey's *Puella* attempts what Gérard Genette ascribes to
literature in general: "It breathes new life into the world, freeing it from the
pressure of social meaning, which is named meaning, and therefore dead meaning, maintaining as long as possible that opening, the uncertainty of signs
which allows one to breathe."[4]

Acknowledging the "uncertainty of signs," we make the critical turn from
identity politics with its delineation of "identity" as fixed, toward a more complex view of the relation between gender, the imagination, and literature. Defend we must Dickey's exploration of the "I" and the "not I" as dimensions of
being, and his imaginative rights to live in Deborah. He places a female speaker
in a mythical and southern landscape, breathing into her his voice: classical
images of Athena springing from the head of Zeus come to mind. But note
that he voices not only the dissolving line between male and female, but also
girlhood and womanhood, past and present, the animate and inanimate,
human and nature, and the actual and mythical. Deborah, somehow, always in

motion, always "veering" into being something else, is a vector. Ungraspable. The challenge then of reading these subtle difficult poems is, "who is speaking?" And as Virginia Woolf further queries in one of her short stories, "when the self speaks to the self, who is speaking?" Is it Deborah? The male poet? Or is it an androgynous voice, both the "male" and "female" self of Dickey in dialogue? And what about the various animate and inanimate voicings that are also part of this speaker?

Different aspects of Deborah, ostensibly the changing, growing speaker, are presented in this collection. Each poem "veers" in another direction, some of them clustering about certain themes like magnetic filings. Dickey imagines Deborah in mythical and cultural relation to her body (menses, sex, death); to her family (mothers, grandmothers); to the house (civilization); to nature (southern landscape, moon, rain, woods/flowers, animals); to sounds (the piano, crows); to the past (heraldry); and to fantasies. In "From Time," Deborah imagines "for Years at the Piano"; in "The Lode," we experience "Deborah's Rain Longing"; in "Tapestry and Sail," "She Imagines Herself a Figure upon Them"; in "The Surround," "Imagining Herself as the Environment, She Speaks to James Wright at Sundown."

The formalist Russian critic Mikhail Bakhtin warns that, resist as we might, social namings are in us, and inscribed in our experience and language. We find in the opaque language of these poems a male presence or sensibility, at times, making it difficult to assess whose "experience" is being represented. In the first poem in the collection, "Deborah Burning a Doll Made of House-Wood," Deborah burns her childhood self symbolized by a doll. She begins,

> I set you level,
> Your eyes like the twin beasts of a wall.
>
> As a child I believed I had grown you,
> And I hummed as I mixed the blind nails
> Of this house with the light wood of Heaven—
> The rootless trees there—falling in love
> With carpenters—their painted, pure clothes, their flawless
> Baggies, their God-balanced bubbles, their levels.

Through Deborah's voice, we encounter metaphors of carpentry. The tools of Deborah's perception that take the measure of the "doll," also her childhood self, are the "level" with its "God-balanced bubble," "the blind nails," "the light wood of Heaven," and "the squared mess of an indoor wood-yard." The poet has breathed language that is gender-marked into Deborah's voice as she watches the dust of her doll, indeed her childhood, bodying "into smoke." This leaves us with a sense that both the male speaker and Deborah intertwine in perception, language, and voice. Deborah continues, and we visually observe a balance in the spacing of the first line below to match Deborah's perception— "leveling" throughout the poem—and then in the fifth line, we observe the steplike lines of the "rungs," the "climbing," and the "domestic ascent" of the doll-child:

> I am leaving: I have freed the shelves
>
>   So that you may burn cleanly, in sheer degrees
>   of domestic ascent, unfolding
>   Boards one after the other, like a fireman
>   His rungs out of Hell
>   or some holocaust
>   whelmed and climbing:

Both the spaces and the words speak and mean in a Dickey poem. Deborah, after this ascent, this levitation of the doll-self, has "the power to see / Pure" and moves on to another aspect of the self in "Deborah, Moon, Mirror, Right Hand Rising." In this poem she observes in a mirror "the moon coming up in my face," and she experiences,

> New Being angled with thresholds.
> Woman of the child
>
> I was, I am shone through now
> In circles, as though the moon in my hand were falling
>
> Concentrically, on the spirit of a tree . . .

Here Deborah is absorbed into both a natural and mythical world through her mirror; comically, "All pores cold with cream." She is moon; she is human, she is tree, even dryad; she is stone. Transparent,

> A woman's live playing of the universe
> As inner light, stands clear,
> And is, where I last was.

All kinds of identities are mystically traversed in her "new being." The poet imagines Deborah in "a body out-believing existence, . . . set going by imaginative laws, emblem eyes, degenerate with symbols" ("The Lyric Beasts"). The landscape of dream and myth, juxtaposed with Dickey's familiar terrain of woods and animals and the physical pleasure of being, leads us to appreciate the deeply felt connection between the man and the changing woman in these poems.

Again, the quality of the writing and perception that one experiences in these poems is "lightness," the feeling that one falls through them sensuously, somehow balanced in flight: and, at times, levitating, rather than just reading them. Italo Calvino in *Six Essays for the Next Millennium,* discusses the virtue that the quality of lightness that removes "weight from the structure of stories and from language" will have, as he projects this quality into the future of literature. He predicts that "the lightness is also something arising from the writing itself, from the poet's own linguistic power, quite independent of whatever philosophic doctrine the poet claims to be following." In choosing an image for the new millennium, he selects one that might well apply to some of Dickey's poetry: "The sudden agile leap of the poet-philosopher who raises himself above the weight of the world showing that with all his gravity he has the secret of lightness."[5]

This lightness is present in even the darkest of Dickey's poems. In one of the most intriguing poems of the collection, "Veer Voices: Two Sisters under Crows," Dickey's voice splinters into the voice of Deborah, her sister, as well as the screeches of the crows—somehow to be heard all through this poem, with "their spirit-shifting splits / Of tongue." Again, we observe the poet traversing different dimensions of "being," not localized in the human, but located mid-way between nature and the human in sound and image. The screech of crows "veer-crying and straining like wire" shadows this poem, the sisters psychically placed under the screeching of the "night-mass of families":

> Sometimes are living those who have seen
> Together   those farthest leaning
> With some dark birds and fielded
> Below them   counter crying and hawing in savage openness
> For every reason. Such are as we, to come out
> And under and balance-cruise,

The spaces of varying length and the placement of words in this description of the dark birds, sisters, together, create a visual veering or change of direction to match the veer-voices of the sisters:

> A crossroads and passing out
> One kind of voice in skinned speeches
> All over the place   leaning and flying
> Passing into
>   flying in and out
> Of each other
>
>   with nothing to tell of
> But the angles of light-sensitive dust
> Between fences leaded with dew,
> You might say back,
>
>   Come with me
> Into the high-tension carry

We both see and hear the voices of the sisters and the crows "flying" in and out, identities blurring in the tense visual field of words and spaces on the page. It is almost as if the "countercrying" crows who "surround" the sisters in nature teach a voice or a knowledge of no human tone, "unfathomable" to human ears. Again Dickey explores the "I" and the "not I": sisters in relation to one another, a man in relation to women, humans in relation to birds and their sounds in nature. Dickey bids the sisters to listen and move into the "high-tension carry" of this other world. Despite the Poe-like ominousness of the invitation, this poem, nevertheless, has a quality of lightness.

"Turning" not only his poetic lines but the dark parable of the two sisters into "lightness," Dickey again reminds us of the paradoxical "lightness" to be found in "gravity." This "lightness" arising from the gravity of the dark intuitions about Deborah's relations, about the relation between the human and natural worlds, then becomes a principle for reading *Puella*. Dickey, the poet, navigating the space of the page as Dickey, the air force pilot, navigated the space of sky in World War II and the Korean War.

In the poem "Deborah in Ancient Lingerie, in Thin Oak over Creek," Deborah asserts all that she can "do" but again the stances and the language somehow suggest a male mirroring. The poet captures the "lightness" of the erotic acrobatics of a man and a woman with the imagery of the aerial beam and "heron-veins" in the landscape of mythic and actual outdoors. The poem and the reader levitate:

> I can do
>
>   gently, just over you:
>
>   balance-beam disdain
>
>   Like heron-veins over the forest
>
>   When my spirit is branching, when I
>
>   Catch it and don't spend it, I can do:
>
>   All kinds of caused shade
>
> I can do, and unparalleled being
>
>   I can do, snake-screaming
>
>   Withering, foster-parenting for animals
>
> I can do
>
>   very gently from just about
>
>   Right over you, I can do
>
>   at no great height I can do
>
>   and bear
>
> And counter-balance and do
>
>   and half-sway and do
>
>   and sway
>
>   and outsway and
>
>   do.

We catch the sensuous rhythm of the erotic from the visual patterning of word and space, as well as the wildness of the sound of "snake screaming." And in the macho tones of words and movements, the repetition of "do" and "gently . . . over you" and "balance-beam disdain" and "catch" and not "spend" and repeated swayings, we sense this is a man—not Deborah—

complicating again our notion of the experience and the speaker represented in these poems. Nevertheless, in the "move" and "do" and "bear" and "sway" and "half-sway" and "outsway," we, as readers, move across the visual space of the page in a choreography of eye and sense, creating a special relationship between the poet and the reader. The spaces of varying length to mark pauses and even a full black page in an earlier poem, "Apollo," for the first manned moon orbit, suggest conceptual, visual, and auditory play in Dickey's poetry. The spaces and blackness are a place, just as Laurence Sterne offered in *Tristam Shandy,* for the participation of the reader.

The "female" companion piece to "Deborah in Ancient Lingerie, in Thin Oak over Creek" may be the glorious poem "RayFlowers." Though it feels like a violation to quote only part of this poem or any of the other poems in this collection because of the importance of Dickey's choreography of space, a part of it will supply the feeling of lightness, and falling, and "consent":

>   As when we all fell all day
>   Consenting
>   Sight-softening   space-massing
>   Time-thickening   time-floating more
>   Light

The repetition of words such as *consenting* (somehow echoing Molly Bloom's "yes, she said yes . . ."), *sown, fall* and lines such as:

>   Come:
>   Muffle   splinter   increase   fill

suggest something, I think, closer to female sensibility. But then we might ask why Deborah says later,

>   Super-nerved with weightlessness:
>
>   All girls of cloud and ego in your time,
>   Smoked-out millennial air-space
>   Empowered with blurr, lie down
>   With bindweed force   with angelic clutter and stillness
>   As I hold out and for you unfold
>   This feather-frond of a bird . . .

Though straining for Deborah's own sexual dawning in this poem, it is, nevertheless, intertwined with the male speaker's prowess, unfolding his "feather-frond of a bird." We shift in different lines to different aspects of sexual experience.

One poem where Dickey crosses over more successfully into female and animal experience and voice is "Deborah as Scion." Deborah at the family cemetery connects with her mothers and grandmothers, traversing the line between the past and the present. In this passage, which is beautiful in its movement and too long to quote, Deborah moves "back, from mother to mother" and is "totally them in the / Breasts, breath and butt." But she is also curiously alive and in touch with whales whose bones have served for the corsets of confinement for them and Deborah:

> I stand now in your closed bones,
> Sucked-in, in your magic tackle, taking whatever,
>   From the stark freedom under the land,
>   From under the sea, from the bones of the deepest beast,
>   Shaped now entirely by me, by whatever
>   Breath I draw.

Identifying with the whales, crossing over from the human to the animal, Deborah and the whales are "paired bones of the deep" joined by the confinement and violation of their bodies. Whatever her own bodily confinements, her being grows as she identifies with and feels the ripping-up and boiling down of the whale "for animal oil." She hears "the weird mammalian bleating of bled creatures" and thinks,

>   This animal
>   This animal   I stand and think
>
>   Its feed   its feel   its whole lifetime on one air:
>   In lightning-strikes I watch it leap . . .

Anyone who has ever watched a "volcanic" whale leaping in the deep knows Deborah's visceral sense of the primeval, and of the mythic proportions of these creatures. Perhaps the volcanic, unconscious structuring of a girl's sexuality into the poem reminds us of Deborah's moving out from cultural restriction into her own experience of sexuality as a woman. "Out-believing" her existence as a woman, entering into the experience of a whale, we again move into a "deepening sense of being" that Laurence Lieberman writes of in a Dickey poem. And we hear, hear, the "weird mammalian bleating of bled creatures" just as we heard the "snake screaming" and the screeching of the crows in earlier poems. And in the penultimate poem, "The Surround," where Deborah imagines herself as the environment speaking to James Wright at Sundown, she is no longer even human but mythically dissolved as a presence in the environment—spiritually sprinkled in nature—to surround and protect the male poet, James Wright, as a beneficent spirit:

>   Stay with me
>   And without me, hearing
>   Your hearing come back in a circle. After midnight no ax
>   Shall be harmful to your wholeness,
>   No blood-loss give life. You are in your rings, and growing
>   In darkness. I quell and thicken
>   Away. I am
>
>   The surround, and you are your own.

In this collection then, Dickey, the male poet, blurs easy distinctions between male and female, man and woman and nature, the animate and the inanimate, the human and the animal, the past and the present, the actual and the mythic, and the landscape of mind and place and page. What is most important is that Dickey attempts (with mixed results) to present a girl-woman, not solely in relationship to other people, but in relation with her girlhood, womanhood, body, life, death, and nature. She does not exist in traditional relation to man, though she is "themed" to meet the male poet. We find her, imperfectly mixed in voice with male sensibility, in relation to the universe. Entering into many dimensions of being and nonbeing, not just the *puella* of the title, Dickey attempts to breathe new and strange life into poetry. He invites the reader into the generous space and dance of words on the page—his *puella,* somehow, in flight.

NOTES

1. Virginia Woolf, *A Room of One's Own* (New York: Harcourt Brace Jovanovich, 1929), 35.
2. Emily Dickinson, *The Complete Poems of Emily Dickenson,* ed. Thomas H. Johnson (Boston: Little, Brown, 1960), 1090.
3. James Applewhite, "Reflections on *Puella,*" *Southern Review* 21 (January 1985): 214–19.
4. Gérard Genette, *Figures of Literary Discourse,* trans. Alan Sheridan (New York: Columbia University Press, 1982), 41.
5. Italo Calvino, "Lightness," *Six Memos for the Next Millennium,* trans. Patrick Creagh (Cambridge, Mass.: Harvard University Press, 1988), 3, 10, 12.

WORKS CITED

Applewhite, James. "Reflections on *Puella.*" *Southern Review* 21 (January 1985): 214–19.
Bakhtin, Mikhail. *The Dialogic Imagination.* Trans. Michael Holquist. Austin: University of Texas Press, 1981.
Calvino, Italo. *Six Essays for the Next Millennium.* Trans. Patrick Creagh. Cambridge, Mass.: Harvard University Press, 1988.
Dickey, James. *Deliverance.* Boston: Houghton Mifflin, 1970.
———. *The Eye-Beaters, Blood, Victory, Madness, Buckhead and Mercy.* Garden City, N.Y.: Doubleday, 1970.
———. *Poems,* 1957–1967. Middletown, Conn.: Wesleyan University Press, 1967.
Genette, Gérard. *Figures of Literary Discourse.* Trans. Alan Sheridan. New York: Columbia University Press, 1982.
Lieberman, Laurence. *The Achievement of James Dickey.* Glenview, Ill.: Scott, Foresman, 1968.
Woolf, Virginia. *A Room of One's Own.* New York: Harcourt Brace Jovanovich, 1929.

James Dickey's Motions

DAVE SMITH

With the death of Robert Penn Warren, the mantle of preeminent Southern poet seems destined to fall to James Dickey. Wendell Berry, Donald
Justice, Eleanor Ross Taylor, and A. R. Ammons are all worthy candidates, but
each has deemphasized a southern identity in ways Dickey has not. Much has
been written about James Dickey that is misinformed, silly, or plainly wrong,
especially in the latter half of his career. The critical profile ranges from a
dismissive, apparently political, condescension to a sycophantic cheering. In *A
History of Modern Poetry,* David Perkins writes tersely of Dickey's "Southern
narratives" and implicitly of the facile local color some readers regard as characteristic of Dickey's poetry. Charles Molesworth and Neal Bowers are more expansive but, essentially, view Dickey as a charlatan and boor, extending Robert
Bly's early attack on Dickey's poetry for what such critics oppose as socially and
politically objectionable opinions. At the other extreme, Robert Kirschten ends
his book *James Dickey and the Gentle Ecstasy of Earth: A Reading of the Poems*
with an unbridled partisan cheer when he writes "Long may James Dickey be
the slugger of creative daring and commitment to poetry so that we may continue our circle and sing."

Whatever the nature of critical response to Dickey, I think a predisposition
to matters "southern" plays a role. To outsiders, southern culture, if those
are not self-contradictory words, remains renegade, bogus, mysterious, often
buffoonish. The South has long and variously paid the cost of its disjunction
from other regions of the United States. Even the election of two presidents
from the South does not easily convince the southerner that equity or respect
has arrived. Just as New Yorkers may imagine a South Carolinian to be fully a
product of swamps and hokum, the South Carolinian—any southerner—
believes *plus ça change* to be the rule. His children, if possible, will be sent as
far northward to college as money and ability permit. His novels will appear in
New York. He will accept, reluctantly, the northern standard as definitive.

The southern poet, like the cottonmouth water moccasin, does not travel
well and thrives mostly at home. James Dickey has often enough been treated
by his press as exactly what Bly called him, a "great blubbery southern toad of

---

Originally published in the *South Carolina Review* 26 (Spring 1994): 41–60. Reprinted by permission.

a poet." Moreover, both in his poetry and out of it, he has confirmed the persistent view of the almost oxymoronic *southern poet,* and not least by playing the role of the redneck sheriff in *Deliverance.* One has only to think of Donald Justice or Archie Ammons to note how different and how melodramatically poetic has been the role Dickey has played.

A Georgian who has lived most of his adult life in South Carolina, Dickey mounted his career in the 1960s and 1970s not merely upon rhythmically fresh and experientially different poems but also on often corrosive opinions of the poets currently favored by one contingency or another. His success, and exuberant pleasure in his success, seemed unrestrained to many at his frequent stops along the poetry reading circuit. Indeed, Dickey's personal conduct on the circuit has generated an apocrypha about him not unlike that of Dylan Thomas. Dickey's advertising-man acumen rightly counted on notoriety to carry his poetry to an audience not often touched by academic meekness, but it may well be that his outlaw image among academics has underwritten the image of the southern poet as inherently inferior and crude. Nevertheless, audiences that have turned out in hundreds to hear him from Portland, Maine, to Portland, Oregon, have found in Dickey a true grit not found in surreal fantasies, metric cosmologies, confession, therapy, or counterculture meetings. Dickey's poetry seemed like life in the last half of the twentieth century—imperiled, dangerous, unprogrammed, abrupt.

Dickey speaks frankly from inside a male, individual, exuberant, and joyous experience. "The Performance," "Walking on Water," "At Darien Bridge," not his most celebrated poems but each standing as a chronological step in his art, are stations toward the roaring joyride of "Cherrylog Road," a ride which reaches apotheosis in "The May Day Sermon to the Women of Gilmer County Georgia, by a Woman Preacher Leaving the Baptist Church." The mystic lift-off from an apparently ordinary dramatic situation that might occur in any reader's life is a formidable trope employed by Dickey. Out of the ashes of momentary, mortal circumstance, Dickey offers the reader what religions have always offered, what "The Salt Marsh" shows: "your supple inclusion / Among fields without promise of harvest, / In their marvelous, spiritual walking / Everywhere, anywhere." It is the joy of those who discover consequence in human connections such as the truck drivers hymned in "Them, Crying" because they feel for *"Those few who transcend themselves, / The superhuman tenderness of strangers."*

Dickey's is a poetry far from ignorant of the dead, the hurt, the maligned, the abandoned peoples who are the common interest of lyric American poetry, but his investigations and his investment have nevertheless been in transcendent joy. His poems seek a good time, and they do it on middle-class terms. They are scarcely marked by the gloom of the American poet's self-conscious rehearsal of personal problems from Lowell's New England dance card to Sharon Olds's sexual abuses. *His* story is upper-tier southern, a bourgeois search for life after success: up from the fens of suburbia, to a university of modest name, discovery of imagination's life, a coven of writers, war and survival, a new and scrupulously-to-be-examined life, books published, a teaching eminence, more books. Had Randall Jarrell played football instead of tennis, he might have been this poet.

Until the publication of *The Whole Motion: Poems, 1945–1992,* there was no abundant evidence in Dickey's books for what Emerson, in his note to Whitman, called a "foreground." The poems gathered under the title "Summons" now show how assiduously Dickey labored to present from his first published work a different sound in his poem. Yet even in the earliest poetry there is little of the historical southern self-awareness and *mea culpa* whose breast-beating, in dark Faulknerian tones, constituted the "burden" of consciousness which would appeal, and does appeal, to generations of specialists. That it might not prove attractive to the educated, general reader, Dickey saw well enough. He set out to transform the pastoral lyric tradition by combining it with a heroic quest for a southern self who would be, as Fred Hobson has described him, "the unburdened Southerner." Hobson, writing specifically of Barry Hannah and young southern fictionists, might be saying of all southern poets what Cleanth Brooks seemed to say in citing the disinclination of lyric to attach to a determinate landscape and purview—that there is no such cat. Hobson says in *The Postmodern Writer in the South* that "not only do family and past mean nothing to him, the South and his identity as Southerner, he insists, mean nothing to him either. The South of his remembrance . . . isn't mysterious, isn't violent, isn't savage, isn't racially benighted, isn't Gothic or grotesque, isn't even interesting."

The trajectory of Dickey's quest, as poems evolved structure, has moved from outside to inside, from emblematic anecdote treated narratively to experienced states of being, known lyrically. The scene, typical of the pastoral poem, has been the wood world or the sea world, nature, because it hosts the unknown and, traditionally, nurtures the spirit. Put bluntly, Dickey like Emerson, like Poe, like Keats, gone outside to find answers to questions echoing on the inside. As with all romantic and lyric poets, the problem was ever how to make intuited consolation, the joy of asserted consequence, credible to readers. What he has done, it now appears in his seventieth year, is to have commanded a formidable rhythmic shift whose expression has baffled as many of us as it may have dazzled.

Whether James Dickey is or is not a "southern" poet may seem irrelevant to the matter of rhythm. The usual definition of the "southern" is a historical consciousness aware of a great civil loss and a fearsomely burdened future; the location of story, as Flannery O'Connor put it, at the intersection of time and place where the clash and consequence of values may most effectively appear; the portrait of people unlikely to benefit from schemes of improvement but driven to suffer them; the environmental effects of rural reality, as the South has known it; the context of violence and violation—these are all to be found in Dickey's poetry. But so, too, is the presence of season, the confident cyclic regularity of living which suffers change and yet endures. The rhythmic nature of being southern, though it may be something much older and deeper, is Dickey's subject and strategy in the work of his most recent decade.

Change continues to occur so fast we scarcely assimilate what it is. The physical landscape of the South has everywhere become an ugly memorial to greed and profit, every town and village marked at ingress and egress by the fecal-like stain of fast food dispensers, gas stations, auto lots, the Arabian knights of neon. Suburbs rise overnight to create instant slums, which themselves breed every conceivable social ill. Yet the evidence of a past still alive is everywhere, too. There are living daughters of Confederate veterans in Richmond, the very last literal connection to that war. My own grandfather, who died at age eighty-eight this past winter, like many worked a lifetime without benefit of a formal education. He became an aeronautical engineer who, as a boy, had hoboed a train to see the first automobiles. Sam Walton, an Arkansas man of the fields, transformed the South by harvesting Wal-Marts everywhere, creating appetites as well as an exchange of goods and ideas whose end we can't guess. The Agrarian ideal that early informed the classics-tutored imaginations of southern poets has been lately expressed by Walter Sullivan who says, "Life lived on the farm is more authentic than life lived in the city, because the rural experience teaches the nature of reality." One end of change much observed by Dickey's poems is the waning of Walter Sullivan's reality.

Freb Hobson is probably correct that writers from the South increasingly attend to a new, urbanized experience, the life they are actually living. But that no South, remembered or lived, is of any interest to contemporary southern writers seems hardly demonstrable in the work of the region's poets. Their South is more, not less, violent, broken, grotesque, disintegrating, *present,* and interesting. It may not even be inhabited as much by southerners—people who want to know what they are, and why; people defined by the consequence of a place. The once stable culture Fugitives found so severely altered remains alongside, not instead of, the South that constituted the "burden." Southern poets, like writers of fiction, feel obligated to examine what is around them, what is inside them. Their interrogation takes a different path, but it remains an interrogation, even literally so in the voice of Robert Penn Warren. Ransom stroked and cooed. Tate fussed. Davidson nattered.

Dickey's voice, from his earliest poems, has possessed remarkable ventriloquial ability and is capable of calibration for effect, at times admonishing, assertive, but also evangelical with a range of wailing, crooning, wall-bursting rhetoric. The cast of characters through whom he has spoken, while not infinite, displays operating range: a king, warrior, hunter, fisherman, fish, bird, wild boar, wolverine, leopard, quarterback, musician, woman preacher, woman-child, lifeguard, and others. Dickey's poems, being mysterious conduits for special speech, give back vital messages to the wobbling world, a message of solidarity and continuity from a scene of human engagement with natural force. Even the most patent "nature" reverie summons its authority for speech

from an intuited scheme of order known both to Milton's "Lycidas" and to
Poe, an order in jeopardy. This visionary role encourages Dickey in a self-
appointed status as the civic voice of his tribe; he urges upon the people virtues
to be celebrated for civilization and for vitality.

This twin-celebratory imperative has, I think, brought Dickey's poetry to
a gulch it has not always transcended. The lyric hasn't the equipment or scope
for a patient portrait of social ills and their remedies. Without being an epic
chronicler of national states (one reason for the contemporary argument about
whether lyric can be successfully political), the lyric poet feels he must contend
against all risk for the biggest stakes. Dickey once told me he hadn't and
wouldn't ever write "anything small." Although *small* may have meant physical
length, I understood it to mean poems not adequately ambitious to speak of
and for the soul of the tribal life. His specifically regional and "big" poems
mark Dickey's "southernness." "Hunting Civil War Relics at Nimblewill
Creek," "Snow on a Southern State," and, later, "Sled Burial, Dream Ceremony," "Slave Quarters," and "Two Poems of Going Home" are variant examples.

The will to assume a civic voice characterizes a number of poems that
began to appear with *The Eye-Beaters, Blood, Victory, Madness, Buckhead and
Mercy* (1970) where the line-tempered and stanza-restrained form Dickey had
refined to award-winning acuteness yielded to poems whose visual dimension
is irregular and whose aural experience one must call, in general, loud.
"Apollo," "The Strength of Fields," "The Olympian," and "For a Time and
Place" reveal Dickey assuming the venerable role of poet for the republic,
broadcaster of answers. It is, I think, the wrong role for Dickey, who seems
here at his most bathetic and transparently bad. He is bad because he loses his
skill for rhythmic delicacy, not because he abandons his narrative gift. He is
bad because he fails to employ language as an act of discovery, a door into that
wood world whose secrets the pastoral poet always unlocks. Dickey bangs dully,
laboring more and more mightily, as if noise will overcome deafness, as in "For
the Running of the New York City Marathon":

I am second
Wind and native muscle in the streets   my image lost and discovered
Among yours: lost and found in the endless panes
Of a many-gestured bald-headed woman, caught between
One set of clothes and tomorrow's: naked, pleading in her wax
For the right, silent words to praise
The herd-hammering pulse of our sneakers,
And the time gone by when we paced
River-sided, close-packed in our jostled beginning,
O my multitudes.

Whitman, of course, would have smiled at this.
Even here, however, is the gist of Dickey's greatness, the seed of "right,

silent words to praise." Dickey is at his best when he abandons pretension to social and cohesive opinion, when he strikes off to find and celebrate the rural life which until his generation was dominant in the South. Indeed, Dickey's interest is most fervent for the pre-rural, wild landscape, the Adamic scene of long scars to our bodies and dark fears to our souls. This may well define the southern poet, and Dickey in particular, as an American example of what Seamus Heaney has called a "venerator." Dickey's quest has been to locate and report the sites of sacred energy which are the unploughed and unknown thickets our myths, legends, and souls regard as compelling, maternal, and tutorial.

The poet-venerator who praises the natural seems inevitably a pastoralist. More often an elegiac than an epic or dramatic writer, he means to concentrate emotive power to evoke immediate and strong response. It is a poetic attitude necessarily more backward-facing than forward, for it laments change that erodes the durable and the good by which we have so long flourished; yet it is also a poetic attitude whose interrogative aspect is less divorced from political and social engagement than we might suspect. To praise the past against a corrupted present is to lodge complaint against the causes and conditions of the corruption. As the portrait moves toward articulated vision, the transcendent and mythical scheme presses more vigorously into the receptive consciousness of the poet. The poem seeks to distill everything to essences beyond which no consciousness can go, the very process undertaken by Dickey's poems in books after the mid-1970s. Two possibilities open for the poet, one formal, one scenic. In evolving toward a poetic sound, Dickey found himself with gifts of the venerator but attracted by the imperatives of a republican voice, a divided duty as it were. The retraining needed to resolve that dilemma results in the characteristic (and not very southern) sound of poetry Dickey has written in the 1980s and 1990s as collected in *Head-Deep in Strange Sounds: Free-Flight Improvisations from the unEnglish* (1979), *Puella* (1982), and *The Eagle's Mile* (1990).

Paul Ramsey, a southern poet whose tastes tend toward the conventionally metric Anglo style, has written, provocatively, that "the metrical history of James Dickey can be put briefly and sadly: a great lyric rhythm found him; he varied it; loosened it; then left it, to try an inferior form." The rhythmic form Ramsey so admired was not found by Dickey so much as forged by him for his need. It flashes in the twenty-five poems of "Summons" with which Dickey opens *The Whole Motion: Collected Poems, 1945–1992*. Stanzas from "For Robert Bhain Campbell" illustrate:

> I like him; I love him,
> I shall soon sit cold in an office,
> Hearing the sea swing, the dead man step:
> The sun at sunset in the mind
> Never falls, never fails.

> There is Berryman's poem, where you were a bird.
> And I, an unsocial man,
> Live working for some kind of living
> In a job where there is no light. But
> I can summon, can summon,
> And your face in my mind is hid
> By a beard I read you once grew.

An intense voice, wanting both intimate and chanting registers, swings through uncertain feet that sound at moments smooth and at moments about to collapse. But the last three lines display what Ramsey had in mind, a mesmerizing rhythm exactly embodied in the line statement, whether trimeter or tetrameter, syllables falling with firm yet delicate motion that is the anapestic shape for which Dickey's poetry would become known. Very shortly, one imagines, Dickey's sense for the line would have revised stanza one this way:

> In an office, hearing
> The sea swing, the dead man
> Step the sun at sunset
> In the mind, never failing.

Dickey's short line with a faintly incantatory quality has a talent for bodying drama *inside* the mind, a consciousness which moves easily backward and forward in time. Aggressive, sensitively receptive, it rocks with a feel of speed but also with grip and vision. By 1962, in *Drowning with Others,* Dickey had learned the subtleties inherent in this form, not least lean, agile stanzas in five and six lines, clusters of perception, and leaps from the real to the mystical, as in "Fog Envelopes the Animals":

> Fog envelopes the animals.
> Not one can be seen, and they live.
> At my knees, a cloud wears slowly
> Up out of the buried earth.
> In a white suit I stand waiting.

While four of the five lines make bold statement, a firm sonic progression of tetrameter creates a background sense of reluctant movement common in confronting the unknown. Each line proceeds as a consequence of the factual line one, though nothing else appears factual because of the shimmery, slightly and oddly formal syntax which makes "and they live" a soft cry of discovery, makes the cloud out of the earth seem a spirit, and makes the white suit of the speaker the ritual dress of the about-to-be-changed. Here, Dickey's trademark anapests create the three-pace phrase which retards an energy always threatening to bolt. Thus "and they live" holds back momentum and permits discovery, as "At my knees" sets it up.

By the mid-1960s Dickey mastered variations of the anapestic rhythm.

They were needed to avoid the inherent monotony of his stichic incantation, a weakness especially troublesome for one of the two kinds of poems he wanted to write. Dickey had from the start an exceptional narrative talent, an ability to bring life to a scene, to color it, expand it, and cinematically make it move. The short line enabled that feel of immersion, the stress pushing ahead and the double drag of anapest retarding. The action of statement was realistic and external, assisting movement, and with it Dickey saw how to tap into moments of mythic reach. Here are two first stanzas that illustrate: "When the rattlesnake bit, I lay / In a dream of the country, and dreamed / Day after day of the river . . ." ("The Poisoned Man"). "Beginning to dangle beneath / The wind that blows from the undermined wood, / I feel the great pulley grind . . ." ("In the Marble Quarry").

Dickey's ability to blow up ordinary scenes into posters of experience, an ability that would force his work farther from the domestic arena and into such wilderness as might be left to an urbanized South, created a need for a line form which did not risk monotony and did not delay progression through temporal and spatial levels. Dickey wanted form capable of what he called, after Whitehead, "presentational immediacy." The poems of *Buckdancer's Choice* (1965), widely seen as his best book, restlessly range through the irregular lines and stanzas (his gap space device appears) of "The Firebombing" to the long-line quintets of "Reincarnation" to the scrupulous sculpted quatrains reminiscent of Herbert in "The War Wound" to the wall of words in "The Shark's Parlor" and "The Fiend."

Dickey had worked himself into possession of many rhythms, none of which sufficed entirely for the tune he wanted to play. Nothing better illustrates Dickey's rhythmic hunt for the sound than his worksheets held by Washington University. Here are the first eight lines of "The May Day Sermon to the Women of Gilmer County, Georgia, by a Woman Preacher Leaving the Baptist Church," in the first draft, then called "Sears."

> The wide-open dance of motes.
> The swinging sand of the motes.
> The wide-open dance,
> The swinging sand of dust.
> That other glory shall pass.
> The stable wanders over the earth.
> And at night, in the animal's sleep,
> The stable wanders over the earth.

The initial lines fumble with that peaceful image of dust as if Dickey can't find a way through tranquillity to his violent tale of paternal and religious abuse, and indeed the struggle lies between potentially soporific iambs and anapests, all jarred by trochees. But by line six a stability arrives as the anapests set a dominant pace, one Dickey will couch in longer lines only in the very last draft before publication. Buried in the lines which seem sculpted by a worshipper's

intensifying in-breath and out-breath, the surge and drag of Dickey's old trimeter works into, parallels, sometimes counters an older tetrameter whose sound
is a rhythmic composite of Anglo-Saxon beats and King James idiom. With this
shift of form, of rhythm, Dickey explodes his poem toward a hybrid and mystical parable of joyful ascension:

> Open to show you the dark where the one pole of light is paid out
> In spring by the loft, and in it the croker sacks sprawling and
>   shuttling
> Themselves into place as it comes   comes   through spiders dead
> Drunk on their threads   the hog's fat bristling   the milk
> Snake in the rafters unbending through gnats to touch the last
>   place
> Alive on the sun with his tongue I shall flickering from my mouth.

Ramsey was certainly correct in observing that Dickey had "loosened" the
rhythm. He did so to liberate the poem from its own success, the solid "click"
of the trimeter lyric as in "The Heaven of Animals." Doubtless, the gain for
Dickey was simply pleasure in stepping outside reader expectations, his own
included. This will to change and change again seems, in retrospect, characteristic of Dickey's writing, as it was of Robert Penn Warren's. Having disguised
and modulated his initial rhythm with the new spread of lines, increasingly
other aspects of Dickey's treatment of language became manifest. In some respects language became his primary subject. He cultivated syntactic reversals,
suspensions, word fusions, print gimmicks, clausal ambiguities, and enjamb-
ments that left comprehension hovering mid-margin like annotation. "The
Eye-Beaters," in fact, employed the poem's margins for authorial commentary.
Dickey transformed verbs into nouns, nouns into adjectives, adjectives into
phrases. He played loose with syllable counts; he truncated sentences to fragments; he made lines of single words. He generally abandoned stanzaic regularity, allowing the words to determine rhythm visually by sometimes sprawling,
sometimes marching, always defining their function in their management of
the white space of the page.

The result of Dickey's improvisations was to move his brand of poem visibly away—as it had already removed itself thematically—from the more conventional contemporary poem. It was not unusual to hear, even among Dickey's
partisans in the late 1970s, that he was becoming hermetic. In truth, because
of their interiority, their will to shift inner and outer forums, Dickey's poems
had never been very accessible, but they became ever more oblique as he cut
the reader's connectors and transitions, offered few clues to relationships, or
left unnamed what he was talking about. Still, his tales spoke more than ever
in the voice of what he had called "the energized man," and nowhere more so
than in *The Zodiac* (1976), a poem about poetry and language as much as it is
about anything. The energized man, as far as Ramsey and traditional formalists

were concerned, was a howler. And was passion enough to justify the willful obliquity of such lines as these from "Root-light, or the Lawyer's Daughter"?

> That any just to long for
> The rest of my life, would come, diving like a lifetime
> Explosion in the juices
> Of palmettoes flowing
> Red in the St. Mary's River as it sets in the east
> Georgia from Florida off, makes whatever child
> I was lie still, dividing.

Dickey made formal experiments jam more and more intense life into the poem, the poem as enactment. Desiring to wed fiction, poetry, and film, Dickey was reflecting a break between himself and his more traditional predecessors in southern poetry. Only Warren evinced anything like the formal trials Dickey attempted, and Warren never escaped the critical estimate of being a fiction writer who traveled in the netherland of poetry. Dickey, with the publication of *Deliverance, Alnilam,* and now *To the White Sea,* runs a similar risk with the southern literature industry. But it is his poetry, surely, and its innovative motions that make him important both as writer and southerner.

Dickey, to use Fred Hobson's word again, is *unburdened* by any great sense of classical obligation. The pressure exerted upon his formal choices comes not from an antiquarian standard but from an attempt to accommodate contemporary experience in a living language. Allen Tate said the problem for the modern was not that he had no form but that he had too many. Dickey's problem has obliged him to understand that his engendered form would have to avoid the monotony his early and middle lyrics seemed headed toward. But the new form must also enable clear shifts away from the direct narratives which undergirded his accomplishment and reputation.

The nature of what constitutes a southern narrative may best be known to the person who receives it as such. If the benchmarks of southern fiction are applied, then one supposes there must be violence, warfare, sexual encounters, pursuit of a wild creature in the wood with an accompanying recalibration of the spirit's experience. If the dominant subjects of the poems are family members, dysfunctional or otherwise, and if the stories invoke the memory that composes a sort of compound of law and expectation for the family, then the grid definition for southern literature may qualify poems as southern narratives. But I see no reason why "In the Waiting Room," Elizabeth Bishop's poem about a visit to the dentist, or Adrienne Rich's "Diving into the Wreck," an undersea divagation, might not be equally southern, excepting, of course, neither poet identifies the landscape employed as southern and, in any regional sense, the landscapes do not function as actors. When there is nothing definitively southern in subject matter, we may wonder to what extent rhythmic patterns define what is southern. Poet James Applewhite has suggested (in

"The Poet at Home and in the South") a relationship clearly southern between tropical weather and slowed, indigenous poetic rhythm.

With landscape as rhythm and a form evolving to minimize the narrative, squeezing it between the lines, Dickey's most recent poetry arrives at a new phase. I mean by rhythm, now, what Warren meant in *Democracy and Poetry* when he wrote that rhythm is "not mere meter, but all the pulse of movement, density, and shadings of intensity of feeling." Dickey's reason for the change, insofar as it may be a personal choice, cannot be known; we can see, though, that his interest in peopled dramas has lessened (though it is not entire abandoned) in favor of an interest in states of being realized through intense, and, after *Puella,* drastically shorter nodes of language. *Puella* is an odd interstice, as I think is *The Zodiac,* for its poems attempt to speak in the voice of Dickey's second wife, Deborah, hence as dramatic monologue, and they attempt the coherence of a bildungsroman or a portrait much like an autobiography, a fictive self self-made.

These poems are unsuccessful heroic quests, narratives of a speaker whose goal must be an emergence from darkness into a treasure-hoard of bright knowledge. For all of Dickey's story skills, neither *Puella* nor *The Zodiac* sustains a beginning-middle-end clarity and progress that we will pay to watch all the way through. I think neither voice is so credibly itself as it is Dickey's, pitched, squeaky, noddingly thrown. The life-plot in each poem is so subordinated to a massing of language appropriate to Dickey's interest in states of passionate being that confusion results. Nor does a lift-off occur, transporting us to revelation. Both poems are never "small" but they try too hard to be "big." In them may be seen the manner of Dickey's late poetry, its richness and a manner arguably southern, observably a different rhythm, and yet visibly the result of a shift meant to realign Dickey's formal strategies with his continued search for an inwardly intensified consciousness and an outwardly pressurized rhythm.

Without study of his worksheets and drafts, no definite date can be assigned for the emergence of the lyric sound characteristic of everything Dickey has published since 1976. The poem of this sound shows a baffling, edged sense of incompleteness, arbitrariness, and rough-born form that some have regarded as proof of a failed talent. Although there is no doubt the late poems are tougher going, I think Dickey's last collections are no less and probably more referential, accessible, and reality-based than John Ashbery's. But the rhythmic pitch is different, as in this excerpt from *Puella:*

> With a fresh, gangling resonance
> Truing handsomely. I draw on left-handed space
> For a brave ballast shelving and bracing, and from it,
>   then, the light
> Prowling lift-off, the treble's strewn search and wide-angle
>   glitter.

In this five-line passage from "From Time," Dickey buries his statement ("I draw on left-handed space") in a haze of unpatterned syllables which make an appositional elaboration, a stretched and gliding poetic sound which features three suspensions or caesuric swirls. Dickey recognizes that his poem resists referential access, so he provides a subtitle ("Deborah for Years at the Piano"). The passage cited is, otherwise, unresolvably ambiguous—yet feels rhythmically persuasive as it works by accretion and momentum, prose principles, and alludes to carpentry, stress forces, and photographic effect all to reinforce a sense of "measuring" in the reader. The laid-in quality of language intense with intention but struggling to maintain movement explains the frequent verbals. To the extent that the lines exist to be commentary on what it *feels like to play piano,* they are registers of inward awareness, slowed thought imitating act and look.

The registration of states of being, of conditions of feeling, as the emphatic enactment of poems appears to migrate toward a form which employs greater ellipsis, compression, and density, all provided for not through symbol so much as through the word-function shifts which Dickey favors, a truncated and often spatially isolated or dramatically enjambed statement for which the usual expectations are frustrated, subverted, and altered. He removes the scaffolding of dramatic circumstance and blurs the occasion of speech, leaving primarily a language of emotive intensity, a sort of curriculum for the soul's exuberant epiphanies. *The Eagle's Mile* (1990) reads, even for a long-immersed Dickey partisan, with a difficulty unmatched by any previous work. But that difficulty has always been a part of Dickey's artistic project, and it seems transient for steady readers.

Head-Deep in Strange Sounds: Free-Flight Improvisations from the unEnglish appeared in 1979, a baker's dozen of poems, each carrying such handrails as "after Alfred Jarry," "near Eugenio Montale," and "from the Hungarian of Attila Joszef, head crushed between two boxcars." Are they translations? Imitations? Some sort of shared composition? I think it matters primarily that they are poems which seek a form-sound in the translation experience of European poets at the same time and in much the same way that James Wright and others did, and do so by breaking the chronological-anecdotal structure, linear and clear as ancestral verse, seeking a dream-fusion of states of being, a braiding in which the inhibitions of usual form and practice may be escaped, and in which looming death-shadows can be cheated by colloquy. It is also a form which permits Dickey to speak of emotion as well as of a citizen's public experiences, about, as he says "the evil / of just living . . ."; or of the magic of the language of numbers "from the frozen, radiant center / Of that ravishing clarity you give. . . ."

Double-Tongue: Collaborations and Rewrites, the final section of *The Eagle's Mile,* contains nine poems very similar to those of *Head-Deep,* each displaying the phrase-making power that has made Dickey a notably epigrammatic poet as well as an image creator with the skills of a jeweler, a power reenfranchised by the brevity, spatial sculpting, and concentration characteristic of this later work. With compressive form, Dickey has vitalized landscapes as historical and evolutionary witnesses. In "Lakes of Värmland," he eulogizes and releases Viking warriors "in water turned to brass" by old wars, his precursors, of whom he says "I wish to gather near them. . . ," a discourse as doomed and moving as that of "The Seafarer," that Anglo-Saxon call to the quest tinged and poignant with late-life's hard wisdom. Indeed, the common landscapes in these poems are rife with danger, with cold, height, inhospitable trials, the blank mercilessness of rooms of air a man comes to—"No side protected, at home, play-penned / With holocaust. . . ." Dickey's late season poetry has left him with a chilling view, sometimes *vistas,* of mortal experience, one which does not always offer consequence for the yearner, though it has cyclical inevitability, which Dickey seems to regard as a sort of master rhythm to which man must seek to fit himself. For that, the poet's pastoral yearning has never been quite enough to satisfy Dickey, though he has deep roots in the agrarian and southern awareness of elemental cycles. Landscapes contain now, it would seem, the full evocation of final ends he wants. In the talky but, perhaps, undeniable "Farmers" he says:

When love gives him back the rough red of his face he dares

To true-up the seasons of life with the raggedness of earth,
    With the underground stream as it turns its water
Into the free stand of the well: a language takes hold

    And keeps on, barely making it, made
By pain: the pain that's had him ever since school,
    At the same time the indivisible common good
        Being shared among the family
Came clear to him: he disappears into fog . . .

His old habit of conducting big matters from the civic podium forces Dickey to assert what he does not dramatize, the noble and exemplary synchronization of environment and manhood, deed and principle. The southerner knows this ordinary farmer, praised into mystical junction with the elements, knows that language of pain and sacrifice; this is an old mainstay in the program of heroes. But Dickey's landscape here has less rhythmic conviction than the Burma Shave rhetoric somewhere behind it.

The new rhythm of landscape, an image strategy, antirational and associational, born of his interest in European modernist poetics, frequently permits Dickey the immediacy and dream-like intensity of consciousness receiving stimuli unmediated. Yet the form also weakens under statements made bluntly, as if they were without need of coloration, extension, appositional naming. "Gila Bend," a memory of pilot gunnery training in World War II, recalls the scene of "a cadaver / On foot" and it is really scene, not human dilemma,

which commands the poem's energy, a desertscape of ". . . small-stone heat /
No man can cross; no man could . . ." survive to "rise face-out"

> Full-force from the grave, where the sun is down on him
>
> Alone, harder than resurrection
>
> Is up: down harder
>   harder
> Much harder than that.

The slight comic bravado in the last line undermines grim memory because the
poet appears manipulative. One is hard-pressed not to feel the trochees, triply
repeated as "harder," slide into lapel-grabbing. The same intensity, however,
leads in *The Eagle's Mile* to an unusual feel of colloquy with natural forces
(often personified), and you feel strongly the renewed energy in elemental and
religious imagery such as that of birds, flight, and upward soaring. Poems praise
yearning for heights. As Dickey says in "Eagles," about ambition, "The higher
rock is / The more it lives." If you feel your suspension of disbelief faltering
before hierarchical ordering which Dickey loves, it is worth recalling that boasts
functioned in our tribal memory and literary heritage to defend against self-
defeat as well as to illuminate destiny. The stance of the aged warrior gazing at
eternals, willing survival, reappears when Dickey writes: "Where you take hold,
I will take / That stand in my mind, rock bird alive with the spirit- / life of
height . . ."

When the heroic imperative wanes and the pastoral waxes, Dickey locates
himself at edges of change. "Circuit," "Daybreak" and "Two Women" are all
poems of beaches, apparently the Atlantic off South Carolina. Dickey's beaches
are sentient forms constantly remaking themselves (as the soul docs) with
"their minds on a perfect connection" which, when you are upon them, allow
you to "meet yourself . . . ," even to make a kind of ultimate prayer: "Stretch
and tell me, Lord; / Let the place talk. / This may just be it." The colloquial
side-of-the-mouth tone of that last half-line has become a staple finishing line
for Dickey, where it cuts against the profound statements of revelation which
he favors.

Perhaps it is elegiac praise for places he views as junctures of meaning and
consequence which is the most southern aspect of Dickey's poetry. Place has
historical consciousness; there he locates rhythmic and final realities. There is
a great sweetness he is adamant to express and a singing quality in these poems,
which Dickey has always had but not pared to such efficient presentation as in
the violent "Night Bird," narcissistic "Daybreak," playful "To the Butterflies,"
and in the second half of "Two Women":

> Early light: light less
> Than other light. Sandal without power
> To mark sand. Softly,
> Her hair downward-burning, she walks here, her foot-touch

> The place itself,
>
> Like sand-grains, unintended,
>
> Born infinite.

The liquid balance that sounds, with *l*'s, the hieratic entry and imagistic power of this woman evokes Genesis, Eve, and Helen. Poe would have approved. With the poetry in *The Eagle's Mile,* Dickey fuses image medallions with compact narrative. The roaring rhythms of his mid-career lyrics slow to write less and get more said. A fine page architect, Dickey's effects range from list to epitaph. Even the civic witness he has long coveted works in "The Eagle's Mile," a poem ode-like in celebrating the masculine and democratic virtues of Justice William Douglas, an outdoorsman and master of Hopkins's "cliffs of the mind." Dickey sees Douglas's spirit riding over the last wilds of North Georgia, making contact with sources of origin that R. P. Warren would certainly have applauded, even if Tate and Ransom might have suspected an Adamic blindness:

> Catch into the hunted
> Horns of the buck, and into the deepest hearing—
> Nerveless, all bone, bone-tuned
> To leaves and twigs—with the grass drying wildly
> When you woke   where you stood with all the blades rising
> Behind you, and stepped out
>   possessing the trail . . .

Beside this man-on-the-trail solitary, Dickey stacks a poetry of tenderness in "Daughter," which few could so convincingly modulate, from a father's gladness at the delivery of his daughter to an exaltation of the guiding powers of life. It begins in the touch of a small finger:

> To him: not father of God, but assistant
> Father to this one. All forests are moving, all waves,
> All lava and ice. I lean. I touch
> One finger. Real God, roll.
> Roll.

Dickey's poetry has turned autumnal, but it is not gloomy. He has lived and lives as an unregenerate warrior in act and in spirit, a joy-seeker, a minister for whatever world he can act for and in. Richard Wilbur's phrase "the mood of manhood" describes what Dickey enacts in poetry. He rejects conventional structures and visions of the contemporary poet who answers only by dim light. Dickey's pastoral depends on heroic enterprise, on out-of-shape Rocky-like runners ("The Olympian"), on a middle-aged man's fantasy of foiling an assault by stripping the thief of his weapon ("Spring-Shock"), on watching a snowfall that may be someone's "very great winning hand" ("Snow Thickets").

In all places and times, Dickey believes, manliness connects to consequence, a way, a courage of behaving by which we can see, as "Expanses" tells us, that "a man comes; / It's true, he's alive. . . ." To know that is to frame acceptance, a submission to the rhythms of being, and finally "Brother: boundless, / Earthbound, trouble-free, and all you want— / Joy like short grass."

Urban America breeds few readers of poetry who favor the old-fashioned man at the heart of *The Eagle's Mile,* a man who forged a life from wilds we don't have much of now, a man for whom the hard scenes of memory speak the unspeakable, one whose destiny is not accusation, guilt, burdened consciousness, but is to live without sophistry. That is Dickey's motion, however, one inseparable from the environmental awareness of his southern experience. In "The Little More," a sort of catechism, he describes the marginal quality of time between boyhood and maturity, the immortal moment that cannot truly be said but may be seen as "Joy set in the bending void / Between the oars" of a rowed craft. Joy, all boys must learn, is the lure of living, the quest's end. It can come only to the boy, Dickey believes, who submits to evolving a competent self. "The Little More" finds Dickey's hero emerged from the wilderness, paternally wise, offering what Dickey has always had in abundance, appetite and the power to "carry," which is simultaneously a metaphor and a faith:

> Boy who will always be glanced-at
>
> and then fixed
>
> In warm gazes, already the past knows
> It cannot invent you again,
>
> For the glitter on top of the current
> Is not the current.
>
> No, but what dances on it is
> More beautiful than what takes its time
> Beneath. Running on a single unreleased
> Eternal breath, rammed
> With carry, its all-out dream and dread
>
> Surging bull-breasted,
> Head-down, unblocked.

The public cadence of exhortation and the private cadence of knowledge—to be and to know—are in the southern poetry of James Dickey, as mysterious as our destiny. From the pastoral to the prayerful to the final "all-out" labors of the heroic athlete, James Dickey praises. It is not athletic success that Dickey covets for us but what he calls an "Eternal breath / rammed with carry," which has to be pregnant destiny, and more, a little more, as he says. He celebrates consequence, the order within all other orders, and motions, which men and women who give their lives to poetry bear upon the page as the issue of life. Life's issue, as he might say, is everything. It is local rhythm. It is many motions braided in one.

Bibliography

WORKS BY JAMES DICKEY

Alnilam. Garden City, N.Y.: Doubleday, 1987.

Babel to Byzantium: Poets & Poetry Now. New York: Farrar, Straus & Giroux, 1968.

Bronwen, the Traw, and the Shape-Shifter. San Diego, New York, and London: Bruccoli Clark and Harcourt Brace Jovanovich, 1986.

Buckdancer's Choice. Middletown, Conn.: Wesleyan University Press, 1965.

The Central Motion: Poems, 1968–1979. Middletown, Conn.: Wesleyan University Press, 1983.

Deliverance. Boston: Houghton Mifflin, 1970.

Drowning with Others. Middletown, Conn.: Wesleyan University Press, 1962.

The Eagle's Mile. Hanover, N.H., and London: Wesleyan University Press and University Press of New England, 1990.

The Early Motion: Drowning with Others and Helmets. Middletown, Conn.: Wesleyan University Press, 1981.

The Eye-Beaters, Blood, Victory, Madness, Buckhead and Mercy. Garden City, N.Y.: Doubleday, 1970.

Falling, May Day Sermon, and Other Poems. Middletown, Conn.: Wesleyan University Press, 1981.

God's Images: The Bible: A New Vision. Birmingham, Ala.: Oxmoor House, 1977.

Helmets. Middletown, Conn.: Wesleyan University Press, 1964.

Into the Stone and Other Poems. In *Poems of Today VII,* ed. John Hall Wheelock. New York: Scribner's, 1960.

Jericho: The South Beheld. Birmingham, Ala.: Oxmoor House, 1974.

This bibliography is based primarily on the bibliography from Gordon Van Ness's *Outbelieving Existence: The Measured Motion of James Dickey* (Columbia, S.C.: Camden House, 1992), and I am grateful to Professor Van Ness and to Camden House for its use.

257

Night Hurdling: Poems, Essays, Conversations, Commencements, and Afterwords. Columbia, S.C., and Bloomfield Hills, Mich.: Bruccoli Clark, 1983.

Poems, 1957–1967. Middletown, Conn.: Wesleyan University Press, 1967.

Puella. Garden City, N.Y.: Doubleday, 1982.

Self-Interviews. Garden City, N.Y.: Doubleday, 1970.

Sorties. Garden City, N.Y.: Doubleday, 1971.

Southern Light. Birmingham, Ala.: Oxmoor House, 1991.

The Strength of Fields. Garden City, N.Y.: Doubleday, 1979.

The Suspect in Poetry. Madison, Minn.: Sixties Press, 1964.

Tucky the Hunter. New York: Crown, 1978.

Wayfarer: A Voice from the Southern Mountains. Birmingham, Ala.: Oxmoor House, 1988.

To the White Sea. Boston: Houghton Mifflin, 1993.

The Whole Motion: Collected Poems 1945–1992. Hanover, N.H.: University Press of New England, 1992.

The Zodiac. Garden City, N.Y.: Doubleday, 1976.

CRITICISM ABOUT JAMES DICKEY

Adams, Percy. "The Epic Tradition and the Novel." *Southern Review* NS 9 (Spring 1973): 300–310.

Adams, Phoebe-Lou. *"Wayfarer."* *Atlantic Monthly* 263 (January 1989): 120.

Anderson, Mia. "A Portrait of the Artist as White-Water Canoeist." *James Dickey Newsletter* 2 (Spring 1986): 11–16.

Applewhite, James. "Reflections on *Puella.*" *Southern Review* 21 (January 1985): 214–19.

Armour, Robert. *"Deliverance:* Four Variations of the American Adam." *Literature / Film Quarterly* 1 (July 1973): 280–85.

Arnett, David L. "An Interview with James Dickey." *Contemporary Literature* 16 (Summer 1975): 286–300.

Aronson, James. *"Self-Interviews."* *Antioch Review* 30 (Fall/Winter 1970–71): 463–64.

Ashley, Franklin. "James Dickey: The Art of Poetry XX." *Paris Review* 65–68 (Spring 1976): 52–88.

Balakian, Peter. "Poets of Empathy." *Literary Review: An International Journal of Contemporary Writing* 27, no. 1 (1983): 135–46.

Barshay, Robert. "Machismo in *Deliverance.*" *Teaching English in the Two-Year College* 1, no. 3 (1975): 169–73.

Bartlett, Lee, and Witemeyer, Hugh. "Ezra Pound and James Dickey: A Correspondence and a Kinship." *Paideuma* 11 (1982): 290–312.

Baughman Ronald. "In Dickey's Latest, Blindness Opens a Man's Eyes to Life." *Philadelphia Inquirer,* 31 May 1987, S1, S8.

———. "James Dickey's *The Eye-Beaters:* 'An Agonizing New Life.'" *South Carolina Review* 10 (April 1978): 81–88.

———. "James Dickey's War Poetry: A 'Saved, Shaken Life.'" *South Carolina Review* 15 (April 1983): 38–48.

———. *Understanding James Dickey.* Columbia: University of South Carolina Press, 1985.

———, ed. *The Voiced Connections of James Dickey: Interviews and Conversations.* Columbia: University of South Carolina Press, 1989.

Beidler, Peter G. "'The Pride of Thine Heart Hath Deceived Thee': Narrative Distortion in Dickey's *Deliverance.*" *South Carolina Review* 3 (December 1972): 29–40.

Bennett, Joseph. "A Man With a Voice." *New York Times Book Review,* 6 February 1966, 10.

Bennett, Ross. "'The Firebombing': A Reappraisal." *American Literature* 52 (November 1980): 430–48.

Berke, Roberta. *Bounds Out of Bounds: A Compass for Recent American and British Poetry.* New York: Oxford University Press, 1981.

Berry, David. "Harmony with the Dead: James Dickey's Descent into the Underworld." *Southern Quarterly* 12 (April 1974): 233–44.

Berry, Wendell. "James Dickey's New Book." *Poetry* 105 (November 1964): 130–31.

Blair, John. "'Breeding Lilacs Out of the Dead Land': James Dickey's *Alnilam* and *Deliverance.*" In Kirschten, *Critical Essays on James Dickey,* 210–19.

Bloom, Harold. "James Dickey: From 'The Other' through *The Early Motion.*" *Southern Review* 21 (January 1985): 63–78.

———, ed. *James Dickey.* New York: Chelsea House Publishers, 1987.

Bly, Robert. "The Collapse of James Dickey." *The Sixties* (Spring 1967): 70–79.

———. "The Work of James Dickey." *The Sixties* (Winter 1964): 41–57.

Bobbitt, Joan. "Unnatural Order in the Poetry of James Dickey." *Concerning Poetry* 11 (Spring 1978): 39–44.

Booklist. "God's Images: The Bible: A New Vision." 74 (15 October 1977): 344.

Bornhouser, Fred. "Poetry by the Poem." *Virginia Quarterly Review* 41 (Winter 1965): 146–52

Bowers, Neal. *James Dickey: The Poet as Pitchman.* Columbia: University of Missouri Press, 1985.

Bowers-Hill, Jane. " 'With Eyes Far More Than Human': Dickey's Misunderstood Monster." *James Dickey Newsletter* 1 (Fall 1984): 2–8.

Bowers-Martin, Jane. *"Jericho* and *God's Images:* The Old Dickey Theme." In Weigl and Hummer, 143–51.

Brewer, Angelin. " 'To Rise above Time:' The Mythic Hero in Dickey's *Deliverance* and *Alnilam." James Dickey Newsletter* 7 (Fall 1990): 9–14.

Bruccoli, Matthew J., ed. *Pages: The World of Books, Writers, and Writing.* Detroit: Gale Research, 1976.

Burnshaw, Stanley. "Star-Beasts of Intellect and Madness: *The Zodiac." Book World,* 21 November 1976, E1.

Calhoun, Richard J. "After a Long Silence: James Dickey as South Carolina Writer." *South Carolina Review* 9 (November 1976): 12–20.

———. " 'His Reason Argues With His Invention'—James Dickey's *Self-Interviews* and *The Eye-Beaters." South Carolina Review* 3 (June 1971): 9–16.

———. "Whatever Happened to the Poet-Critic?" *Southern Literary Journal* 1 (Autumn 1968): 75–88.

Calhoun, Richard J., and Robert W. Hill. *James Dickey.* Boston: Twayne, 1983.

Calhoun, Richard J., ed. *James Dickey: The Expansive Imagination: A Collection of Critical Essays.* DeLand, Fla.: Everett/Edwards, 1973.

Carnes, Bruce. "Deliverance in James Dickey's 'On the Coosawattee' and *Deliverance." Notes on Contemporary Literature* 7 (March 1977): 2–4.

Carroll, Paul. "James Dickey as Critic: *Babel to Byzantium." Chicago Review* 20 (November 1968): 82–87.

———. *The Poem In Its Skin.* Chicago: Big Table Publishing Company, 1968.

———, ed. *The Young American Poets.* Chicago: Big Table Publishing Company, 1968.

Cassity, Turner. "Double Dutch: *The Strength of Fields* and *The Zodiac." Parnassus: Poetry in Review* (Spring/Summer 1981): 177–93.

Cavell, Marcia. "Visions of Battlements." *Partisan Review* 38, no. 1 (1971): 117–21.

Chappell, Fred. "Dickey Novel Wordy, but Not Boring." *The (Columbia, S.C.) State,* 21 June 1987, 6F.

———. "Vatic Poesy." *The (Columbia, S.C.) State,* 9 December 1991, 5F.

Christian Century. "Books of the Season." 94 (14 December 1977): 1173.

Clausen, Christopher. "Grecian Thoughts in the Home Fields: Reflections on Southern Poetry." *Georgia Review* 32 (Summer 1978): 283–305.

Connell, Evan S. *"Deliverance."* New York Times Book Review, 22 March 1970, 1, 23.

Corrington, John William. "James Dickey's *Poems 1957–1967:* A Personal Appraisal." *Georgia Review* 22 (Spring 1968): 12–23.

Covel, Robert C. "The Metaphysics of Experience: James Dickey's 'The Scarred Girl.'" *James Dickey Newsletter* 1 (Spring 1985): 24–30.

———. "'A Starry Place': The Energized Man in Dickey's *Alnilam."* James Dickey Newsletter 5 (Spring 1989): 5–17.

Davis, Charles E. "The Wilderness Revisited: Irony in James Dickey's *Deliverance."* Studies in American Fiction 4 (Autumn 1976): 223–30.

Davison, Peter. "The Difficulties of Being Major: The Poetry of Robert Lowell and James Dickey." *Atlantic Monthly* 220 (October 1967): 116–21.

DeCandido, GraceAnne A. *"God's Images: The Bible—A New Vision."* Library Journal 103 (15 January 1978): 154.

De La Fuente, Patricia, ed. *James Dickey: Splintered Sunlight.* Edinburg, Tex.: Pan American University, 1979.

DeMott, Benjamin. "The 'More Life' School and James Dickey." *Saturday Review* (28 March 1970): 25–26, 38.

Dickey, William. "Talking About What's Real." *Hudson Review* 18 (Winter 1965–66): 613–17.

Dillenberger, Jane. *"God's Images: The Bible: A New Vision."* Theology Today 35 (January 1979): 507–11.

Donald, David Herbert. "Promised Land or Paradise Lost: The South Beheld." *Georgia Review* 29 (Spring 1975): 184–87.

Donoghue, Denis. "The Good Old Complex Fate." *Hudson Review* 17 (Summer 1964): 267–77.

Doughtie, Edward. "Art and Nature in *Deliverance."* Southwest Review 64 (Spring 1979): 167–80.

Duncan, Robert. "Oriented by Instinct by Stars." *Poetry* 105 (November 1964): 131–33.

Edwards, C. Hines. "Dickey's *Deliverance:* The Owl and the Eye." *Critique: Studies in Modern Fiction* 15, no. 2 (1973): 95–101.

———. "Initiation Ritual in 'The Shark's Parlor.'" *James Dickey Newsletter* 7 (Spring 1991): 19–23.

Elledge, Jim. "James Dickey between Wars: An 'Appreciation' of the *Gadfly* Poems." In Kirschten, *Critical Essays on James Dickey,* 78–89.

———. *James Dickey: A Bibliography, 1947–1974.* Metuchen, N.J.: Scarecrow Press, 1979.

———. "James Dickey: A Supplementary Bibliography, 1975–1980: Part I." *Bulletin of Bibliography* 38 (April–June 1981): 92–100, 104.

———. "James Dickey: A Supplementary Bibliography, 1975–1980: Part II." *Bulletin of Bibliography* 38 (July–September 1981): 150–55.

Endel, Peggy Goodman. "Dickey, Dante, and the Demonic: Reassessing *Deliverance*." *American Literature,* 60: 4 (1988): 611–24. Rpt. in Kirschten, *Critical Essays on James Dickey,* 175–86.

Evans, Eli N. "The South the South Sees: *Jericho*." *New York Times Book Review,* 9 February 1975, 4–5.

Eyster, Warren. "Two Regional Novels." *Sewanee Review* 79 (Summer 1971): 469–74.

Filler, Louis, ed. *Seasoned Authors for a New Season: The Search for Standards in Popular Writing.* Bowling Green, Ohio: Bowling Green University Popular Press, 1980.

Fraser, G. S. "The Magicians." *Partisan Review* 38 (1971–72): 469–78.

Friedman, Norman. "The Wesleyan Poets—II." *Chicago Review* 19 (January 1966): 55–67, 72.

Glancy, Eileen. *James Dickey: The Critic as Poet.* Troy, N.Y.: Whitson, 1971.

Gregor, Arthur. "James Dickey, American Romantic." In Calhoun, *James Dickey: Expansive Imagination,* 77–80.

Greiner, Donald J. "The Harmony of Bestiality in James Dickey's *Deliverance*." *South Carolina Review* 5 (December 1972): 43–49.

Guillory, Daniel L. "Myth and Meaning in James Dickey's *Deliverance*." *College Literature* 3 (1976): 56–62.

———. "Water Magic in the Poetry of James Dickey." *English Language Notes* 8 (December 1970): 131–37.

Guttenberg, Barnett. "The Pattern of Redemption in Dickey's *Deliverance*." *Critique: Studies in Modern Fiction* 18, no. 3 (1977): 83–91.

Harmon, William. "Herself as the Environment" [review of *Puella*]. *Carolina Quarterly* 35 (Fall 1982): 91–94.

Haule, James M. " 'The Thing Itself Is in That': Closure in the Poetry of James Dickey." In De La Fuente, 31–44.

Heilbrun, Carolyn. "The Masculine Wilderness of the American Novel." *Saturday Review* (29 January 1972): 41–44.

Heylen, Romy. "James Dickey's *The Zodiac:* A Self-Translation?" *James Dickey Newsletter* 6 (Spring 1990): 2–17. Rpt. in Kirschten, *Critical Essays on James Dickey,* 187–200.

Hill, Robert W. "James Dickey: Comic Poet." In Calhoun, *James Dickey: Expansive Imagination,* 143–55.

Hodge, Marion. "All that Religious Stuff He Had Learned How to Say: Camouflage, Ritual, and Writing in *To the White Sea.*" *James Dickey Newsletter* 11 (Fall 1994): 12–19.

———. "James Dickey's Natural Heaven and the Tradition." *James Dickey Newsletter* 7 (Fall 1990): 15–21.

———. "The New King at Dover." *James Dickey Newsletter* 2 (Fall 1985): 17–20.

Hollahan, Eugene. "An Anxiety of Influence Overcome: Dickey's *Puella* and Hopkins' *The Wreck of the 'Deutschland.'*" *James Dickey Newsletter* 1 (Spring 1985): 2–12.

Holley, Linda Tarte. "Design and Focus in James Dickey's *Deliverance.*" *South Carolina Review* 10 (April 1978): 90–98.

Howard, Richard. "On James Dickey." *Partisan Review* 33 (Summer 1966): 414–28, 479–86.

Italia, Paul G. "Love and Lust in James Dickey's *Deliverance.*" *Modern Fiction Studies* 21 (Summer 1975): 203–13.

Jameson, Fredric. "The Great American Hunter, or, Ideological Content in the Novel." *College English* 34 (November 1972): 180–97.

Johnston, Albert H. *"God's Images: The Bible—A New Vision."* *Publishers Weekly* 212 (15 August 1977): 63.

———. *"Tucky the Hunter."* *Publishers Weekly* 214 (31 July 1978): 88.

Jolly, John. "Drew Ballinger as 'Sacrificial God' in James Dickey's *Deliverance.*" *South Carolina Review* 17 (Spring 1985): 102–8.

Jones, Betty Ann. *"Jericho:* The Marketing Story." In Bruccoli, 248–53.

Kalstone, David. *"Sorties."* *New York Times Book Review,* 23 January 1972, 6, 24.

Keesey, Douglas. "James Dickey and the Macho Persona." In Kirschten, *Critical Essays on James Dickey,* 201–10.

Kennedy, X. J. "Joys, Griefs, and 'All Things Innocent, Hapless, Forsaken.'" *New York Times Book Review,* 23 August 1964, 5.

———. "Sometimes It's the Sound That Counts." *New York Times Book Review,* 15 July 1962, 4.

Kerley, Gary. "Dickey Delivers Second Novel." *Gainesville Times,* 19 July 1987, 5E.

———. "Understanding 'This Hunter Made Out of Stars': The Myth of Orion in James Dickey's *Alnilam.*" *James Dickey Newsletter* 4 (Fall 1978): 15–22.

———. "Unifying the Energy and Balancing the Vision: Nature, Man, and Quest in James Dickey's *Deliverance* and *Alnilam.*" *James Dickey Newsletter* 5 (Spring 1989): 17–26.

Kirkus. "*Bronwen, The Traw, and the Shape-Shifter.*" 54 (15 August 1986): 1289–90.

———. "*Tucky the Hunter.*" 46 (15 August 1978): 917.

Kirschten, Robert. "*Approaching Prayer*": Ritual and the Shape of Myth in the Poetry of A. R. Ammons and James Dickey. Baton Rouge: Louisiana State University Press, forthcoming.

———, ed. *Critical Essays on James Dickey.* New York: G. K. Hall, 1994.

———. "Form and Genre in James Dickey's 'Falling': The Great Goddess Gives Birth to the Earth." *South Atlantic Review* 58 (May 1993): 127–54. Rpt. in Kirschten, *Critical Essays on James Dickey,* 153–74.

———. *James Dickey and the Gentle Ecstasy of Earth: A Reading of the Poems.* Baton Rouge: Louisiana State University Press, 1988.

———. "James Dickey's 'Approaching Prayer': Ritual and the Shape of Myth." *South Atlantic Review* 61 (Winter 1996): 27–54.

———. "The Momentum of Word-Magic in James Dickey's *The Eye-Beaters, Blood, Victory, Madness, Buckhead and Mercy.*" *Contemporary Literature* 36 (Spring 1995): 130–63.

Korges, James. "James Dickey and Other Good Poets." *Minnesota Review* 3 (Summer 1963): 473–91.

Kostelanetz, Richard. "Flyswatter and Gadfly." *Shenandoah* 16 (Spring 1965): 92–95.

Kunz, Don. "Learning the Hard Way in James Dickey's *Deliverance.*" *Western American Literature* 12 (February 1978): 289–301.

Landess, Thomas. "Traditional Criticism and the Poetry of James Dickey." *Occasional Review* 3 (Summer 1975): 5–26.

Lask, Thomas. "Serene and Star-Crazed." *New York Times,* 22 January 1977, 19.

Laurence, Patricia. "James Dickey's *Puella* in Flight." *South Carolina Review* 26 (Spring 1994): 61–71.

Leibowitz, Herbert. "The Moiling of Secret Forces: *The Eye-Beaters, Blood, Victory, Madness, Buckhead and Mercy.*" *New York Times Book Review,* 8 November 1970, 20, 22.

Lensing, George. "James Dickey and the Movements of Imagination." In Calhoun, *James Dickey: Expansive Imagination,* 157–75.

———. "The Neo-Romanticism of James Dickey." *South Carolina Review* 10 (April 1978): 20–32.

Lieberman, Laurence. *The Achievement of James Dickey.* Glenview, Ill.: Scott, Foresman, 1968.

————. "Erotic Pantheism in James Dickey's 'Madness.' " *South Carolina Review* 26 (Spring 1994): 72–86.

————. "Exchanges: Inventions in Two Voices: *The Strength of Fields.*" *Sewanee Review* 88 (Summer 1980): lxv–lxvi.

————. "James Dickey—The Deepening of Being." In Lieberman, *The Achievement of James Dickey,* 1–21.

————. "Notes on James Dickey's Style." *The Far Point* 2 (Spring/Summer 1968): 57–63.

————. "The Worldly Mystic." *Hudson Review* 20 (Autumn 1967): 513–20.

Lindborg, Henry J. "James Dickey's *Deliverance:* The Ritual of Art." *Southern Literary Journal* 6 (Spring 1974): 83–90.

Literature as Revolt and Revolt as Literature: Three Studies in the Rhetoric of Non-Oratorical Forms. Minneapolis: Proceedings of the Fourth Annual University of Minnesota Spring Symposium in Speech-Communication, 1969.

Logue, J. D. "Books About the South." *Southern Living* 9 (February 1974): 184, 186.

————. "Books About the South." *Southern Living* 14 (January 1979): 68.

Longen, Eugene M. "Dickey's *Deliverance:* Sex and the Great Outdoors." *Southern Literary Journal* 9 (Spring 1977): 137–49.

Ludvigson, Susan. "A Radical Departure for James Dickey" [*on Puella*]. *The (Columbia, S.C.) State,* 31 October 1982, G6.

Macaulay, David. *"Bronwen, the Traw, and the Shape-Shifter."* New York Times Book Review, 8 March 1987, 31.

Maloff, Saul. "Poet Takes His Turn as Critic: *Babel to Byzantium.*" *Book World,* 30 June 1968, 10.

Mapp, Joy E. "James Dickey's 'The Eye-Beaters': The Savage Spear of Salvation." *James Dickey Newsletter* 8 (Spring 1992): 27–35.

Marin, Daniel B. "James Dickey's *Deliverance:* Darkness Visible." *South Carolina Review* 3 (November 1970): 49–59.

Markos, Donald W. "Art and Immediacy: James Dickey's *Deliverance.*" *Southern Review* NS 7 (Summer 1971): 947–53.

Marty, Martin E. "God and Man: *God's Images.*" *New York Times Book Review,* 18 December 1977, 13.

Martz, William J. "A Note on Meaningless Being in 'Cherrylog Road.' " In Calhoun, *James Dickey: Expansive Imagination,* 81–83.

Mason, Kenneth C. "A Book to Relish." *Prairie Schooner* 54 (Winter 1980–81): 107–8.

McGinnis, Wayne D. "Mysticism in the Poetry of James Dickey." *New Laurel Review* 5, nos. 1–2 (1975): 5–10.

McHughes, Janet Larsen. "From Manuscript to Performance Script: The Evolution of a Poem." *Literature in Performance* 2 (November 1981): 26–49.

McNamara, Eugene. "James Dickey's 'The Eye-Beaters': Poetry of the Burning Bush." *James Dickey Newsletter* 3 (Fall 1986): 20–24.

Medwick, Cathleen. "Moby Dickey." *Vogue* (June 1987): 118, 120.

Meredith, William. "A Good Time for All: *Poems 1957–1967.*" *New York Times Book Review,* 23 April 1967, 4, 46.

Metz, Violette. "The Blessed Beasts and Children: An Examination of Imagery in James Dickey's *Poems 1957–1967.*" In De La Fuente, 45–55.

Mills, Ralph J. *Creation's Very Self: On the Personal Elements in Recent American Poetry.* Fort Worth: Texas Christian University Press, 1969.

———. *Cry of the Human: Essays on Contemporary American Poetry.* Urbana, Chicago, and London: University of Illinois Press, 1975.

———. "The Poetry of James Dickey." *TriQuarterly* 11–14 (Winter 1968): 231–42.

Mitgang, Herbert. "Man, Nature and Everyday Activities in Verse." *New York Times,* 27 October 1990, 16.

Mizejewski, Linda. "Shamanism Toward Confessionalism: James Dickey, Poet." *Georgia Review* 32 (Summer 1978): 409–19.

Monk, Donald. "Colour Symbolism in James Dickey's *Deliverance.*" *Journal of American Studies* 11, no. 2 (1977): 261–79.

Morris, Christopher. "Dark Night of the Flesh: The Apotheosis of the Bestial in James Dickey's *The Zodiac.*" *Contemporary Poetry* 4, no. 4 (1982): 31–47.

Morris, Harry. "A Formal View of the Poetry of Dickey, Garrigue, and Simpson." *Sewanee Review* 77 (Spring 1969): 318–25.

Nemerov, Howard. "Poems of Darkness and a Specialized Light." *Sewanee Review* 71 (Winter 1963): 99–104.

Niflis, N. Michael. "A Special Kind of Fantasy: James Dickey on the Razor's Edge." *Southwest Review* 57 (Autumn 1972): 311–17.

Norton, John. "Ego-tripping with James Dickey." *Osceola* (23 May 1972): 10–11.

Oates, Joyce Carol. "Out of Stone into Flesh: The Imagination of James Dickey." *Modern Poetry Studies* 5, no. 2 (1974): 97–144.

Pair, Joyce. " 'Dancing With God': Totemism in Dickey's 'May Day Sermon'." In Kirschten, *Critical Essays on James Dickey,* 135–52.

———, ed. *James Dickey Newsletter.* DeKalb College, Dunwoody, Ga. 30038.

———. "Postmodernism and *To the White Sea,*" *James Dickey Newsletter* 12 (Spring 1996): 19–23.

Palmer, R. Barton. "Narration, Text, Intertext: The Two Versions of *Deliverance*." *James Dickey Newsletter* 2 (Spring 1986): 2–10.

Parini, Jay. "James Dickey's Massive and Mystifying *Alnilam*." *USA Today,* 29 May 1987, 70.

Peterman, Gina. "The Clothing Metaphor in James Dickey's 'Springer Mountain' and 'Falling.' " *James Dickey Newsletter* 7 (Spring 1991): 12–18.

Peters, Robert. "The Phenomenon of James Dickey, Currently." *Western Humanities Review* 34 (Spring 1980): 159–66.

Pierce, Constance. "Dickey's 'Adultery': A Ritual of Renewal." *Concerning Poetry* 9, no. 2 (1976): 67–69.

Playboy. "Review of *Alnilam*." 34 (August 1987): 25.

Preiss, David. "Art Books." *American Artist* 41 (November 1977): 26.

Prescott, Peter S. "Lost in the Stars: *The Zodiac*." *Newsweek* 88 (6 December 1976): 89.

Ramsey, Paul. "James Dickey: Meter and Structure." In Calhoun, *James Dickey: Expansive Imagination,* 177–94.

Reeves, Garland. "Poet's Perspective Journal Criticizes Works of Others." *Birmingham News,* 13 February 1972, E7.

Rose, Maxine S. "On Being Born Again: James Dickey's 'May Day Sermon to the Women of Gilmer County, Georgia, by a Woman Preacher Leaving the Baptist Church.' " *Research Studies* 46 (December 1978): 254–58.

Rosenthal, M. L. *The New Poets: American and British Poetry Since World War II.* New York: Oxford University Press, 1967.

Rubin, Louis D. "Rituals of Risk." *New York Times Book Review,* 3 June 1984, 23.

Schechter, Harold. "The Eye and the Nerve: A Psychological Reading of James Dickey's *Deliverance*." In Filler, 4–19.

Schmitt, Ronald. "Transformations of the Hero in James Dickey's *Deliverance*." *James Dickey Newsletter* 8 (Fall 1991): 9–16.

Seale, Jan. "Narrative Technique in James Dickey's 'May Day Sermon.' " In De La Fuente, 24–30.

Shaw, Robert B. "Poets in Midstream." *Poetry* 118 (July 1971): 228–33.

Silverstein, Norman. "James Dickey's Muscular Eschatology." *Salmagundi* 22–23 (Spring/Summer 1973): 258–68.

Skinner, Izora. "A Fun Poem by James Dickey." In De La Fuente, 56–58.

Skipp, Francis. "James Dickey's *The Zodiac*: The Heart of the Matter." *Concerning Poetry* 14, no. 1 (1981): 1–10.

Sloan, Thomas O. "The Open Poem is a Now Poem: Dickey's 'May Day Sermon.' " In *Literature as Revolt and Revolt as Literature: Three Studies in the Rhetoric of Non-Oratorical Forms,* 17–31.

Smith, Dave. "James Dickey's Motions." *South Carolina Review* 26 (Spring 1994): 41–60.

———. "The Strength of James Dickey." *Poetry* 137 (March 1981): 349–58.

Smith, Mack. "James Dickey's Varieties of Creation: The Voices of Narrative." *James Dickey Newsletter* 1 (Spring 1985): 18–22.

Smith, Raymond. "The Poetic Faith of James Dickey." *Modern Poetry Studies* 2, no. 1 (1972): 259–72.

Spears, Monroe. *Dionysus and the City: Modernism in Twentieth-Century Poetry.* New York: Oxford University Press, 1970.

———. "James Dickey as a Southern Visionary." *Virginia Quarterly* 63 (Winter 1987): 110–23.

Sporborg, Ann. *"Bronwen, the Traw, and the Shape-Shifter." James Dickey Newsletter* 4 (Fall 1987): 25–28.

Starr, William W. "James Dickey's Novel Explores Father and Son Relationships." *The (Columbia, S.C.) State,* 17 May 1987, 1F, 10F.

———. "The Title Fight." *The (Columbia, S.C.) State,* 16 October 1988, 1F, 8F.

Steadman, Venson. "A Skillful Tribute, Nothing More: *Jericho: The South Beheld." Osceola* (14 February 1975): 9.

Steinberg, Sybil. *"Alnilam." Publishers Weekly* 231 (17 April 1987): 65.

Stepanchev, Stephen. *American Poetry Since 1945.* New York: Harper and Row, 1965.

Strange, William C. "To Dream, To Remember: James Dickey's *Buckdancer's Choice." Northwest Review* 7 (Fall/Winter 1965–66): 33–42.

Strong, Paul. "James Dickey's Arrow of Deliverance." *South Carolina Review* 11 (November 1978): 108–16.

Suarez, Ernest. *James Dickey and the Politics of Canon: Assessing the Savage Ideal.* Columbia: University of Missouri Press, 1993.

———. "Buckdancer's Choice." In Frank N. Magill, ed., *Masterplots II: Poetry, 1992* (Pasadena: Salem Press, 1993), 301–3.

———. *"Deliverance:* Dickey's Original Screenplay." *Southern Quarterly* 33 (Winter/Spring 1994–1995): 161–69.

———. "Dickey's Literary Reputation." *South Carolina Review* 26 (Spring 1994): 141–54.

———. "Dickey on Melville." *South Carolina Review* 26 (Spring 1994): 115–26.

———. "Emerson in Vietnam: Dickey, Bly and the New Left." *Southern Literary Journal* 23 (Spring 1991): 77–97. Rpt. in *Critical Perspectives in American Literature* (New York: G. K. Hall, 1994), 105–22.

———. "Falling." In Frank N. Magill, ed., *Masterplots II: Poetry, 1992* (Pasadena: Salem Press, 1993), 724–26.

———. "Interview with James Dickey." *Contemporary Literature* 31 (Summer 1990): 116–32.

———. "An Interview with James Dickey: The Novels." *Texas Review,* forthcoming.

———. "James Dickey." In Frank N. Magill, ed., *Critical Survey of Poetry* (Pasadena: Salem Press, 1992), 310–16.

———. "James Dickey and David Bottoms: Interpreting Influence." *James Dickey Newsletter* 13 (Fall 1996): 10–17.

———. "James Dickey and the Politics of Canon: A Literary Civil War." *James Dickey Newsletter* 9 (Fall 1992): 2–11.

———. "James Dickey at Seventy" *Dictionary of Literary Biography Yearbook: 1993* (Bloomfield Hills, Mich., and Columbia, S.C.: Bruccoli-Clark, 1993), 136–38.

———. "James Dickey's Literary Reputation: Romanticism and Hedonism in *To the White Sea* and *Deliverance.*" *South Carolina Review* 26 (Spring 1994): 141–55.

———. "Real God, Roll'': Muldrow's Primitive Creedo" *James Dickey Newsletter* 10, (Spring 1994): 3–14.

———. "Review of *The Whole Motion.*" *James Dickey Newsletter* 9 (Fall 1992): 24–29.

———. "Review of *James Dickey: A Descriptive Bibliography.*" *Analytical and Enumerative Bibliography* 5, no. 1 (1991): 62–64.

———. "The Southern Writer and the Politically Correct." *Contemporary Literature* (Spring 1992): 157–62.

———. "Towards a New Southern Poetry." *Southern Review* 33 (Winter 1996): 181–96.

———. "The Uncollected Dickey: Pound, New Criticism and the Narrative Image." *American Poetry* 8 (Fall 1990): 128–45.

Taylor, Chet. "A Look into the Heart of Darkness: A View of *Deliverance.*" In De La Fuente, 59–64.

Taylor, Welford D. "Dickey Pursues Universal Truths in *Alnilam.*" *Richmond News Leader,* 2 September 1987, 15.

Tillinghast, Richard. "James Dickey's *The Whole Motion.*" *Southern Review* 28 4 (Autumn 1992): 971–80.

Towers, Robert. "Prometheus Blind." *New York Times Book Review,* 21 June 1987, 7.

Tucker, Charles C. "Knowledge Up, Down, and Beyond: Dickey's 'The Driver' and 'Falling.' " *CEA Critic* 38, no. 4 (1976): 4–10.

Van Ness, A. Gordon. " 'The Lonely Self-Watchful Passion': Narrative and the Poetic Role of Robinson Jeffers and James Dickey." *James Dickey Newsletter* 11 (Spring 1995): 2–15.

———. " 'Stand Waiting, My Love, Where You Are': Women in James Dickey's Early Poetry." *James Dickey Newsletter* 6 (Fall 1989): 2–11.

———. "Steering to the Morning Land: The Poet as Redeemer in Dickey's *The Zodiac.*" *James Dickey Newsletter* 2 (Fall 1985): 2–10.

———. "To Splinter Uncontrollably Whole: Circularity and the Philosophic Subtext in James Dickey's *The Eagle's Mile.*" In Kirschten, *Critical Essays on James Dickey,* 220–32.

———. "The Voicing of the Perception: James Dickey and the Image of Stone." *James Dickey Newsletter* 12 (Fall 1995): 2–8.

———. "*Wayfarer: A Voice from the Southern Mountains.*" *James Dickey Newsletter* 5 (Spring 1989): 31–33.

———. " 'When Memory Stands without Sleep': James Dickey's War Years." *James Dickey Newsletter* 4 (Fall 1987): 2–13.

Varn, Jim. "Primordial Reunions: Motion in James Dickey's Early Poetry." *James Dickey Newsletter* 5 (Fall 1988): 4–14.

Waggoner, Hyatt H. *American Poets: From the Puritans to the Present.* Boston: Houghton Mifflin, 1968.

Wagner, Linda. "*Deliverance:* Initiation and Possibility." *South Carolina Review* 10 (April 1978): 49–55.

Warren, Robert Penn. "A Poem about the Ambition of Poetry: *The Zodiac.*" *New York Times Book Review,* 14 November 1976, 8.

Weatherby, H. L. "The Way of Exchange in James Dickey's Poetry." *Sewanee Review* 74 (Summer 1966): 669–80.

Weigl, Bruce, and T. R. Hummer, eds. *The Imagination as Glory: The Poetry of James Dickey.* Urbana and Chicago: University of Illinois Press, 1984.

Whalin, Kathleen D. "*Bronwen, the Traw, and the Shape-Shifter.*" *School Library Journal* 33 (October 1986): 173.

Wimsatt, Margaret. "*Self-Interviews.*" *Commonweal* 93 (19 February 1971): 501–3.

Winchell, Mark Royden. "The River Within: Primitivism in James Dickey's *Deliverance.*" *West Virginia University Philological Papers* 23 (January 1977): 106–14.

Winton, Calhoun. "James Dickey at Vanderbilt." In Kirschten, *Critical Essays on James Dickey,* 69–77.

Yardley, Jonathan. "A Colossal Ornament?: *Jericho: The South Beheld.*" *New Republic* (30 November 1974): 43–44.

Zweig, Paul. "Bel Canto, American Style: *The Strength of Fields.*" *New York Times Book Review,* 6 January 1980, 6, 17.

Contributors

Lee Bartlett is a professor of English at the University of New Mexico. He is the author of *Benchmark and Blaze: The Emergence of William Everson; William Everson: The Life of Brother Antoninus;* and *Kenneth Rexroth.* He has edited *Earth Poetry: Selected Essays and Interviews of William Everson; William Everson: A Descriptive Bibliography, 1934–1976;* and *Karl Shapiro: A Descriptive Bibliography, 1933–1977.*

Ronald Baughman is the director of graduate studies for the University of South Carolina's Media Arts Division. He has written *Understanding James Dickey,* edited *The Voiced Connections of James Dickey: Interviews and Conversations,* and contributed the Dickey entry to *Dictionary of Literary Biography Documentary Series, Volume 3: James Dickey, Robert Frost, and Marianne Moore.*

Clifford Gallo was a drama critic for the *Los Angeles Daily News.*

John Gallogly, managing director at Theatre West, is also on the directing faculty at the American Film Institute in Los Angeles. He is an award-winning director and has appeared as an actor on Broadway, at the New York Shakespeare Festival and at American Place Theatre and Manhattan Theatre Club, as well as at various regional theaters and in television and film.

Thom Gunn is the author of many books of poems, including *Jack Straw's Castle and Other Poems, Positives: Verses by Thom Gunn,* and *Collected Poems.* His books of criticism include *The Occasions of Poetry: Essays in Criticism and Autobiography* and *Shelf Life: Essays, Memoirs, and an Interview.*

Bridget Hanley, an award-winning actress whose career has spanned thirty years of theater and film, is best known for her starring roles in the television series *Here Come the Brides* and *Harper Valley PTA.* Affiliated with Women in Film, listed in *Who's Who in America, Who's Who in American Women, World Who's Who of Women,* she is a lifetime member of the Actor's Studio.

William Harmon has taught at the University of North Carolina at Chapel Hill since 1970 and is currently James Gordon Hanes Professor of English. His writing has appeared in *Poetry, PMLA, Parnassus, American Anthropologist,* and *Carolina Quarterly* and in several reviews—*Agni, Antioch, Sewanee, Partisan,* and *Kenyon.* His books of poetry include *Treasury Holiday; Legion: Civic Choruses; The Intussusception of Miss Mary American; One Long Poem;* and *Mutatis Mutandis.* He is also the author, co-author, or editor of *Time in Ezra Pound's Work, The Oxford Book of American Light Verse, A Handbook to Literature, The Concise Columbia Book of Poetry* (republished as *The Classic Hundred: All-Time Favorite Poems*), and *The Top 500 Poems.*

Malcolm Jones Jr. is a general editor at *Newsweek,* where he writes about arts and culture, mostly about books. Before joining *Newsweek* in 1989, he worked for newspapers around the South from 1972 to 1989. He is the co-author, with Van Dyke Parks, of *Jump!,* a retelling of Brer Rabbit stories.

Robert Kirschten is an assistant professor of English at The Ohio State University. He is the author of *James Dickey and the Gentle Ecstasy of Earth: A Reading of the Poems; "Approaching Prayer": Ritual and the Shape of Myth in the Poetry of A. R. Ammons and James Dickey;* and *Old Family Movies* (poems). He has edited *Critical Essays on James Dickey* and *Critical Essays on A. R. Ammons.*

Patricia Laurence is a professor of English at City College of New York and deputy director of the Center for the Study of Women in Society, Graduate Center, C.U.N.Y. She specializes in modernism and has written widely on Virginia Woolf. Her book *The Reading of Silence: Virginia Woolf in the English Tradition* was published in 1991.

Laurence Lieberman is professor of English at the University of Illinois at Urbana-Champaign. He is the author of nine books of poetry, including *The Creola Mephistopheles; New and Selected Poems; The St. Kitts Monkey Feuds;* and *Dark Songs: Slave House and Synagogue.* His books of criticism include *The Achievement of James Dickey; Unassigned Frequencies;* and *Beyond the Muse of Memory.*

Janet Larsen McHughes is a co-author of *Theatres for Literature: A Practical Aesthetics for Group Interpretations.* Her study *A Phenomenological Analysis of Literary Time in the Poetry of James Dickey* was published in 1987.

Harry Morris is the author of several books of poems, including *The Snake Hunter; Birth, Copulation, and Death;* and *The Sorrowful City.*

R. Barton Palmer is currently Calhoun Lemon Professor of Literature at Clemson University. He also serves as executive director of the South Atlantic Modern Language Association. An award-winning translator and editor of medieval poetry, he has written several books on film, including *The Cinematic Text, Hollywood's Dark Cinema,* and *Perspectives on Film Noir.*

Robert Peters is the author of *Gauguin's Chair: Selected Poems, 1967–1974; Goodnight, Paul: Poems; Hunting the Shark: A Compendium of New Poetic Terminology; The Crowns of Apollo: Swinburne's Principles of Literature and Art;* and *Zapped: Two Novellas.*

Harold Schechter is a professor of English at City University of New York in Queens. He is the author of *The New Gods: Psyche and Symbol in Popular Arts; Film Tricks: Special Effects in the Movies;* and *The Bosom Serpent: Folklore and Popular Art.* He has edited *American Voices: A Thematic/Rhetorical Reader* and *Discoveries: Fifty Stories of the Quest.*

Dave Smith's most recent books are *Fate's Kite: Poems of 1991–1995* and *Night Pleasures: New and Selected Poems.* He is a co-editor of the *Southern Review* and a professor of English at Louisiana State University.

Monroe Spears is a professor emeritus of English at Rice University. He is the author of *Dionysus and the City, The Poetry of W. H. Auden: The Disenchanted Island, American Ambitions,* and *One Writer's Reality.* He has also edited *Auden: A Collection of Critical Essays.*

William C. Strange is a professor emeritus of English at the University of Oregon. He is the co-editor of *Perspectives on Epic.*

Richard Tillinghast is a professor of English at the University of Michigan. He is the author of *Robert Lowell's Life and Work: Damaged Grandeur* and several books of poems, including *The Knife, and Other Poems, Our Flag Was Still There, Sleep Watch,* and *The Stonecutter's Hand.*

Lewis Turco is a professor of English at the State University of New York at Oswego. He is the author of *Awaken, Bells Falling: Poems 1959–1967; A Cage of Creatures: Poems; The Shifting Web: New and Selected Poems; The New Book of Forms: A Handbook of Poetics;* and *Visions and Revisions of American Poetry.*

Louis Untermeyer is the editor of *The Book of Living Verse* and *The Golden Treasury of Poetry.* He is the author of *Edwin Arlington Robinson: A Reappraisal; The Forms of Poetry; Emily Dickinson; For You with Love: A Poem;* and *Long Feud: Selected Poems.*

Hugh Witemeyer is a professor of English at the University of New Mexico. He is the author of *The Poetry of Ezra Pound: Forms and Renewal, 1908–1920* and of *George Eliot and the Visual Arts.* He is the editor or co-editor of *William Carlos Williams and James Laughlin: Selected Letters,* of *Ezra Pound and Senator Bronson Cutting: A Political Correspondence, 1930–1935,* and *Pound/Williams: Selected Letters of Ezra Pound and William Carlos Williams.*